"In his enlightening new work, Hernandez masterfully challenges the conventional emotive approach to poverty with a refreshing and intellectually rigorous exploration of Catholic Social Teaching. This book brilliantly uncovers the often overlooked yet crucial role of individual agency and market participation in alleviating poverty. By rejecting the stale 'Petrarchan conceits' of crisis and urgency that dominate traditional discourse, Hernandez advocates for a more inclusive and practical solution where the poor are not mere recipients of aid but active participants in creating sustainable economic value. A must-read for anyone serious about the real solutions to poverty that respect the dignity and potential of every human being."

—Andreas Widmer
Director of the Arthur & Carlyse Ciocca Center
for Principled Entrepreneurship
The Catholic University of America

"What is poverty? It's the wrong question. In *Rethinking Charity*, Ismael insists we ask something else. What is exceptional in the person? What is the basis of human dignity? What causes human flourishing? From a foundation of philosophy and years of real-world experience, Ismael thoughtfully and thoroughly answers these questions. Lofty 'solutions' motivated by redistributionist ideology are ruined leaving the reader with a narrow but effective path forward to truly help his neighbor in need. This book should be required reading for every social science student, policy intern, and seminarian. No one walks away from this read without seeing the next person in poverty as a radiant image-bearer with grand potential, to be crowned with dignity."

—James Whitford
Co-founder and CEO
True Charity

"There is a recurring myth that those who favor free markets are motivated by base desires, such as greed and selfishness, and that those who favor state control are motivated by compassion and benevolence. In this captivating book, Ismael Hernandez dares to bust many such myths about wealth, poverty, compassion, and Christianity. Given God's good creation and the grace he shows to all his creatures every day, why should we merely focus on redistributing material goods as if that would satisfy the demands of justice? Hernandez points to a much more compelling and comprehensive vision, one grounded in the dignity of the human person created in God's image, a dignity shared alike by rich and poor, male and female, Christian and non-Christian. If we are to effectively engage the perennial problems of poverty in its full dimensions—spiritual and relational as well as material—then we need those who see clearly and are willing to speak the truth that they see. Hernandez sees clearly, and he is courageous enough to proclaim the truth that he sees. We would all do well to listen to him."

—Jordan J. Ballor
Director of Research
Center for Religion, Culture & Democracy at First Liberty Institute

"As Christians we have an irrefutable call to care for the poor. Compassion alone is not enough; making our compassion effective is necessary. Rather than de-humanizing the poor by fostering dependency, our responsibility lies in helping them permanently escape poverty. Free markets, rather than being the culprit, are the antidote. Ismael Hernandez has written a persuasive and must-read book that compels us to put the human person at the center of our efforts."

—Anne Bradley
Vice President of Academic Affairs
The Fund for American Studies

"Ismael Hernandez is that rare combination: an original thinker and someone who acts. This shines through every page of *Rethinking Charity.* Bringing together good philosophy, sound economic theory, and the insights of years of experience, Hernandez shows readers how it is possible to help those on society's margins in ways that affirm rather than undermine their dignity. This is the type of intellectual leadership needed in our time."

—Samuel Gregg
Friedrich Hayek Chair in Economics and Economic History
American Institute for Economic Research

"Ismael Hernandez challenges the assumptions of standard left-leaning textbooks and offers a thoughtful alternative for smart undergraduate and graduate students, especially those who are Catholic. *Rethinking Charity* sees the poor not as capitalism's puppets but as real people often held back by those who see any emphasis on personal responsibility as 'blaming the victim.'"

—Marvin Olasky
Chairman
Zenger House

"Ismael Hernandez is a noble advocate for those who struggle materially. He understands their full humanity as persons with dignity and he recognizes their innate capacity for responsibility. He writes with authority because he has walked in their shoes. In this book, he teaches others how to walk with our brothers and sisters during their times of need. Hernandez instructs that the key to meaningful charity is authentic love of neighbor."

—Seana Sugrue
Ambassador Michael Novak Chair of Politics
Ave Maria University

"Read this book and you'll come away thinking more clearly about how to achieve positive change in the world."

—Matt Warner
President
Atlas Network

"The challenge of thinking well about living well will always be with us, and so we're in need of expert guides to lay out what is at stake with not only what human flourishing looks like but what practical steps will actually get us closer to those ideals. Ismael Hernandez is such a guide, and in this book he seamlessly draws from the fields of economics, philosophy, political science, theology, and more to show us how we can promote the good effectively without falling into the ditches of utopianism on the one side or pessimism on the other. This work is judicious, convictional, readable, and hopeful. I highly recommend it."

—Micah J. Watson
Henry Institute
Calvin University

RETHINKING CHARITY

ISMAEL HERNANDEZ

RETHINKING CHARITY

RESTORING DIGNITY TO POVERTY RELIEF

ACTON INSTITUTE

Rethinking Charity: Restoring Dignity to Poverty Relief

ISBN 979-8-218-44104-3 (paperback)
ISBN 978-1-880595-77-0 (ebook)

Cover image is derivative of an untitled image sourced from Body Stock/Shutterstock.com.

ACTON INSTITUTE

98 E. Fulton
Grand Rapids, Michigan 49503
Phone: 616.454.3080
Fax: 616.454.9454

Interior composition by Judy Schafer
Cover design by Angel K. Will

Printed in the United States of America

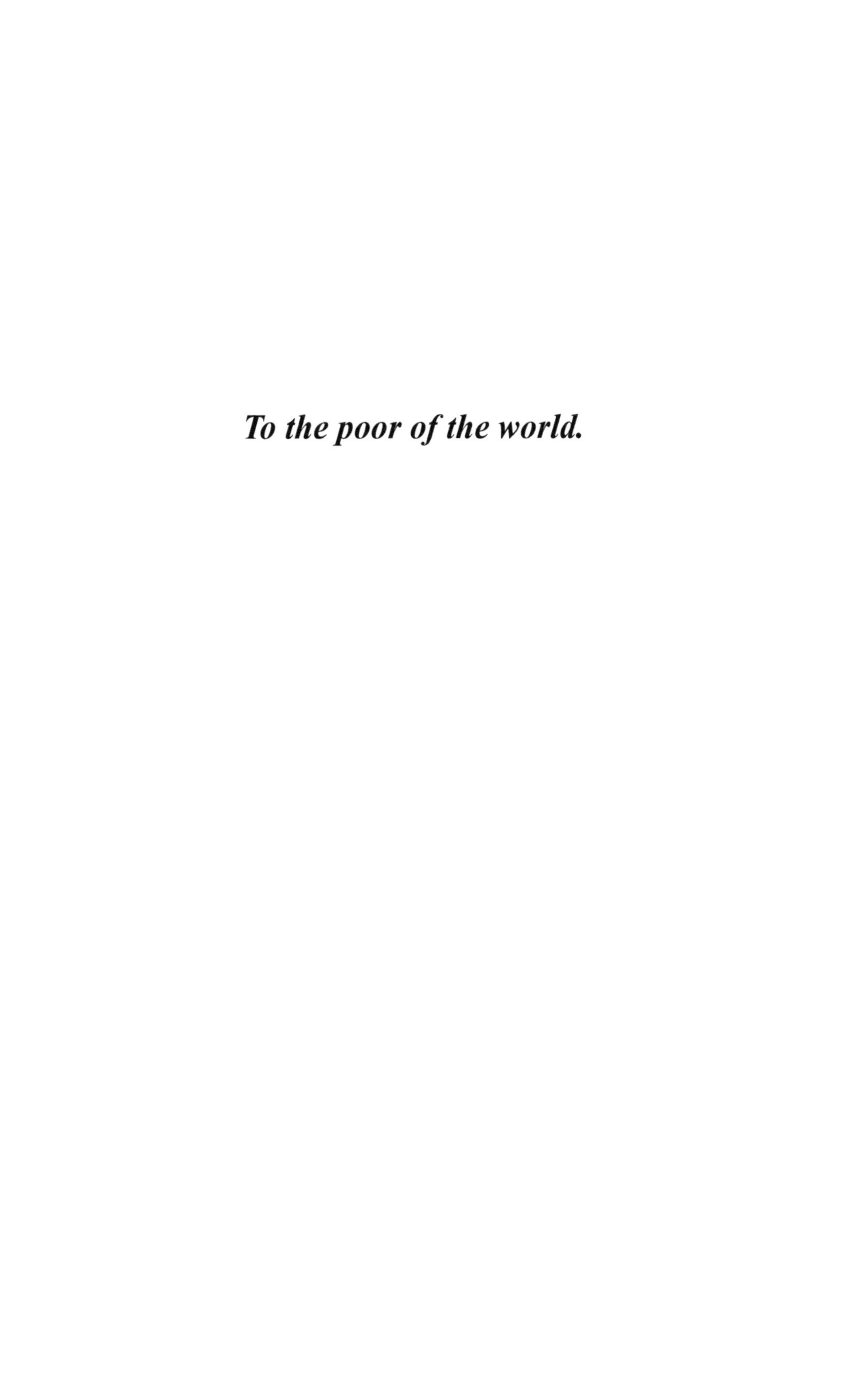

To the poor of the world.

Contents

FOREWORD

In our desire to help those in need, we can often turn poor people into objects of charity, pity, or compassion instead of seeing people as the protagonists of their own development and flourishing. Ismael Hernandez has been a consistent voice and reminder that we must never lose sight of the agency, potential, and creative capacity of each person no matter their circumstances. His life and work are examples of true charity and solidarity—that is, seeking the good of the other and helping to create the conditions for human and social flourishing. Over the last decades a shift has taken place from charity to humanitarianism. It is a subtle shift, but the impact is profound. As distinct from charity, which takes into account long-term flourishing, humanitarianism focuses primarily on providing material comfort. As Hernandez explains, this has led to cultures of dependency on state relief that robs people and communities of their self-reliance.

A backdrop to Hernandez's book is a long debate over two competing visions of how to address poverty in the United States. One is associational, community-led, and decentralized, rooted in mutual aid and enterprise. The other sees large-scale, government-led social programs as the necessary means to solve such a pressing problem.

The dominant model of poverty alleviation over the last century has been this large-scale, expert led, government-centered approach. In a sense, this was understandable. Inspired by the achievements of the physical sciences, the industrial revolution, and management ideas of people like Frederick Taylor, and especially the impressive technical and social engineering accomplishments that led to military victory in World War II, the idea was: we've won the war, now let's apply all that energy, money, and technical expertise to end poverty. This vision came to full fruition in the 1960s with the Great Society, the War on Poverty, urban renewal, massive housing projects, and a multiplicity of government welfare programs to assist those in need.

Despite great optimism, this scientific approach to the management of people—specifically poor people—led to the breakdown of natural communities and relationships that enable people to flourish. Poverty became more concentrated in certain areas, creating a kind of multiplier effect for existing cultural and social weaknesses. To be sure, we cannot blame federal government programs for all the social ills of our time; but the social engineering of people, combined with regulations and policies that undermined local organizations and weakened family ties, led to a breakdown of relationships in poor communities and what Seth Kaplan has called "fragile neighborhoods."[1] As Hernandez writes:

> The legacy of the Great Society was not the elimination of poverty but the institutionalization of welfare and the definitive federalization of poverty alleviation efforts. Long gone was the initial residualist conception of welfare, whereby helping those in need was a function primarily of families, churches, and private charities. The institutional conception, where the nation-state provides a broad range of social services and economic protections, was here to stay.[2]

A prime example of this was the combination of new highway construction, urban renewal, housing projects, and welfare regulations that discouraged marriage and saving. There were communities—poor no doubt, but filled with neighborhoods, families, shops, churches, schools, and community life—that were leveled to make room for new highway construction or other urban renewal projects. The area known as "Black Bottom" in Detroit is just one example of a vibrant community that was destroyed as a part of transportation policy and urban renewal. Displaced people were often moved into high density towers in park projects inspired by modernist architects and planners like Le Corbusier. Examples include Robert Taylor Homes and Cabrini Green in Chicago, the infamous Pruitt-Igoe apartments in St. Louis, the Forrest Houses in the Bronx, and Brewster-Douglass Housing

---

[1] See Seth D. Kaplan, *Fragile Neighborhoods: Repairing American Society, One Zip Code at a Time* (New York: Little, Brown Spark, 2023).

[2] Ismael Hernandez, *Rethinking Charity: Restoring Dignity to Poverty Relief* (Grand Rapids: Acton Institute, 2024), 115.

Projects in Detroit. Many have since been demolished. These housing projects became centers of crime, drugs, and other social pathologies. And if that was not enough, housing and welfare benefits were often tied to income and a woman's marital status. If a woman saved too much, she could lose her benefits. Social workers would visit to make sure there was no man in the house. This incentivized the breakdown of marriage which is a prime predictor of poverty. These programs concentrated the poor into isolated communities, and compromised family cohesion which had an especially negative impact on poor African Americans.

It is often said that these were unintended consequences of well-intended social planners. Perhaps. But a better description is they were *unpredicted* consequences, because they were based on reductionist and mechanistic theories and models of the social planners that ignored the complexity and nature of human society and relationships. Part of it was an error, part was hubris and failure to listen to critics. These planners were, in the words of anthropologist James Scott, "seeing like a state." They focused on "formal order," looking at society from the outside, and missed the layers of complexity, relationships, tradition, and informal order that Scott calls "functional order":

> These rather extreme instances of massive, state-imposed social engineering illustrate, I think, a larger point about formally organized social action. In each case, the necessarily thin, schematic mode of social organization and production animating the planning was inadequate as a set of instructions for creating a successful social order. By themselves, the simplified rules can never generate a functioning community, city, or economy.[3]

Another important contribution of *Rethinking Charity* is the combination of theory and practice. Hernandez pays special attention to theory and the proper mental models of how to think about poverty. This is not simply an academic debate. Theory impacts practice. The proper vision of the human person as a unique, unrepeatable individual with a social nature, born into a family and community; the proper role of government; the importance of local communities and charities; economic incentives; the proper division of social responsibilities are ideas that—whether you get them right or wrong—have real world consequences. Hernandez is not simply a theoreti-

[3] See James C. Scott, *Seeing Like a State: How Certain Schemes to Improve the Human Condition Have Failed* (New Haven: Yale University Press, 2020), 310.

cian. He has spent years helping people in a variety of situations and has seen first-hand the results of how good or bad theory helps or harms real people, families, and communities.

Two key themes in Hernandez work are the principles of solidarity and subsidiarity.

Solidarity and subsidiarity are often presented as opposing principles where solidarity is viewed as responsibility of the state while subsidiarity is the practice of local, smaller scale activity. But this is incorrect. They are mutually reinforcing principles. Every part of society, from the largest state to the individual, has responsibilities of solidarity and subsidiarity. These duties come from the nature and function of the particular group or community. Solidarity is the inspiration for the practice of subsidiarity, and subsidiarity is the arena where solidarity is lived out and grows.

Solidarity is social charity. It is Christian love played out in society where we treat our neighbors as ourselves. Indeed, the state has a role in promoting solidarity, but it is through the practice of subsidiarity that solidarity is primarily lived out. One way to understand subsidiarity is the division of social responsibility. Those closest to the problem should handle it. The federal government has specific responsibilities that a local township does not. A local township has responsibilities that a church or community organization does not. The church has responsibilities that the family does not, and the family has responsibilities that the church or the state cannot claim. There are times when smaller associations need assistance. This should always be temporary and with the goal of reestablishing independence. It is a breakdown of subsidiarity when a larger association takes to itself the rights of another. Hernandez quotes a famous passage from *Quadragesimo Anno*:

> Just as it is gravely wrong to take from individuals what they can accomplish by their own initiative and industry and give it to the community, so also it is an injustice and at the same time a grave evil and disturbance of right order to assign to a greater and higher association what lesser and subordinate organizations can do. For every social activity ought of its very nature to furnish help to the members of the body social, and never destroy and absorb them.[4]

It is essential to note that subsidiarity is not the devolution of power. Families do not receive their authority from the state but have authority and

[4] Pius XI, encyclical letter *Quadragesimo Anno* (May 15, 1931), §79.

responsibility that derive from their nature and function. Similarly, while it is true that those closest to the problem are generally the most efficient at handing it, efficiency alone is not the determining value. An inefficient family or community center is better for the common good than a hyper-efficient, distant bureaucratic approach that undermines natural communities.

These theories may sound academic, but they have profound practical impact. As Hernandez stresses, solidarity cannot be outsourced to someone else. Neither can self-reliance. A community grows in solidarity when it works together to solve problems and create the conditions for flourishing. Analyzing our work through this lens can be very instructive from the family to the federal government. This has special relevance and practical application for working with people in poverty. Every charity, government agency, church, and non-profit should be asking whether their projects align with the principle of subsidiarity and respect human agency.

- Are we doing for someone what they can and should be doing for themselves?
- Are we helping people become self-reliant, or creating the conditions for dependency?
- Does our work or service usurp the role of someone else who should be the main person helping our client?
- Who are the most important relationships in the life of the person we are trying to help? Are we engaging with those people or perhaps standing in their way?

If we are running an after-school program tutoring children, how involved are the parents or the extended family of the child? Are the fathers invited to participate? Are there programs that might involve and benefit the whole family? If we are building homes in a poor area, are we hiring or at least involving people in the neighborhood? Using the principle of subsidiarity as a guide can help avoid weakening social solidarity and harming the common good by alienating people from their friends, families, neighbors and others who have the potential for the most long-term positive impact.

I am grateful to Ismael for his work and insight over the years on effective compassion, self-reliance, mutual aid, and the entrepreneurial spirit. I have learned a great deal from him, and he has been an inspiration to the PovertyCure initiative and the formation of the Acton Institute's Center for Social Flourishing which promotes local, participatory, and enterprise solutions to material and social poverty, the principle of subsidiarity, and encourages and supports locally-led institutions and enterprise solutions to poverty.

Rethinking Charity is essential reading for anyone who wants to help people create prosperity, opportunity, as well as human and social flourishing in their own families and communities.

—Michael Matheson Miller
Director, Center for Social Flourishing
Acton Institute

Acknowledgments

This book had its beginning decades ago, as its ideas can be traced back to my life in the poverty of 1960s Puerto Rico. I want to express my thanks to many.

To all those who lived in *Barriada Garnier* (the Garnier section) of the city of Mayagüez and the town of Isabela and experienced with me the sorrows and great joys of childhood, thank you.

To my parents, Socorro and Juan, for all the lessons; and to my brothers Augusto, Bolivar, and Jorge, for all the laughs and moments.

To my loving wife, Crystal, and our children Lael, Mateo, and Miriam, for revealing to me the meaning of love as the disinterested gift of self.

To all those who worked side by side with me in many ministry settings in poor communities in Southwest Florida and elsewhere. To the people of the African Caribbean American Center where I worked and to those who followed me as we began and continue the new journey of the Freedom & Virtue Institute.

To the many scholars who assisted me with their knowledge through the years as I first learned the Marxist catechism and later the ideas of freedom: Michael Novak, Samuel Gregg, Robert P. Gorge, Thomas Sowell, Ludwig von Mises, F. A. Hayek, and so many others.

To the many inspiring people I have met throughout the years as they engaged in all types of activities to help the poor. I have learned everything from their steadfast commitment to better the lives of others.

To Father Robert Sirico and the Acton Institute for helping me as I was on a journey of discovering new ideas.

To Kevin Schmiesing for his invaluable scholarly advice and editing support.

—Ismael Hernandez
May 2, 2024

Introduction

Conceits are figures of speech in a sonnet, a fourteen-line rhyme scheme invented by the fourteenth-century Italian Renaissance poet Petrarch. Petrarchan conceits often consist of suffering lovers using fanciful and hyperbolic metaphors for their beloved, such as comparing a woman's eyes to the sun or the ocean.[1] By the seventeenth century, however, Petrarchan conceits came to be seen as highly emotional conventions, trite and melodramatic comparisons that eventually induced boredom and indifference.

Much of the language of compassion and poverty in America has become a sort of Petrarchan conceit of emotive conventions, stirring the heart toward action that eventually becomes stale. These conventions work intuitively, using emotion as the measure to discern courses of action. What feels right becomes the right thing to do. The images used are crucial because they go straight to the heart and can help to create unfalsifiable demands. We must do something, anything, to fix the problem. The images are there to create impact but, as with movie special effects, we are eventually desensitized. Often, the solution proposed by the image gravitates toward already existing, prefabricated, transactional answers. The hyperbolic notion of "crisis" is a preferred conceit—we must act now, or doomsday will befall us. Another is "justice" as a descriptor for virtually

[1] A good example is Spencer's poem "Epithalamion," where he describes a lover's lips as being "like cherries charming men to bite" and says that her cheeks are "like apples which the sun hath rudded." Edmund Spencer, "Epithalamion," Poetry Foundation, https://www.poetryfoundation.org/poems/45191/epithalamion-56d22497d00d4.

any campaign or claim of rights. The fragility of the poor is highlighted, and they are depicted as marionettes of happenstance.[2] The enthusiastic, cherry-picking use of "Aha!" statistics to move the will toward a preconceived goal, often consisting of the transfer of resources, is another preferred conceit, one based on rationalizations; that is, emotions that sound like reasons but admit no alternatives.[3]

Other types of poetic conceits are called metaphysical instead of Petrarchan. These are literary devices appealing to the intellect, not only the emotions, by way of analogies tying an entity's spiritual qualities with an object in the physical world. They merge emotions and reasons to reveal deeper truths present in the mundane. Metaphysical conceits can be vulgar or even blasphemous, as in John Donne's "Batter My Heart," which uses the shocking conceit of comparing God to a sexual aggressor.[4] Our political and cultural discourse is full of vulgar metaphysical conceits that either lionize or malign. Designations such as "fascist" or "communist" are offered with abandonment, and the adjective "heroic" is employed for what was once understood as normative. Analogies to evil forces are used for those who dare to challenge the given transactional paradigm of charity, perhaps the most insidious being "uncaring." The use of language has become a powerful weapon in a cultural and political war for the heart of our civilization, and it deeply affects how we understand the problems related to poverty. As F. A. Hayek observed, not only wisdom but also folly lives implicitly in words.[5]

Like Petrarchan conceits, the metaphysical ones also seem strained by their continual repetition throughout a sonnet. Over and over these stale comparisons are used until their effect is exhausted. Every year at certain times we hear the calls for more donations, because the problems are always getting worse. It is Thanksgiving, Christmas, or the coming new school year, and truly caring people must respond to *our* campaign to save *our* children. After enduring so many such litanies, we grow numbed and uninterested.

---

[2] See Theodore Dalrymple, "The Knife Went In," *City Journal* (Autumn 1994), https://www.city-journal.org/article/the-knife-went-in.

[3] See Thomas Sowell, *The Vision of the Anointed: Self-Congratulation as a Basis for Social Policy* (New York: Basic Books, 1995), chap. 4.

[4] See Christopher Ricks, ed., *Selected Poems of John Donne* (New York: Penguin Classics, 2006), 183.

[5] F. A. Hayek, *The Fatal Conceit: The Errors of Socialism* (1988; repr., Chicago: University of Chicago Press, 1991), 106.

The poor become a sonnet, a theme, an instrument. We may or may not donate based on the cleverness of the message or the power of a particular analogy, but the giver and the receiver are like elements in a poetic conceit, whose relation to each other, as Samuel Johnson wrote of the metaphysical conceit, seem "yoked by violence together."[6]

My life as a poor child in Puerto Rico seems discordant with the charity conceit. Like many others, I did not know that I was poor. We had some food on the plate, a roof over our heads, and parents at home. They were good parents who valued education and sound character. My father, a committed Marxist, was an intellectually sophisticated, avid reader who taught us to love learning. Our oppressed condition, he insisted, was imposed on us by the "Yankees," but we should study hard, for one day that reality would disappear within the great utopia to come. My mother, who couldn't have cared less about politics, also insisted that we should learn, her vicarious motives streaming from a childhood experience of poverty. By the end of the third grade, she had to stay home and work to help sustain the family when all she wanted to do was to go to school. Yes, there was a latrine in the backyard of our various rented homes, not many presents at Christmas, and we never owned a car. However, that seemed normal in an environment where everyone had the same lifestyle. One thing was certain: *we had hope and hope is everything*. In great part that hope was based on that instilled love for learning and the loving embrace of an intact family.

There was something else that in many places has virtually disappeared from our twenty-first-century ethos: *an abhorrence of dependency*. Yes, most people received some federal assistance in the form of occasional bags of free cheese, milk, and other items from the Puerto Rico Emergency Relief Administration—*La Prera*, as everyone called it. "*¡Llegó la Prera!*" (The relief has arrived) was the slogan often shouted at the sight of the government truck carrying the loot. I also remember my mom counting the food stamps she received. She hated the sight of those bills. Seared in my memory is the day my father finally got a good job at the tuna factory and my mother, full of joy, dressed up my older brother and me to take us to the government food stamps office. "Take me off that list!" For three or four years we had needed much help as my father lost one job after the other due to his consistent attempts at communist-organizing in the workplace;

---

6 Samuel Johnson, "Crowley," in *The Lives of the English Poets*, vol. 1 (Leipzig, 1858), 12.

he was even involved in court cases for terrorism. Likewise, the tuna job was soon lost, and my mother hated going back on the dole.

As I write, I have beside me my father's COINTELPRO FBI file, a witness to over thirty years of radical activity.[7] One day I would join the Socialist Party with him to fight America, the "Guts of the Monster."[8] Later, I joined the Jesuit order in great part because they were assigning me to Sandinista Nicaragua to study philosophy and also because I wanted to merge my double consciousness as a Catholic and Marxist-Leninist. The Catholicism part was one imbued in the culture and incentivized by my mother sending us to church on Sundays with neighbors. But my journey never happened. Weeks before my trip to Sandinista-land, seven Jesuits were murdered in El Salvador and the order decided not to send us there. That put an end to my Jesuit life, and I ended up in Mississippi of all places. I landed in Dixie!

For the first time, I had to face a challenge to my safe assumptions about the meaning of life and of poverty. Was my poverty a curse imposed by forces outside my control, or was there a different possibility? One thing that dawned on me as I studied at the University of Southern Mississippi was that what Americans called "poverty" was a joke, compared with my

[7] See "Puerto Rican Groups," at FBI Records: The Vault, accessed COINTELPRO in vault.fbi.gov. Retrieved January 12, 2024, https://vault.fbi.gov/cointel-pro/puerto-rican-groups. According to the summary at this site, "The FBI began COINTELPRO—short for Counterintelligence Program—in 1956 to disrupt the activities of the Communist Party of the United States. In the 1960s, it was expanded to include a number of other domestic groups, such as the Ku Klux Klan, the Socialist Workers Party, and the Black Panther Party. All COINTELPRO operations were ended in 1971. Although limited in scope (about two-tenths of one percent of the FBI's workload over a 15-year period), COINTELPRO was later rightfully criticized by Congress and the American people for abridging first amendment rights and for other reasons."

[8] The great eighteenth-century Cuban patriot José Martí coined the phrase "Guts of the Monster" (*Las Entrañas del Monstruo*). Martí lived in New York for fourteen years and had a complex relationship with America. Initially, Martí's stance toward the United States was one of admiration. As the idea of purchasing Cuba from Spain spread, Martí's stance shifted. A revolutionary who wanted Cuba's independence, he arrived back in Cuba in 1895 and died in the Dos Ríos Battle against Spanish forces. The phrase was written by him in a letter to a friend the day before his death, only one month after his arrival in the island. The phrase was coopted by the Marxist Cuban Revolution of Fidel Castro and adopted by communist revolutionaries all over Latin America, including the Socialist Party I belonged to.

life in Puerto Rico. "Give me some of that!" I thought. This book is in great part a reflection on poverty after years of experiencing it, researching it, and serving among the poor. I came to realize that the most significant part of my experience of poverty was the importance of family, encounter, and true compassion. Compassion and help during the crises I much later learned about—as our parents protected us from their miseries—came mostly from the extended family and neighbors.

There is no doubt that most Americans are compassionate, as compassion has been primarily understood for quite some time. They donate generously and volunteer.[9] But there is a systemic sonnet ringing within our ears and narrowing the alternatives we have within the constraints of transactional systems of care that misuse that immense good will. The main false assumption is that the state has the primary responsibility for the care of the poor. There seems to be a unitary vision of society that elevates the state as the soul of compassion for the nation, with basic communities within society taking a secondary role and even becoming subsidiaries of the state. Those invested with a strong and wholesome desire to help those in need have a task. They should convince themselves that *the creation of wealth is a spiritual exercise.*[10] In principle, wealth creation does not need a corrective in voluntarism or taxation, although our lives need a corrective as we engage all areas of social reality. Wealth creation is a calling, a vocation, not a concession to man's imperfection. Wealth creation ought to be the task for both givers and receivers, and it is in that context that we must understand ministry to those in need.

Callings have four characteristics, as the great Michael Novak taught. First, it is unique to the individual. This feature rejects collectivist and identitarian ideologies, as the uniqueness of each calling cannot be subsumed. Second, it

---

[9] See Una Osili, Chelsea Clark, and Jon Bergdoll, *The 2021 Bank of America Study of Philanthropy: Charitable Giving by Affluent Households*, Indiana University Lilly Family School of Philanthropy, September 2021; and Nathan Dietz and Robert T. Grimm, Jr., "Understanding Generosity: A Look at What Influences Volunteering and Giving in the United States," Do Good Institute, School of Public Policy, University of Maryland, November 2023, https://dogood.umd.edu/sites/default/files/2023-10/UnderstandingGenerosityReport_DoGoodInstitute_11.2023.pdf.

[10] See Theodore Roosevelt Malloch, *Doing Virtuous Business: The Remarkable Success of Spiritual Enterprise* (Nashville: Thomas Nelson, 2008), 3; and Michael Novak, *Business as a Calling: Work and the Examined Life* (New York: Free Press, 1996).

comes with preconditions, requiring talents and not just desires. The second precondition is fascinatingly important. It requires love—not just love of the activity it involves but also love of drudgery. We must understand that embracing the struggle is an essential element of any calling. Those called to help the poor must embrace the suffering it involves for themselves, as compassion is to suffer with the poor and to allow the poor to struggle, for in that loving process they will find their calling.

A calling also brings a sense of satisfaction and renewed energies. Transactional processes lack this energizing element, apart from the momentary high experienced by the giver. In effect, they often confer a dreadful sensation of shame. Finally, callings are not easy to discover. Wealth creation as a calling is consistent with such trial and error and painful setbacks, which the poor *have a right to endure*, with us right there suffering with them.[11] Yet, as Thomas Sowell eloquently puts it, "One of the sad signs of our times is that we have demonized those who produce, subsidized those who refuse to produce, and canonized those who complain."[12]

According to Hayek, civilizations grew and prosperity ensued with the advent of *extended order*; that is, free market economies.[13] He showed that the dispersed and uncontrolled knowledge of the many as they engage in millions of incessant economic decisions—with all the tacit knowledge of skills, experience, wisdom, and insight—defeats the hubris of control. Hayek made us aware of a third type of conceit, the narcissistic hubris of statist control. The fatal flaw of socialism is its insistence on the superiority of purposefully designed systems of economic control. The fatal flaw of charity is similar. It consists in ignoring the subjectivity of the poor and their capacity to engage in risky but rewarding economic activity while favoring the control that comes with transactional systems of care. These systems transfer benefits as an attempt to simplify the complexity of poverty-alleviation efforts, while the poor remain as passive recipients of magnanimity. In such an attempt to control we necessarily gravitate toward meeting biological needs, depersonalizing the individual person into a client, and focusing on resources as the key to success. This common human tendency to simplify is what we know as *bureaucracy*. In the

[11] Novak, *Business as a Calling*, 34–36.

[12] Thomas Sowell, *Ever Wonder Why? and Other Controversial Essays* (Stanford, CA: Hoover Institution Press, 2006), 328.

[13] Hayek, *Fatal Conceit*, 6.

economy, prices are the tokens of recognition or information-rich icons offering necessary signals for economic decision-making. They are means of enabling each economic decision to attend to the economic calculation problem. In charity, that token is *encounter*.

An additional element that complicates things is the existence of *paradigms* and *ideologies* seeping into our social consciousness. In the early chapters of this book, I discuss them and how they impinge on the question of charity. They are important because they are built, as we will see, on skeptical, reductionist, and determinist conceptions of the human person that render a choice toward the good of the other mute. Their reductionism ends in a vying for power among competing actors who, in the end, are moved by instinct, without the radical capacity of changing their lives by the choices they make. Power decides, because all affirmations of knowledge and all truth-claims are merely value-laden social constructs expressed through language and culturally disseminated. Today, the cynical, deconstructive nit-picking at Western civilization is provided by postmodernism. The impetus to burn it all to the ground is Marxist. As scholars Helen Pluckrose and James Lindsay tell us, we experience the rejection of both the smallest unit of social reality, the individual, and the largest, humanity. What is left? Identity groups vying for power.[14] Such cultural constructivism is the greatest enemy of true love for the poor.

A love and concern for the poor informs the heart of Christianity, attended the birth of our nation, and has been a component of American civic life from the beginning. From its earliest days, Christian faith was identified with the poor, as St. James tells us: "Religion that is pure and undefiled before God and the Father is this: to care for orphans and widows in their affliction and to keep oneself unstained by the world" (James 1:27). Alexis de Tocqueville placed philanthropy and the care of the poor within the spectrum of proliferating American associations. He spoke with admiration about the flourishing of private organizations that extended democracy beyond electoral confines. This characteristic is highlighted when he describes how Americans helped each other: "I have seen Americans making great and sincere sacrifices for

[14] Helen Pluckrose and James Lindsay, *Cynical Theories: How Activist Scholarship Made Everything about Race, Gender, and Identity—and Why This Harms Everyone* (Durham, NC: Pitchstone, 2020), 42.

the key common good and a hundred times I have noticed that, when needs be, they almost always gave each other faithful support."[15]

The ahistorical ideologies destroy the American ethos of compassion that for long was cultivated in our society. The later chapters of this book present a practical framework to rediscover and actualize it today. This ethos, based on the free encounter of free individuals who make a conscious decision to help others, is worth preserving.

In 1370, ill health prevented Petrarch from traveling to Rome, where Pope Urban V had summoned him. He died in 1374 while working in his study, his head resting on a manuscript of Virgil. He was in the vanguard of the Renaissance, the advance of a humanistic approach to life. Such humanism could go in the direction of denying Providence and become the hallmark of a false anthropology, or it could affirm God's superintendence over his creation by placing at its center the human person, the image-bearer of the Creator. Petrarch's humanism considered that man's reason and creative powers had been given by God so that he could achieve his fullest potential. He valued the study of human thought and action. The past is a great teacher, and those who ignore its wisdom falter. Recovering the wisdom of the past in the sacred task of helping those in need can help us to avoid charity's fatal conceit.

[15] Alexis de Tocqueville, *Democracy in America and Two Essays on America* (1840; repr., London: Penguin Books, 2003), 594–95.

Part 1

The Theoretical Foundations of Charity

1

The Instinct of Charity

In his book *The Fatal Conceit*, the twentieth-century economist and philosopher F. A. Hayek captured the perennial contrast between instinct and reason, impulse and deliberation. A behavior is instinctive if it is performed in the absence of learning and without much reflection based on experience. Instinct is different from reflex, as instinct is more complex and can be modified by human choice. Yet instinct remains an expression of innate biological factors.

According to Hayek, early thinkers examined society using a theory of human action (a praxeology) with little space for deeper reflection based on a priori information. As an example, Hayek appealed to Aristotle's understanding of a city in the Greek philosopher's *Nicomachean Ethics*. Aristotle could not fathom the existence of a city with one hundred thousand inhabitants. "You cannot make a city of ten men, and if there are a hundred thousand it is a city no longer."[1] For him, a realm of human activities beyond the confines of small communities was impossible. Human life was constrained to the familiar and adjacent, to the reach of the voice of a messenger. What would he have thought of Tokyo and its thirty-seven million people? Aristotle was reflecting with limited experience. As Hayek adds, however, even in the very lifetime of Aristotle what he thought impossible had already happened. But Aristotle, and other early thinkers with him, understandably spoke within the limitations of their historical context. Their

[1] Aristotle, *Nicomachean Ethics*, 9.10, trans. W. D. Ross, Internet Classics Archive, http://classics.mit.edu/Aristotle/nicomachaen.9.ix.html.

surroundings informed the limitation of the order of things to the voice of the herald, to the realm of instinct.[2]

As prescient and bright as early thinkers were, they still reflected on lives lived within narrower experiential confines. Even earlier, in prehistoric times, interactions and behaviors steered cooperation to accomplish common ends among exceedingly small cadres of people. Under such circumstances instinct sufficed to know how to act, when getting fed on a given day or finding cover against the intemperance of the climate were the only tasks at hand. Solidarity within a roving band was informed by a desire to survive and sufficed to accomplish ends. Human needs were discerned as collective needs in a condition where there was no such thing as the individual, isolated from the context of the clan. Long-distance travel was virtually impossible for most people, as it was costly and full of hardships due to the condition of roads and dangers such as hunger, dehydration, disease, and assault by humans or animals.[3] For most people, life was confined to a perimeter encompassing a few miles from their place of birth.

There seemed to be an order of easily apprehended immediate needs, a biologism to human survival that informed human action. Most acts were restricted to tribal life, and the decisions were made by the collective for the members. As the Harvard sociologist Orlando Patterson shows, in earlier times the idea of individual freedom was conceived in the human heart, but it never took on institutional life. Independent life was *social suicide* and almost always also physical death. A space for autonomy was found in full integration within the corporate polity, as all of existence was dependent on the kin group.[4] The antithesis to slavery was not individual autonomy as we know it but only a reduction of marginality.[5] These natural and social

[2] Hayek, *Fatal Conceit*, 11–12.

[3] Trade motivated the earlier instances of longer travel, one that was first facilitated by rivers. In Egypt, trade developed along the Nile River, and in today's Iraq it developed via the Tigris and the Euphrates. Long-distance land travel was supplementary. Soon, conquest became a reason for such travel, and there is also evidence for religiously motivated long-distance travel. See Lionel Casson, *Travel in the Ancient World* (Baltimore: Johns Hopkins University Press, 1994), 23, 31–33.

[4] See Orlando Patterson, *Freedom in the Making of Western Culture* (New York: Basic Books, 1991), 22–23.

[5] See Suzanne Miers and Igor Kopytoff, eds., *Slavery in Africa* (Madison: University of Wisconsin Press, 1977), 17.

constrains made instinct the main voice of knowledge in satisfying human needs.

The totalism of instinct would eventually dissipate as society became more complex. Interestingly, instinct resurfaces often, as it is a powerful force informed by desires that are positive. Often, this reign of instinct is not totalistic but hierarchical, occupying the central place informing human action. It can be said that the reign of instinct contained earlier in human history remains alive and well in charity work. It is expressed in the sincere desire to help those in need but only scratches the surface of an encounter with the poor because biologism persists as its main target. We have drawn Plato's "divided lines"[6] of affections and can only see those which are, to refer to his other famous analogy, "shadows" of the deeper human need.

The divided line analogy pictures an unequally bisected line further bisected into four resulting segments. Each of the four segments represents a separate "affection" of the inner self. The lower two segments (AB and BC) represent that which is *visible*, while the higher two (CD and DE) are said to represent what is *intelligible* or understandable.

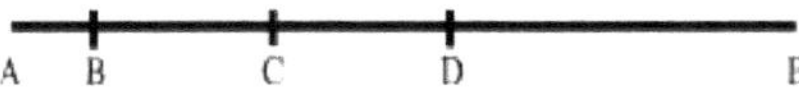

As we move further from segment to segment, we encounter correspondingly increasing levels of reality and truth. At the end, there is full understanding, which Plato calls the Form of the Good. You work your way up to this stage through thought until you grasp the Form of the Good. Everything starts at the level of initial perception, at the lower level of imagination, but it must proceed further. Then, everything is illuminated. These levels proceed from conjecture to belief to thought and finally to understanding. We go from objects of perception to objects of understanding and knowledge.

The schema of these affections of the psyche in *The Republic* serves us well to visualize how those invested in attending to the needs of the poor often miss what lies ahead and fail to grasp the truths that inform the lives of human beings. We bisect the lives of the poor and often remain in the segment of understanding shaped by the immediate visual need but miss the full scope of dignity: illumination escapes us. It is as if we remain deep in the cave of encounter, where the shadows are dim. The first level, the AB segment, gives us a shallow perception of *who* those we are trying to help

[6] See Plato, *The Republic*, bks. 6 and 7.

are as we *imagine* them to be; while the BC segment puts us in contact with their biological needs as they are or as we imagine them to be.

Here is where we form *a belief* about what the needs are, which often remain merely biological needs. This is the world of pinto beans cans, rice pudding, and paid water bills. The world of items. The world of transactions. This physical world of need, apprehended through our senses and readily classified by instinct, remains the closest encounter many have with the poor. It is where many stay, within the shadows arising from the label of "poverty" as a mirage informing their activity, followed by the tangible world of items and services to be provided. Beliefs about things at these levels are generally reliable but always incomplete—there is much more that escapes the weak gaze of instinct.

This world is also the world of emotion, feelings, and abstractions. From the shadows we perceive we form *a conjecture*; that is, a determination based on incomplete information arising from the images, described by Plato as "first shadows, then reflections in water and in all compacted, smooth, and shiny materials."[7] Yes, our assumptions about poverty are the conjectures that arise from limited encounters. They appear coherent, smooth, and true, but they are a mirage. Remaining there gives us a very low encounter with reality and truth but also a hallucination—it seems as if there is success as transactions occur, because there is an apparent immediate success. People are fed and clothed, and that seems to be the purpose of it all. We can now prepare the brochure with the stats and the illusions.

But there is a world beyond our proximate, shallow passing through the lives of the poor. This is the CD segment, a world of intelligibility and understanding of true self, the world of flesh-and-blood people, with names and histories, with hopes and aspirations, with capacities and potentialities built into their very nature. This is also the world of trouble, angst, sin, and deflection. The world of imperfect beings struggling to find meaning and purpose, at times in the wrong direction of integral fulfillment.

Because this world is real and reality is struggle, we often try to avoid it. It is easier to romanticize the abstraction of "poor people." The deeper we proceed into the segments of intelligibility, the more we transition from conjectures based on incomplete information into the world of *thought* and *reflection*, that is, the world of *practical reason*, a knowledge of what is true and good geared toward human action. We pause to think deeply not

[7] Kenneth Dorter, *The Transformation of Plato's Republic* (Lanham, MD: Lexington Books, 2006), 191.

only about poverty but about the deeper human need. We go from a world of illusions and shadows into a world of reason, trying to discover what is authentic.

This is the world of *Dianoia*,[8] that is, the world of cognition, deep thinking, and penetration into the mystery of man concealed by a veil of ignorance. This attempt gets us closer to the most authentic love, the *agape*, as we see in Luke 10:27.[9] This deeper knowledge in Plato's thought still falls short of the deepest knowledge possible. Yet, as a necessary step, it moves us closer to a sustained encounter with the poor and the satisfaction of authentic human goods. These goods are aspects of human well-being worth pursuing.

In Plato, to truly understand, we must enter into the world of ideas; the world of the essence or nature of things; the world of forms that lies beyond physical objects.[10] However, there is a limitation in Plato's divided line analogy. According to him, forms (essence, nature) can only be accessed through philosophical inquiry, as they are purely intelligible. That is, these *Platonic forms* exist separately from the things that exist in our material world.[11] You see a dog and there might be a form or essence of "dog" somewhere out there in the sky. It is with Aristotle that we see a different conception, whereby the form or essence of all things in this world exist *in the things themselves*. In Aristotle's view, "For all things that have a function or activity, the good and the 'well' is thought to reside in the function."[12] Aristotle's claim is that in achieving its end, one that is within itself, an object achieves its own good.[13] Every object is teleological, with

[8] See Simon Blackburn, "Dianoia," in *The Oxford Dictionary of Philosophy*, 3rd ed. (Oxford: Oxford University Press, 2016).

[9] Luke 10:27 reads: "He said in reply, 'You shall love the Lord, your God, with all your heart, with all your being, with all your strength, and with all your mind, and your neighbor as yourself.'" The term *Dianoia* is used here for "mind" or reason.

[10] See Gail Fine, "Knowledge and Belief in Republic V–VII," in *Plato: I Metaphysics and Epistemology* (Oxford: Oxford University Press, 1999), 217–48.

[11] See Robert P. George, *In Defense of Natural Law* (Oxford: Oxford University Press, 1999), 103.

[12] Aristotle, *Nicomachean Ethics*, bk. 2, trans. H. Rackham, Perseus Digital Library, http://www.perseus.tufts.edu/hopper/text?doc=Perseus%3Atext%3A1999.01.0054%3Abook%3D2.

[13] See Andrew Fisher and Mark Dimmock, "Aristotelian Virtue Ethics," in *Philosophical Thought: Across Cultures and Through the Ages*, 4th ed., https://open.library.okstate.edu/introphilosophy/chapter/virtue-ethics/.

a built-in thrust that is manifested in its function. When this idea is applied to human beings, our only response is reverence and awe at every encounter we have with people. When you encounter those in poverty, remember that you are encountering a spark of the divine, a being before whom the most adequate response is respect.

All the things we see around us are composed of both matter and form, with the form making them what they really are—that is, nature tells us what a thing is.[14] The poor person we encounter is a composite of matter and form. He is a human being with a nature that goes beyond the matter that can be empirically detected.[15] To enter fully into the knowledge of the truth about any and every person we must *transcend* the Platonic forms, as there is a segment beyond point E in Plato's divided line. That is where we discover and act toward *basic human goods*, which are, as philosopher Robert P. George describes them, "those intrinsic aspects of well-being and fulfillment of flesh and blood human beings in their manifold dimensions" that provide to us "*reasons for action*."[16] These reasons for action are at a lower level instrumental, because it is good to discern the most effective means to meet human needs. Efficiency has its place. But these reasons become noninstrumental or intrinsic when we approach people as such, because persons are worthwhile for their own sake. These reasons for action constitute the first principles of morality, pointing toward *integral human fulfillment*. It should be clear by now that mere satisfaction of biological needs misses the person. When we come to that full understanding and actualize it in acts of choice that go beyond abstraction and conjectures, we have moved in the direction of a fuller knowledge of loving God by authentically loving our neighbor.

Churches, ministries, secular charities, government agencies, international organizations, and NGOs are admired for their good intentions and their good deeds. Our body politic, thankfully, is imbued with support for the notion of service. These intentions seem innate, a fixed pattern of behavior

---

[14] This is what is called *hylomorphism*. For an examination of the concept, see Christopher Shields, "Aristotle's Psychology," *Stanford Encyclopedia of Philosophy* (Winter 2020 Edition), ed. Edward N. Zalta, https://plato.stanford.edu/archives/win2020/entries/aristotle-psychology/.

[15] St. Thomas Aquinas, *On the Principles of Nature*, trans. R. A. Kocourek, cc. 8–9, Aquinas 101, https://aquinas101.thomisticinstitute.org/aquinas-on-the-principles-of-nature-cc-89.

[16] George, *In Defense of Natural Law*, 103.

signaling what a good person ought to do. Yet, as Robert Lupton tells us, "Good intentions can translate into ineffective care or even harm."[17] Charity work often only scratches the surface of encounter, because it maintains a transactional spirit and comes with no strings attached. It seems noble and righteous, but its underbelly is not informed by reflection. It is as if we transport ourselves anachronistically to the nomadic roving band, expressing solidarity with those whose whole existence revolves around finding the next meal.

Lupton adds, "Relationships built on need do not reduce need. Rather, they require more and more need to continue."[18] Why do we tend to act in this way? *Because it is much easier.* When needs are reduced to easily discernible biological ones, reflection about how to attend them is reduced to utilitarian calculation. Challenges to such an understanding are often portrayed as a lack of zeal for justice or a lack of empathy. We often feel that time is of the essence and all we need is greater resources and a willingness to spend more, which increases over time as it is the token or recognition of a workable relationship. Moreover, reducing compassion to meeting biological needs is easier to do because they are *quantifiable*. They require a minimum of acquaintance, and the avoidance of intimacy is easily attained and often necessary—the relationship is with the system of care. The most important figures within an organization spend their lives far away from the poor: in cubbyholes working with data or writing grants, or at restaurants wining and dining public officials.

Quantifiable charity provides the opportunity to offer highly emotional rationalizations that come with the illusion of success. As there is the immediate effect of transferred resources, we can point to the fact that people needed food or shelter, and these needs are being met. The activism of the giver is mixed with the passivity of the receiver in a common cause informed by instinct. If poverty is simply a lack of certain material resources, their provision becomes the point of the relationship. We get tasks fulfilled, and these become the metric of encounter.

When you ask poor people about their poverty, however, they deviate from the narrative of empty holes of need. As Brian Fikkert and Steve Corbett put it in their analysis of a World Bank study about how the poor describe poverty, "Poor people typically talk in terms of shame, inferiority,

[17] Robert D. Lupton, *Toxic Charity: How Churches and Charities Hurt Those They Help (And How to Reverse It)* (New York: HarperCollins, 2011), 2.

[18] Lupton, *Toxic Charity*, 61.

powerlessness, humiliation, fear, hopelessness, depression, social isolation, and voicelessness."[19] Yet, seldom do those engaged in traditional forms of poverty-alleviation efforts ask what the poor bring with them as gifts. They remain silent witnesses of our good instincts, with nothing to offer but a grocery list.

Blaming the Victim?

At times some are offended at the thought of charity that looks on both sides of the relationship. It is characterized as "blaming the victim."[20] The phrase was coined by sociologist Willam Ryan, who described it as "a brilliant ideology for justifying a perverse form of social action designed to change, not society, as one might expect, but rather society's victims."[21] In this view, the poor are already doing all they can, and questioning what they can bring with them feels like an imposition, another injustice. The paradigm of understanding poverty in a way that avoids blaming the victim has become commonplace in social work and charity efforts. Sociologists Herbert and Irene Rubin, for example, tell us that "blaming the victim is a form of social control that disempowers by denying people a legitimate focus of complaint."[22] What causes poverty and is at the heart of individual problems is what another sociologist, William Brueggemann, calls "institutional deviance." Society "concentrates on the social deviant but fails to look at the conditions that may cause people to become deviant."[23] Sociologist C. Wright Mills was accurate in 1959 in telling us that "perhaps the most

[19] Cited in Peter Greer, "'Stop Helping Us': A Call to Compassionately Move Beyond Charity," in *For the Least of These: A Biblical Answer to Poverty*, ed. Anne R. Bradley and Art Lindsley (Grand Rapids, MI: Zondervan, 2014), 232.

[20] The classic account of victimization was offered by William Ryan, who coined the phrase "blaming the victim" as a rejection of an emphasis on personal behavior as a cause for poverty. See William Ryan, *Blaming the Victim* (New York: Vintage Books, 1976).

[21] Ryan, *Blaming the Victim*, 78.

[22] Herbert J. Rubin and Irene S. Rubin, *Community Organizing and Development*, 3rd ed. (Boston: Allyn & Bacon, 2001), 81.

[23] William Brueggemann, *The Practice of Macro Social Work* (Belmont, CA: Brooks/Cole, 2002), 41–43. In his work, Brueggemann describes the various models concisely and accurately, advising prospective practitioners to learn about all models, including the individualist and the systems models.

influential distinction with which the sociological imagination works is between 'the personal troubles of milieu' and the 'public issues of social structure.'"[24] His words remain true, though it seems as if the social structure understanding has won the day. The individual is fading as a meaningful element in understanding social behavior, as we are seen now as pieces within a puzzle of group identity and the social stigmatization of minorities and the poor that is at the heart of interpersonal pathologies. From the inability to form relationships and the failure to become good parents to suffering high blood pressure, all maladies are traceable to group stigmatization.[25]

Orlando Patterson points out a crucial problem with such reasoning: the problem of *determinism*. The moral cost of such a response is high. "By its very nature, a deterministic framework accentuates the moral superiority of the victimizer. As long as one is in the position where one has to appeal to the moral sense and mercy of another person, one remains, almost by definition, morally compromised."[26] Patterson argues elsewhere, "To hold someone responsible for his behavior is not to exclude any recognition of the environmental factors that may have induced the problematic behavior in the first place."[27] The cry of victimization reduces the person (or the group) to an object moved by forces outside their control. It offers to those under the grip of deterministic assumptions only the world of *Ananke*, the Greek goddess who was the personification of the world of compulsion, necessity, and inevitability.[28] As there is always a human tendency to protect our own psyche, when the entire enterprise of care is informed by *Ananke* the temptation is to find an alibi and ignore our subjectivity.

[24] See C. Wright Mills, *The Sociological Imagination* (London: Oxford University Press, 1959), 8.

[25] See Ismael Hernandez, *Not Tragically Colored: Freedom, Personhood, and the Renewal of Black America* (Grand Rapids, MI: Acton Institute, 2016), 99–100; Richard Delgado and Jean Stefancic, eds., *Critical Race Theory: The Cutting Edge* (Philadelphia: Temple University Press, 2000), 131–33.

[26] See Orlando Patterson, *The Ordeal of Integration: Progress and Resentment in America's Racial Crisis* (New York: Basic Books, 1998), 95.

[27] Orlando Patterson, "A Poverty of the Mind," *New York Times*, March 26, 2006.

[28] Editors, "Ananke," *Britannica*, rev. October 10, 2007, https://www.britannica.com/topic/Ananke-Greek-mythology. The Greek term *Ananke* is derived from the common Ancient Greek noun ἀνάγκη, meaning "force, constraint or necessity." See Robert Paul Beeks, *Etymological Dictionary of Greek*, Leiden Indo-European Etymological Dictionary Series, vol. 10 (Boston: Brill, 2009), 97.

The alternative often leads to meaningless activism or self-pity. If I am an absolved victim of forces out there, the world of alternatives shrinks. Instead, why not present the world of *érgon*, the world of *work* and activity that accomplishes something.[29] The world of *érgon* leads to what Aristotle in his *Nicomachean Ethics* called *eudaimonia*, a world of "human flourishing" and "blessedness," informed by "*aretê* ("virtue" or "excellence") and the character traits that human beings need in order to live life at its best."[30] Yet, as Thomas Sowell has stated, "Among the many disturbing signs of our times are conservatives and libertarians of high intelligence and high principles who are advocating government programs that relieve people of the necessity of working to provide their own livelihoods."[31]

The "blaming the victim" paradigm has taken hold because victimhood offers a sort of alternative moral universe, and siding with the victim is what being "woke" means. Siding with the victim is different from recognizing the dignity of every individual whose worth is intrinsic and untransferable. The victim in this case is a specimen of a group whose worth resides in the label of victimhood. The highest virtue for the woke is political action against the oppressors of a group. This is the new victimhood culture. This is why we see the rise of the "microaggressions" mindset, as the victim finds a moral right in every action of others toward him and the woke ally affirms the soft skin of victimization.[32] This parasitic relationship validates the moral worth of the patron and strengthens the sense of being the object of oppression in the victim. As Noelle Mering puts it, "Woke ideology en-

---

[29] Richard Parry and Harald Thorsrud, "Ancient Ethical Theory," *Stanford Encyclopedia of Philosophy* (Fall 2021 Edition), ed. Edward N. Zalta, https://plato.stanford.edu/archives/fall2021/entries/ethics-ancient/.

[30] Richard Kraut, "Aristotle's Ethics," *Stanford Encyclopedia of Philosophy* (Fall 2022 Edition), ed. Edward N. Zalta and Uri Nodelman, https://plato.stanford.edu/archives/fall2022/entries/aristotle-ethics/. See Aristotle, *Nicomachean Ethics*, bk. 4.

[31] See Thomas Sowell, "Is Personal Responsibility Obsolete?" *Creators*, June 7, 2016, https://www.creators.com/read/thomas-sowell/06/16/is-personal-re-sponsibility-obsolete.

[32] See the discussion on the victimhood culture in the thought of sociologists Bradley Campbell and Jason Manning in Noelle Mering, *Awake, Not Woke: A Christian Response to the Cult of Progressive Ideology* (Gastonia, NC: Tan Books, 2021), 62–64.

courages the behavior of the mob but takes the posture of the scapegoat."[33] The mob launches at the very communities they purport to defend while playing victim of forces in society. It is truly a scandal that many churches and ministries aspire to being known as woke.

Others do not emphasize the victimology paradigm but appeal to a sort of Rawlsian "anti-perfectionist" political theory that affirms the infliction of injuries to human autonomy and fundamental justice if a moral expectation is attached to social benefits, either from the state or other institutions.[34] This is an influential view in liberal society, called nonjudgmental toleration. As philosopher Michael Sandel defines it, nonjudgmental toleration "permits some practice on grounds that take no account of the moral worth of the practice in question."[35] Our welfare system has historically offered aid based on financial means-test criteria, without any type of categorization or judgment based on its doctrine of the equal protection of the law. Two individuals with different lifestyles and values are to be treated the same way. The law brackets questions of substantive moral norms or expectations in providing aid. Philosophers have often called this type of Kantian bracketing, "voluntarist toleration."[36] The law must treat all persons equally for the sake of treating all as free and independent persons choosing their ends for themselves.

Another popular form of toleration is the "minimalist" one that affirms the need for neutrality concerning the law, so as to allow for social cooperation in the face of disagreements on morality and ultimate ends.[37] A good

[33] Mering, *Awake, Not Woke*, 110.

[34] See John Rawls, *A Theory of Justice* (Cambridge, MA: Harvard University Press, 1971), 327–30. For a critique of anti-perfectionism see George, *In Defense of Natural Law*, chap. 11.

[35] See Michael J. Sandel, "Judgmental Toleration," in Robert P. George, ed., *Natural Law, Liberalism, and Morality* (Oxford: Oxford University Press, 1996), 107.

[36] According to Kant autonomy defines human beings. The autonomous man is responsible and arrives at moral decisions which constitute for him imperatives. In a sense, man becomes a law unto himself. He is self-legislating. It follows to Kant that the autonomous man is not subject to the will of another or to laws that contain moral norms. He is in the political sense *free*. The totally voluntarist condition follows: man may conform to a law by assessing it by his own reason, not because the state has authority

[37] Sandel, "Judgmental Toleration," 108–9.

portion of charity work has followed the same model. It might indeed be the case that the state is not qualified to pass certain judgments, but that notion has also permeated charity work dependent on public funds and all charity work that uses only one aspect of the doctrine of human dignity, that of intrinsic dignity. Providing relief without asking questions is often the norm in charity organizations.

Anti-perfectionism and nonjudgmental toleration are amply explored in questions of jurisprudence, but they are also applied to social problems and the task of aiding those in need. When it comes to the service of those in need, both types of toleration have done great harm. The voluntarist does harm by affirming that there is no objective set of moral norms that apply to human perfection in general and that each person creates his own set of norms and hierarchies, leading to limiting service to the transfer of goods and services without expectations. The minimalist focuses strictly on practical questions of efficiency, afraid of passing judgment or being "controversial."

Interestingly, although a minimalist approach pretends neutrality, it cannot attain it, as in the process of bracketing certain moral responses it necessarily affirms others, such as the notion that benefit is granted without expectations, severing the tie between reward and accomplishment. There is no neutral ground, because, using Michael Sandel's rendition, political conceptions of justice are "parasitic on a certain view of the controversies it would bracket."[38] Pretentions of neutrality in jurisprudence attempt to separate politics from philosophy, and in the world of charity they separate service from the types of character-forming expectations that are the only ones that remain with people and shape their character once the physical object given or the service provided are long gone. Poverty alleviation should not be about how to build the best supermarket ministry.

Those in service of the poor, believers or not, ought to apply a different notion of toleration: following Thomas Aquinas, "*judgmental toleration.*"[39] They must remain partial on the side of certain moral expectations and willing to pass judgment on how, when, and what kind of aid is given. What I

[38] Sandel, "Judgmental Toleration," 110.

[39] Aquinas presents heresy and unbelief as great sins and prima facie unworthy of toleration. However, just as God "allows certain evils to take place in the universe which He might prevent, lest without them greater goods might be forfeited, or greater evils ensue," so the law might tolerate certain evils. Likewise, in service, we use the same criteria of judgmental toleration. St. Thomas Aquinas, *Summa Theologica* II-II, q. 10, a. 11.

mean here is not that those adhering to minimalist or voluntarist toleration approaches are not judgmental. They are, because it is not possible to refrain from judgment in the social exchange between giver and receiver. They *implicitly* affirm a certain conception of the human person, while deluding themselves about being neutral. On the other hand, judgmental toleration is *explicit* about its commitments to a certain conception of the human good. This judgmentalism is tolerant, however. That is, certain evils are tolerated as the giver and the receiver enter a relationship of mutual trust. People are not discarded *prima facie* on account of where they are in life but are helped in various ways in an attempt to help them discover on their own the route toward the authentic human good. We must tolerate certain vices so as not to lose the relationship with those we are trying to assist, as losing that relationship is a greater and intolerable evil.

The sociologist Arthur C. Brooks is correct in stating that the majority of Americans embrace the concept of a *safety net* administered by the state.[40] Conservatives and liberals tend to differ in terms of how to administer that safety net in a fiscally responsible way and also in terms of what sphere of government (federal or state) has the constitutional duty to maintain it. However, there is no question that both have maintained support for the safety net in general and have attended to its incremental growth.

Regardless of your position on that specific question, there are more basic questions at stake. Can the federal government change its welfare system by encouraging second-order activities requiring a certain conception of the good? Isn't that against nonjudgmental toleration? As Brooks correctly states, conservatives complain because the system as currently administered "does not equip citizens to build meaningful dignified lives of their own making."[41] Such expectations would indeed demand a new and better metric, that of how many people no longer need subsistence support. A rejection of nonjudgmental toleration must form the basis for such expectations, which by definition offer a very specific conception of the good—it is better to live lives of effort and independence, informed by the willingness to take risks without any expectation of success. The safety net must permit some unsafe expectations. Another problem with the state operating with such a new metric is that the very nature of state action as a political enterprise creates great temptations to introduce ideology and electoral goals into the

[40] See Arthur C. Brooks, *The Conservative Heart: How to Build a Fairer, Happier, and More Prosperous America* (New York: Harper Collins, 2015), 18.

[41] Brooks, *Conservative Heart*, 19.

process by benefiting certain entrepreneurial enterprises but not others, as has happened with benefits provided to so-called green energy.[42] The state wants to be a player, not the referee.

Still others see welfare and private relief as a political right. For example, British sociologist T. H. Marshall pioneered the concept of "social citizenship," which transcended that of "political citizenship" and included the rights to material resources and social services.[43] Marshall said, "The claim of the individual to welfare is sacred and irrefutable and partakes of the character of a natural right … but the citizen of the welfare state not only has the right to pursue welfare: he has the right to receive it."[44] If that is the case, that receiving services and material support is a natural right, it exists by virtue of being human and no moral expectation or requirement can be allowed to intrude in its reception. Then there exists an absolute political and natural right to relief, and private charity collapses into the affairs and institutions of the state, as the state is the social entity whose jurisdiction encompasses the entire collection of citizens. If private charity exists, it exists only as a *mechanistic proxy* for the redistribution of resources. Many larger charities actually do function, in practical terms and at least partially, as such proxies. What could be the substance of private charity if welfare is an inviolable natural and political right? Is it that Christians smile more widely while giving stuff away?

---

[42] Take the billions of dollars poured into the Inflation Reduction Act or so-called Clean Air Act under President Joe Biden, the Solyndra loans under the Barack Obama Administration, and billions for "climate change" companies under the George W. Bush Administration. See Max Zahn, "Biden Climate Law Spurred Billions in Clean Energy Investment. Has It Been a Success?" ABC News, January 29, 2023, https://abcnews.go.com/Business/biden-climate-law-spurred-billions-clean-energy-investment/story?id=96632120; Ivan Penn, "Expansion of Clean Energy Loans Is 'Sleeping Giant' of Climate Bill," *New York Times*, August 22, 2022, https://www.nytimes.com/2022/08/22/business/energy-environment/biden-climate-bill-energy-loans.html; see "Energy Security for the 21st Century," The White House, 2011, https://georgewbush-whitehouse.archives.gov/infocus/energy/.

[43] For a description of Marshall's thought see Ben Jackson, "T. H. Marshall," *Britannica*, November 25, 2023, https://www.britannica.com /biography/T-H-Marshall.

[44] See T. H. Marshall, *Class, Citizenship, and Social Development* (New York: Doubleday, 1965), 258–59.

2

Sound Thinking about Poverty Alleviation

For those using political philosophy to claim a right to relief, the notion of *redress* is preeminent.[1] Unequal outcomes or even inequalities of intellectual or social endowment are grievances that deserve remedy or compensation to be achieved through direct, top-down, intervention by the state or other institutions of civil society. Again, the logic is clear: if relief is a political right of the citizen and some citizens lack certain goods and services, then something must be wrong with the political structure or with the grand design of the universe when these goods are not delivered in abundance. As affirmation of the need for redress is parasitic to belief in an expanded human intellectual capacity to accomplish it, it highlights the hubris of the intelligentsia. Thomas Sowell aptly calls this hubris "cosmic justice," a type of unattainable justice in eternal antagonism with reality. It is also a concept irreconcilable with individual freedom, the rule of law, and an objective assessment of human capacities to rearrange the order of things.[2]

Meeting Deeper Needs

In reality, economic inequality persists because human beings are not equal in every way, and because the human capacity to realign the stars does not

[1] The principle of redress is presented by John Rawls thus: "the principle that undeserved inequalities call for redress." Rawls, *Theory of Justice*, 86.

[2] For a detailed examination of the concept of "cosmic justice," see Thomas Sowell, *The Quest for Cosmic Justice* (New York: Touchtone, 1999).

exist. Unequal outcomes are not grievances but necessary results from facts of human nature. As human beings are more than constructs of the political system or biological organisms with determined organic features, it follows that removing the moral demands from welfare will spell failure. These failures, however, are often used to increase claims for greater political power to finally make it work.

My experience with having been poor and later working with the poor moves me to believe that there are deeper human needs people carry with them. The most important one is the need for a recognition of their subjectivity. The apparent need is but a step the poor take toward encounter and involvement. As Hilaire Belloc said long ago, "Man, like every other organism, can only live by the transformation of his environment."[3] Yet, unlike every other organism, man cannot live without working and engaging in second-order activities that transcend his environment and give him an inward movement of the will and the intellect. This basic human constitution and the activities that flow from it are pre-political: they are natural in the human constitution and their existence is revealed through human work. That is, working to gain sustenance is a sort of spontaneous order.[4] They reveal order in the mind of God as he created human beings, order in the natural state of those created, and order in human action. Human societies cannot function well if they go against the spontaneous order of things. This order is not the result of what Hayek calls, using a German term, *Machbarkeit*, which might be rendered into English as "manufacturability." Yet, we can "secure the assistance of some very general conditions" to facilitate it.[5]

[3] Hilaire Belloc, *The Servile State* (1913; repr., Indianapolis: Liberty Fund, 1977), 45.

[4] A spontaneous order is an order in nature that is revealed through human action but not created by the human mind. It affirms the limitations of our rationality and seeks to explain the emergence of practices and institutions as the unintended consequences of multiple individual actions. See Daniel Luban, "What Is Spontaneous Order?" *American Political Science Review,* 114, no. 1 (February 2020): 68–80, https://doi.org/10.1017/S0003055419000625.

[5] For Hayek, a spontaneous order is a feature of evolutionary processes. There is no God behind such ordering. As a Christian, I reject his agnostic conclusion. However, Hayek was on to something important in positing that an order can be brought about only if humans cause it. The uncaused, uncontrolled, dispersed action of individuals in most interpersonal exchanges reflect the reality that our powers

We must then go deeper than a mere assertion of political rights. Those political rights are invariably asserted against the labor and production of other human beings with the same human constitution and inclinations to actualize their subjectivity. The "servile state"[6] is a result of the politization of the question of the economic and social welfare. This is the state where positive law intervenes to force some people to labor for the advantage of others, corrupting the whole social order with this imposition. The servile state becomes the "intrusive state," where positive law forces some to labor for others and both positive law and private institutions encroach significantly on the lives of the poor, infringing their right to act on their own behalf and stamping society with the mark of paternalism. Confiscatory paternalism is an injury to the whole body politic and especially to the poor themselves.

Now, is abject or extreme poverty a justification to intervene in people's lives? Can a man in extreme hunger claim a right to relief. Yes. The scholastic distinction between domain and use might help us understand how it can be that I have a right to my property, yet another might have a right to use it under certain conditions—with a distinction between consumption and durable goods.[7] The Late Scholastic theologians understood that if I am starving, in a desperate situation of imminent serious harm, and there is fruit hanging from a tree, I can make use of that fruit. I do not, however, take ownership or dominion over the tree. Yet, as the owner of the tree also owned the fruit, how could I consume the fruit without at the same time taking dominion over it? The answer lies in the fact that the moment I consume the fruit, I incur debt. At least in principle, I owe the one with dominion over the fruit. I might not be in a position to immediately repay, or even ever repay, but the debt exists. This moral norm is not onerous. In fact, it sees the poor as having dignity, as being subject to basic moral norms just as others are. It also sees the owner of property as called to compassion and generosity. Our duty toward the person in such a desperate situation is restorative. We must journey with him as he moves toward meeting the standards of morality and in the process assist him to reach a point where he will no longer find himself in such a predicament.

---

to control are limited and the best we can do is first respect the natural order of things. See Hayek, *Fatal Conceit*, 83.

[6] Hayek, *Fatal Conceit*, 50.

[7] See Alejandro A. Chafuen, *Faith and Liberty: The Economic Thought of the Late Scholastics* (Lanham, MD: Lexington Books, 2003), 42–44.

If there is a primary area for attention on the question of poverty in the American context, it is not in finding clever schemes for more programs meeting *unmet needs*. The most important activity before us is the changing of the narrative of victimization that prevents the poor from seeing themselves as the protagonists of their own development whose primary right is to engage in productive activity on their own behalf. The narrative of penury and pauperism does not fit American poverty, because the context for economic and social advancement is there, greater than any other place on earth. Regulation of the poor, even with the lofty language of human flourishing and political rights, is an enemy. It incentivizes passivity in the realm of economic activity and activism in the realm of political intervention by patrons. It goes even further, demanding an entire restructuring of our vision of the place of the individual person in the configuration of society.

We must see the task of walking side by side with those in need as a journey whose destination is uncertain precisely because it requires risk. The greater risk is that of renouncing our dominion over the lives of the poor, as if they are so fragile that they cannot fail to crack without our benevolent management. Arthur Brooks often speaks of *earned success* not merely as a practical possibility but as a moral imperative.[8] We must create systems with critical components that highlight positively the capacities of the poor to engage in free and creative economic activity. An environment of profound respect for the poor demands free-market economic activity, with all its glories and warts.

As theologian Jordan Ballor points out, those in the developing world are now more confident about free markets than those in developed countries that benefited from free markets. One reason is human corruption in the marketplace. Another is what I call the boredom of affluence, which leads us to take such benefits for granted. Yet another is an intelligentsia invested in ideas contrary to free enterprise. I also believe that a problem is that we do not see the economic sphere as being part of a system that supports the poor. We see charity here and the market there. We see volunteering as a corrective of earned success. In so doing, we impede movement toward authentic love. As Ballor eloquently puts it, "A system within which service is

---

[8] See Arthur C. Brooks, *The Road to Freedom: Howe to Win the Fight for Free Enterprise* (New York: Basic Books, 2012).

valued, stewardship is expected, and sustainability is pursued is that which will tend to produce a more accurate earthly reflection of heavenly *shalom*."[9]

Accompanying, Not Intervening

The cloak of invisibility engulfing the poor remains in place because we have become cowards with a smile and a bag of rice to hand out. An authentic Christian response rejects subsuming the primary responsibility of individuals toward their basic communities—especially the church—within the role of the state (or charities and ministries) as it moves to grant welfare the status of a "sacred" political right. It also rejects the idea that welfare is a political right whose main enforcer is the state (and its subsidiaries) as it fosters the common good of the community within its jurisdiction.

A problem we have in grasping this essential understanding is that the target community for state action is the entirety of society within its jurisdiction. As the target is the whole, it is easy to believe that the state has plenary authority over the whole. It is important to affirm, however, that having the community at large as the target does not give the state a comprehensive role; it merely identifies its target without conferring expansive powers. The power of the state is as limited as the power of any other community. Identifying the role of each community is crucial. No one has expressed this truth better than the late Pope John Paul II:

> By intervening directly and depriving society of its responsibility, the Social Assistance State leads to a loss of human energies and an inordinate increase of public agencies, which are dominated more by bureaucratic ways of thinking than by concern for serving their clients, and which are accompanied by an enormous increase in spending. In fact, it would appear that needs are best understood and satisfied by people who are closest to them and who act as neighbors to those in need. It should be added that certain kinds of demands often call for a response which is not simply material, but which is capable of perceiving the deeper human need.[10]

---

[9] Jordan Ballor, *Get Your Hands Dirty: Essays on Christian Social Thought (and Action)* (Eugene, OR: Wipf & Stock, 2013), 97.

[10] John Paul II, encyclical letter *Centesimus Annus* (May 1, 1991), §48.

Our lack of courage and discernment incentivizes what Frédéric Bastiat called "a fatal tendency of mankind" to live and prosper at the expense of others. "This fatal desire has its origin in the very nature of man—in that primitive, universal, and insuppressible instinct that impels him to satisfy his desires with the least possible pain."[11] The least possible pain in what we may call *biologistic charity* is seen in the already mentioned admixture of *activism with passivity*. The giver avoids the pain in the effort to establish a relationship, while the receiver has some immediate physical pain relieved for a while. Living and prospering at the expense of others does not refer only to the receiver. The giver may experience a semblance of psychological prosperity in the reign of instinct that informs the transactions that occur when resources pass hands. A type of comforting paternalism offers those helping the poor a measure of satisfaction with the least possible accompanying pain.

The alliance between the state and the church in the American context, where the state is the one with the purse and the hand on the cradle, threatens the church as an independent and vibrant institution. As Alexis de Tocqueville warned of what he observed in the European context, "European Christianity has allowed itself to be intimately united with the powers of this world. Now that these powers are failing, it is as if it were buried under their ruins. A living being has been tied to the dead; cut the bonds holding it and it will arise."[12] What we need is the courage to sever the tie.

The "outsider's dilemma" must be addressed if we are to avoid the condescension of paternalism. Study after study shows that aid does not work. As economist Dambisa Moyo puts it, "The idea that aid aimed at economic development helps to alleviate systemic poverty is a myth."[13] Atlas Network president Matt Warner describes the dilemma as the question of how to help without interfering. How can we foster personal responsibility for one's future and idiosyncratic solutions to poverty while avoiding the type of interference that nullifies agency? The Atlas Network has found a response

[11] Frédéric Bastiat, *The Law* (Irvington-on-Hudson, NY: Foundation for Economic Education, 1998), 5–6.

[12] Alexis de Tocqueville, *Democracy in America* (New York: Harper Perennial, 1969), 301.

[13] Dambisa Moyo, *Dead Aid: Why Aid is Not Working and How There Is a Better Way for Africa*, as quoted in Matt Warner, Poverty & Freedom: Case Studies on Global Economic Development (Arlington, VA: Atlas Economic Research Foundation, 2019), 16.

when it comes to international aid and philanthropy: Philanthropists must agree to become subsidiary supporters of the research, advocacy, and initiative of local scholars and advocates. The focus ought to be the expansion of indigenous institutional space for local economic initiative informed by economic freedom and market-oriented solutions.[14]

A similar thesis applies to domestic efforts to end poverty, where helpers imagine that enough money poured into local communities and the work of agencies, nonprofit organizations, and philanthropists will have the effect of solving poverty at that level. This is the same kind of "magical thinking" that has been the norm in justifying foreign aid in Africa and other regions.[15] Interventionist powers are often government agencies disbursing direct aid to individuals but also churches, ministries, and other relief organizations that act upon local communities with good intentions but without the insight provided by people within these communities.

Even when these institutions are located within these very communities, they may have an interventionist mindset. The hubris of expertise and planning remains embedded in processes that attempt to fabricate solutions instead of strengthening local institutions such as the family and fraternal aid organizations while supporting local entrepreneurs and entrepreneurial initiatives. Moreover, these solutions often bypass the need for individuals to not only participate in the process beyond being clients but also to have a leadership role in the process.[16] We need fewer agencies and more support for those in the local community who stand for freedom, especially the aid of churches and other indigenous organizations who see themselves in the same light of subsidiary assistance to individuals and families. In other words, a local organization might not be the best to change the face of a community if the core vision of that organization is interventionist.

The hubris of central planning is at the heart of interventionism. The arrogance of interventionism is accompanied by the hubris of what I call *tokenistic love*. In society at large, but especially among believers, there is always the temptation of loving-sounding religious verbiage or perfunctory or symbolic efforts that avoid a deep commitment based on a consistent striving to actualize principles. We must be careful of unwittingly transforming the poor into a kind of religious currency, with them becoming

[14] Warner, *Poverty & Freedom*, 15.

[15] Warner, *Poverty & Freedom*, 16–17.

[16] Warner, *Poverty & Freedom*, 17–20.

a sort of token of authenticity, with not much more value than checking a box that needs to be filled. If we have a church, the thinking goes, we must also have an addendum of services for the poor—some service, any service. Very often we have a food pantry, help people with paying bills, welcome state agency services to our premises, and conduct drives and events. These are justified by way of biblical passages referring to poverty or instinctively accepted as something Christians are supposed to do. Almost invariably they provide something tangible to clients. Mobilization heightens during holidays and other events such as school openings, and they decrease in between celebrations. We have a plan of activities that provide something we find important for the poor at that moment.

Yet, as James Schall asks in *On Christians and Prosperity*, "If we love our neighbor because we are 'commanded' to love him, do we really love him?"[17] Or, as Steve Corbett and Brian Fikkert add in their influential book *When Helping Hurts*, "What truly motivates you? Do you really love poor people and want to serve them? Or do you have other motives?"[18] Are we objectifying the poor for the sake of scoring brownie points with God or of garnering the accolades of society?

The temptation to romanticize the poor and love poverty instrumentally is always there. That is, poverty becomes the occasion to fulfill some command by doing the minimum necessary to satisfy the command. At times, the poor become a symbol that advances an ideology. It seems as if our attitudes toward poverty float between *utopianism*, with a call to end poverty by the redistributive activity of the non-poor or via the revolutionary activism of movements to change structures, and *instrumentalism*, with the poor becoming an abstraction out there in the outskirts of our existence. We can "love" them by sending a donation, supporting certain redistributionist policies, or giving away some food through the small bureaucracies of compassion we have created in our churches and charitable institutions.

Have we given some thought to the possibility of loving the poor because they are persons with dignity and skills, becoming ourselves secondary aides for the expansion of economic activity initiated and led by the poor themselves? It has always bothered me that we use certain phrases, such

[17] See James V. Schall, *On Christians and Prosperity* (Grand Rapids, MI: Acton Institute, 2015), 16.

18 Steve Corbett and Brian Fikkert, *When Helping Hurts: How to Alleviate Poverty without Hurting the Poor... and Yourself* (Chicago: Moody Publishers, 2009), 61.

as "our children," to justify increases in spending for failing public schools or to justify transactional events where the poor receive items. If they are really "our children" instead of individual persons with the moral capacity for self-realization and the children of their actual parents, then we must reflect on how good parents treat their own children. Granted, good parents love their children by directly providing for them. But they love them the most by challenging them, expecting much from them, assisting them in developing the habits of virtue, and allowing them to struggle at times. We allow the struggle because it is good for them. They are not our pets; they are our offspring. Our instinct is to immediately intervene. Right reason invites us to discern.

Further insight is found in Bastiat's *Broken Window* story. Although applied to economics in his example, there is also much to learn about failed instincts. After the son of the bourgeois Jacques Bonhomme broke a window, his neighbors advised him of some salutary effects from the boy's mischief. After all, "Good comes out of everything. Accidents like this keep production moving. Everyone has to live. What would happen to glaziers if no window panes were ever broken?"[19] Highlighted in the advice is *what is seen*, that is, a broken window and a window maker getting paid to repair it. "The conclusion is reached," Bastiat continues, "that it is a good thing to break windows, that this causes money to circulate and therefore industry in general is stimulated."

Good comes from everything … Let's do anything as long as we are doing something. What do we see when a transactional process ensues in charity work? A bag of food was in my hands and now it is in yours. A shipment of rice was in our port and now it has just arrived at the shore in Port-au-Prince. We see a rally for "justice" and against capitalism or increases in funding for this or that agency. Just like Bastiat in his story, I must say to you, "'Stop!' Your theory has stopped at what is seen and takes no account of what is not seen."[20] In Bastiat's example, what is not seen is the economic activity that did not occur because I now must pay for a repair. I had a window and money to spend elsewhere. Later, I have a new window, but my money disappeared. In charity work what is not seen is

[19] Frédéric Bastiat, "What is Seen and What Is Not Seen, or Political Economy in One Lesson," in *Economic sophisms; and, What is seen and what is not seen* (Indianapolis: Liberty Fund, Inc., 2016), 405.

[20] Bastiat, "What is Seen and What Is Not Seen, or Political Economy in One Lesson," 405–6.

the damage to the dignity of the poor who remain as scenery in the drama of our good intentions.

What is not seen is the dignity of the giver making the determination not to intervene in a depersonalized fashion and choosing to suffer alongside the poor. What is not seen is the actualized potentiality of the poor who might not take the tiny step his agency and circumstances permitted because I, moved by instinct, took it from him. What remains unseen is the possibility of a fruitful life informed by economic activity through which we expand circles of exchange. Tom Nelson tells us in *The Economics of Neighborly Love* that "human fruitfulness is manifested in the kind of people we are becoming, because our inward character transformation profoundly influences the fruitfulness we produce outwardly."[21] That fruitfulness often never materializes, being lost in an ocean of fiery interventionism moved by instinct. Bastiat said, "Destruction is not profitable."[22] Not in the world of instinct. If you have a food distribution project whose aim is to provide more and more, what do you need for your budget to grow, more hungry people or less? In that world, destruction pays.

[21] See Tom Nelson, *The Economics of Brotherly Love: Investing in Your Community's Compassion and Capacity* (Downers Grove, IL: IVP Books, 2007), 53.

[22] Bastiat, "What is Seen and What Is Not Seen, or Political Economy in One Lesson," 406.

3

Religion and Reason

Over the course of human history, the initial reliance on instinct became less tenable. It is not that easy to ascertain a course of action when men have more developed needs within societies more complex than the herd. We live now in a space between instinct and reason, reflection and inclination. As Hayek surmises, "Mankind achieved civilization by developing and learning to follow rules (first in territorial tribes and then over broader reaches) that often forbade him to do what his instincts demanded, and no longer depended on a common perception of events."[1] It turns out that there was another herald, another messenger with something to say about the affairs of men. This herald, however, was coming from within the human heart. In effect, civilization evolved as men gathered and questioned. They began to reflect on things beyond the immediate dictates of appetite. The herald was reason. Interestingly, the religious nature of man was aligned with reason *from the beginning*.

For a long time, anthropologists assumed that religion evolved as a useful instrument to solve the social problems of clans. As hunter-gatherers encamped and settled, they began to create small, tight-knit village communities and, by 1200 BC, there were developed cities throughout the world. The members of small groups then conceived of gods that looked out for their welfare, and religion provided a structure and stability to the developing villages, tribes, cities, and civilizations. Once villages emerged and nomadic bands settled down, more complex problems and aims arose.

[1] Hayek, *Fatal Conceit*, 12.

Only then earlier religious practices such as burying the dead evolved into a common unifying vision of tribal religious practices. Religion, so goes the theory, assisted in the development of social cohesion, with leaders seen as having a special connection with the gods who manifested themselves in nature.

However, new insights suggest that religion existed prior to and brought about civilization, and not the other way around. As Charles C. Mann tells us, "There is evidence that organized religion could have come before the rise of agriculture and other aspects of civilization. It suggests that the human impulse to gather for sacred rituals arose as humans shifted from seeing themselves as part of the natural world to seeking mastery over it."[2] This view is consistent with the proposition that, embedded within the fabric of humanity, there was a capacity to transcend *from the beginning*. From the outset, when dust was made into man, there was this capacity to go beyond the proximate instincts of survival to ponder and question, to reason about the ultimacy of existence, and to master his environment as a steward of creation and a creator of new things—even if the full realization and actualization of this capacity occurred gradually.

Natural Law

It is not until the advent of Christianity that we see a more careful exploration of reason as another herald of insight into human action. Christian thinkers defined natural law as *lex indita*, a law imprinted in our being by God. Thomas Aquinas offered the better-known classical definition of natural law: the "participation in the eternal law by the rational creature."[3] Aquinas saw our rational nature as providing "the rule and measure of human acts."[4] In the Thomistic tradition, the eternal law is the highest law that expresses God's plan of order in his mind for the entire universe. Human beings possess an imprint of that plan within them, ordering us toward certain ends. Since that is the case, our behavior must conform to our rational nature and pursue certain things, certain goods. Moral law derives from the nature of human

---

[2] Charles C. Mann, "The Birth of Religion," *The Revealer*, June 1, 2011, https://therevealer.org/the-birth-of-religion/.

[3] Aquinas, *Summa Theologica*, I-II q. 91 a. 2; see also q. 93 a. 6.

[4] Aquinas, *Summa Theologica*, I-II, q. 90, a. 1.

beings as human.[5] There are three centers of attention when we reflect on human action: an order in the human mind, an order in nature, and an order in the divine mind. Harmonizing the three is important to understanding the full scope of human action.

As there are certain goods we must pursue and certain actions we must shun to attain fulfillment, men are moral beings. That is, our actions have external consequences within our social context and internal consequences within our very beings. When *homo sapiens* came into being, human beings became moral entities; that is, they discovered the demands of a greater order of things that instinct could not satisfy. An existential call, with its demands and angst, came into being with them. Human affairs exist along the lines of persistence and existential change, instinct *and* reasoning.

With this quantum leap in the beginning (Genesis 1:1) came a new set of problems to be solved. In a sense, we must thank God that such is the case, as that angst and those problems involve surprise and wonder, an existence that speaks of a deeper human need. We long for encounter and participation. It is essential to understand that every person we encounter is a moral being, capable of acting for himself. If not, we reduce natural law to mere biological necessity, which sends us back to instinct. We reduce the person to the boring examination of organic processes.

What does it mean to say that through the natural law we *participate* in the moral law of God? We find the origin of the notion of participation in Neoplatonic metaphysics. In Neoplatonism there is a mysterious way by which a lower order of being shares with a higher order. In Christian theology we refer to this sharing as being in the image and likeness of God. That participation goes beyond physical states of affairs or mental constructs created by us; that is, it is not a physical necessity. We participate in the eternal law via our intellect and all our "natural inclinations," including the biological, psychological, intellectual, and spiritual inclinations. Biological processes are included, but they do not exhaust our participation in the moral law of God.[6] Yet, those who want to help the poor tend to act as if all they need is intuition to fulfill authentic human needs. If they have the inner inclination

[5] See Kenneth Einer Himma, *Natural Law*, Internet Encyclopedia of Philosophy, accessed January 23, 2024, https://iep.utm.edu/natlaw/.

[6] See Robert Kraynak, "The Natural Law Jurisprudence of Russell Hittinger," *The Imaginative Conservative*, March 24, 2017, https://theimaginativeconservative.org/2017/03/natural-law-jurisprudence-russell-hittinger-robert-kraynak.html.

to help and can identify certain needs, they mobilize. Because they "know" by instinct what the poor need, they move into action without much reflection. It is as if primitive instinct is supposed to reign over reason and reflection. Reflecting on needs beyond such urgent desires ends up being seen as an excuse to not do what we need to do in the urgency of the now. Our approach mirrors our attitude toward nonhuman life, with its biologistic urges and classification of needs. If we already know what people need (they need food and shelter, just like my pet), what are we waiting for? We seem to reject the fact that, as Hayek pointed out, "restraints on instinctual demands serve to coordinate the activities of larger numbers."[7] But more importantly, we ignore the fact that authentic human life is more than biological existence, that human beings are more than mouths to be fed, bodies to be clothed, and problems to be solved. Our society is not made of small roving bands of hominids looking to satisfy the next immediate urge. Even when serving small numbers of people, we must remember that in transcending the early reign of instinct we discovered the reign of reason and what is asked of us is deeper.

This problem is more important when Christians are the ones engaged in activities with the poor. When Christian charity is informed by instinct, by our "good intentions" without much reflection on ultimate ends, we can forget that the very emergence of religion as such reflected a rejection of purely instinctual pondering. There is a betrayal of authentic Christian service when we prefer the facile transactional system of filling every hole of need without regard to a serious consideration of deeper and authentic human needs.

When we succumb to the dreadful temptation of reducing human needs to biological needs we run the risk of missing the great mystery of man. Possibly primitive hominoids were guided strictly by concrete and immediate needs, and coordination of aims was simple and easily discernible.[8] Modes of cooperation depending heavily on necessity, solidarity, and altruism

[7] Hayek, *Fatal Conceit*, 13.

[8] My reference here is not an embrace or a rejection of any scientific theory of origins. The point also obtains with a more literalistic reading of Genesis.

developed among members of small clans and these modes sufficed. But human beings have a built-in urge for transcendence, and reason emerged as the herald of more than desire-satisfaction. *Instinctual animalism* gave rise to *rational animalism*. Even on such purely theoretical evolutionary terms, which the reader need not accept, we can see that the satisfaction of purely biological needs is not the essence of authentic human life in the context of the development of higher types of human society.

Wealth Creation

If poverty-alleviation organizations were to begin with the right questions, instead of the right feelings or a ready-made script providing answers, the exercise would prove fruitful. One of those questions is *how to create wealth*.

The question of wealth creation takes us back to the great marginalist revolution of the 1870s. In the decades prior to that date, the industrial revolution was in the full force of its initial stages. Karl Marx observed those stages while he developed his theories living in England. He was correct in stating that wealth was growing and concentrating in the hands of the rich while the incomes of the workers or *proletarians* did not keep pace.[9] Marx projected an imminent global centralization of capital in the hands of fewer and fewer owners through expansionary cycles. This seemed unjust as, after all, of the three factors of production recognized initially by the classical economists (land, for which rents are paid; labor, for which wages are paid; and capital, for which interest is paid) only labor was the source of economic value. Although value was produced by the worker, *surplus value*

[9] See, for example, Karl Marx, *Capital*, vol. 1, sec. 5, Marx/Engels Library, https://www.marxists.org/archive/marx/works/1867-c1/ch25.htm#S5a.

The term *proletarian* in Marxist theory refers to the class of industrial revolution factory workers who sell their labor but do not own the means of production. They were so poor that their only possession was said to be their children, or *prole*. These were differentiated from other oppressed classes, such as peasants or farmers living in the countryside as well as the *lumpenproletariat,* a class consisting of beggars, thieves, prostitutes, and all sorts of marginalized people living in the outskirts of the great industrial revolution centers.

went to the capitalist.[10] The capitalist pays the worker a subsistence wage, far below the value of the labor the worker adds to the goods he produces.[11]

In developing his understanding of labor and the value of goods, Marx was following the classical economic Labor Theory of Value (LTV), mostly associated with David Ricardo but with precursors going all the way back to John Locke.[12] Marx believed that what he was observing in the 1830s and 40s was the maturity of capitalism, its entire cyclical structure. This maturity revealed its Achilles' heel, an inability to prevent the concentration of capital at one extreme of society while the masses at the other extreme earned less and less, with an accompanying vacuum in between. This *alienation*, as economist Hernando de Soto puts it, was a "fertile field for class confrontation."[13] The worker, whose labor is stolen, sees himself

---

[10] Surplus value in Marxian theory arises when the industrialist pays the worker less than the value that his labor has added to the goods he produces. The compensation that the worker receives, however, is insubstantial, mere crumbs to enable him barely to subsist (a notion derived from David Ricardo's "Iron Law of Wages," which proposed that real wages tend to gravitate toward a minimum subsistence wage), and only a meager portion of the total worth of the worker's labor. The uncompensated portion is called "surplus labor," and the value it produces is called "surplus value." Capitalism is exploitative, Marx believed, because the capitalist confiscates surplus value, which becomes his profit.

[11] "Socially necessary labor" is the total work required to produce a good or render a service. It follows that if the worker is the one who adds this element, which determines the value of a good, then surplus value belongs to him.

[12] The Labor Theory of Value (LTV) held that an item's value derives from the work used to produce it and not from its ability to satisfy human needs and wants. In other words, the economic value of a good is determined by the total amount of "socially necessary labor" required to produce it. It follows that the value is objective. Fixed and variable costs are involved in calculating the objective value in the production of goods or services. LTV is associated with classicists such as Adam Smith, David Ricardo, and later, Karl Marx.

[13] *Alienation* is the English word for two German terms: *Entfremdung* (estrangement) and *Entäußerung* (externalization), whose origins reside in Hegel's philosophy, specifically in his book *Phenomenology of Spirit*. Karl Marx, however, is the one who popularized the term in his manuscripts of 1844. In Marx, the proletarian is first alienated from the fruit of his labor and the worker becomes merely a factor of production. See Allen W. Wood, "Alienation," *Routledge Encyclopedia of Philosophy*, 1998 https://www.rep.routledge.com/articles/thematic/alienation/v-1

objectified or commoditized as a mere factor of production, a process called reification in Marxist theory.[14]

We should not underestimate the power of Marx's narrative. It provides the poor with a very tangible enemy and a worthy cause promising relief from their condition. The whole capitalist system is based on theft. The worker is commoditized as merely another factor of production and his wealth is stolen. Behind this theory we can find the "utopian syndrome," which leads to extremism in solving human problems by finding a comprehensive and ultimate solution. Once this all-embracing solution is discovered, activism is in essence pursuit of its actualization. The syndrome can take different variants, from the "introjective," where the adherent to the solution, recognizing how daunting and unattainable it is, withdraws from engaging life, to the "projective," by which one assumes a righteous stance and missionary purpose. In utopianism the cause becomes reality and the premises sustaining it cannot be false.[15]

At the turn of the1870s, however, the LTV was challenged by a group of economists. Carl Menger in Austria, Stanley Jevons in England, and Léon Walras in France, working independently, developed the Theory of Marginal Utility.[16] What they discovered challenged the idea that value resides strictly in the labor applied to produce a good. These and other nineteenth-century economists realized that price was in part determined by utility—that is, by the capacity of a good to satisfy a consumer's needs and desires.[17] Why is this important in the question of poverty alleviation? If the value of goods is subjective, the value resides in that which satisfies a human need, regardless of the costs of production or the labor needed

---

Hernando de Soto, *The Mystery of Capital: Why Capitalism Triumphs in the West and Fails Everywhere Else* (New York: Basic Books, 2000), 212.

[14] See Titus Stahl, "Georg [György] Lukács," *Stanford Encyclopedia of Philosophy* (Winter 2023 Edition), ed. Edward N. Zalta and Uri Nodelman, https://plato.stanford.edu/archives/win2023/entries/lukacs/.

[15] See Paul Watzlawick, John Weakland, and Richard Fisch, *Change: Principles of Problem Formation and Problem Solving* (New York: W. W. Norton, 1974), chap. 5.

[16] The "revolution" was spearheaded by this marginalist school between 1871 and 1874, with the publications of Menger's *The Principles of Pure Economics*, Jevons's *The Theory of Political Economy*, and Walras's *Elements of Pure Economics*.

[17] See Editors, "Marginal Utility," *Britannica*, March 20, 2016, https://www.britannica.com/money/topic/marginal-utility.

to produce goods.[18] In other words, the value of a good is to be discerned phenomenologically. Our consciousness is involved, and value relates to how an object appears to the subject. Our lived experience and appreciation of the relative worth of things is essential in determining value—value is in the eye of the beholder. Phenomenology is an account of subjective experience, of "worldly things considered in a certain way."[19] Max Borders furnishes a good personal example of subjective value:

> I was living in an apartment complex with a coin laundry. One day, when I put the quarters in to dry the laundry, I found myself $0.25 short. I was in a hurry. I couldn't wear my sweats to dinner. I needed clean, dry slacks. Fortunately, a man with a basketful of whites and a Ziploc bag, quarters jingling, wandered into the laundry room. I fished a dollar bill from my pocket.
>
> "Excuse me, sir," I said. "Would you take a dollar for one of those quarters?" He smiled. "Sure, no problem." At that time, in that context, from my perspective, his quarter was worth at least a dollar to me. That afternoon I wore clean, dry pants. Could I have made a better choice? And, if so, by whose lights? Certainly not mine.[20]

We must use reason and insight to search our environment and discern the needs of others, in order to satisfy those needs. If we are to sell products or offer a service, we must become *other-regarding*. The marginalists had this insight, and with it they discovered another factor of production: *the entrepreneur*—the one who searches the horizon of human wants and needs and creates (and risks) with his mind.[21] Value goes his way if he

---

[18] See William Luckey, *Wealth Creation: The Solution to Poverty* (Grand Rapids, MI: Acton Institute, 2017), chap. 6.

[19] David Woodruff Smith, "Phenomenology," *Stanford Encyclopedia of Philosophy*, ed. Edward N. Zalta, December 16, 2013, https://plato.stanford.edu/entries/phenomenology/.

[20] See Max Borders, "Subjective Value," *Foundation for Economic Education*, October 24, 2012, https://fee.org/articles/subjective-value/. Max Borders is also cofounder of the Voice & Exit event and former editor at the Foundation for Economic Education (FEE).

[21] The word *entrepreneur* is found as early as the thirteenth century, with a French word referring to undertaking a task, *entreprendre.* By the sixteenth century it had come to mean someone who undertakes a business project or speculation. In the nineteenth century, French economist Jean-Baptiste Say described the entrepreneur

sends subjective value in the direction of his fellow human beings. This is why socialism cannot work, as it disregards the value of the entrepreneur. This is also why many charity initiatives fail: they miss the creative power of entrepreneurial initiative. There is no more important task than to side with those in poor communities searching for the subjective value of things to satisfy their own communities' needs. In a sense, failing to recognize the entrepreneur, both in socialism and in bad interventionist charity, is an anthropological error. This observation is also that of Pope John Paul II in *Centesimus Annus*: "The fundamental error of socialism is anthropological in nature. Socialism considers the individual person simply as an element, a molecule within the social organism, so that the good of the individual is completely subordinated to the functioning of the socio-economic mechanism."[22]

Marx was a prisoner of his time. He equated an initial phase of the industrial revolution with its essential nature. As de Soto states, "Much of Marx's thought is outdated because the situation today is not the same as in Marx's Europe."[23] The early stages of industrial revolution were attended by the need to build fixed capital of the needed factories, raw materials extraction, machinery, transportation channels, and other elements necessary for production. At the time, only a few people had the wealth to finance such an enterprise, and yet their wealth was also fixed, as they could not initially generate profits from fixed capital. Fixed capital investment grew at the expense of circulating capital, the kind of capital that is gained through market activity of buying and selling products. Salaries remained low and even depressed initially, as only those who invested more in fixed capital had an opportunity to survive early competition. The industrialist who decided to raise salaries too early would have less to invest in the fixed capital necessary for production, leading to his eventual elimination from the market and leaving workers unemployed. Those who invested more in fixed capital early on produced more and made workers more productive, thus surviving the first stages of industrial revolution. As labor became more

---

as one who "shifts economic resources out of an area of lower and into an area of higher productivity and greater yield." He is the only early classical economist to concede importance to the entrepreneur in economic theory. See the chapter on Say in Gilbert Faccarello, ed., *Studies in the History of French Political Economy* (London: Routledge, 1998).

[22] John Paul II, *Centesimus Annus*, §13.

[23] Soto, *Mystery of Capital*, 216.

productive and fixed capital was created, costs began to fall, productivity increased, and so did circulatory capital, that is, profits.

At this juncture, the industrial revolution entered a different stage, with a new set of incentives and requirements. These movements were independent of the goodwill of the capitalist. Salaries began to grow as those who survived the initial stages by investing more in fixed capital and less in paying salaries, made better products, gained greater earnings, and expanded their enterprises. Competition moved toward getting more skilled workers. At this stage, we also see the advent of new economic actors entering the market. By the second half of the nineteenth century in England we see salaries increase, with a corresponding bettering of the lives of workers. The gap between the extremes began to be filled from the ranks of the workers, and the beginnings of a middle class were evident. This was something that Marx said could not happen. Revolution was supposed to come, as society alienated more and more. Marx, and many early economists, missed the entrepreneur and how ideas and insight could produce wealth.

As the German economist Wilhelm Röpke put it, the market economy offers challenges and variety, and "its stress on individual action and responsibility, and its elementary freedoms, is still the source of powerful forces counteracting the boredom of mass society and industrial life which are common to both capitalism and socialism." The problems of "enmassment"—the tendency of modern society to subsume the individual within mass institutions and movements—are not unique to capitalism. Yet, in the socialist paradigm there is no escape valve. Its boredom is, in Röpke's view, "irresistible," as its thrust toward centralization and top-down control "blunts all the instincts of independence and responsibility."[24] To foster a poverty-alleviation project built on a glorious economic and anthropological vision that counters the boredom of existence is worth trying.

In the process of expanding opportunity an important element for economic success is the foundation of a legal system that defends private property and extends property rights. Potential capital eventually stopped being the privilege of the few, and after Marx's time the West created a legal framework providing expanded access to property and the tools of production. Yet, around the world, the poor often live in extra-legal circumstances that prevent them from entering the world of wealth creation. They have things but not capital. Fighting for a rule of law that benefits them is

[24] Wilhelm Röpke, *A Humane Economy*, 3rd ed. (Wilmington, DE: ISI Books, 1998), 87.

a sacred task. In America, there are still certain legal constraints that need attention, but for the most part our problem is that we gravitate toward the redistribution of goods and services rather than promoting the productive activity of individuals with ideas. Long ago, Leonard E. Read told us of an important lesson we ought to heed: "Leave all creative energies uninhibited. Merely organize society to act in harmony with this lesson."[25] The best direct intervention is usually nonintervention.

Even a religiously agnostic thinker such as Hayek understood that in the development of men as such there was a leap of consciousness that transcended instinct and biology into the realm of reason and economic activity. He understood that men created civilization and with it rules of conduct "handed on by tradition, teaching and imitation, rather than by instinct, and largely consisting of prohibitions (shalt not's) that designate adjustable domains for individual decisions.... Mankind achieved civilization by developing and learning to follow rules ... that often forbade him what his instincts demanded.... These rules in effect constituting a new and different morality..."[26]

It follows that to treat human beings as truly human we must transcend transactional systems of care and institutional approaches informed by bureaucracy by going back to a tradition of service and rules of conduct that places the person at the center. We must embrace new approaches that reflect the human condition as it is in the state of civilization. How easy it is to forget these important lessons when we mobilize ourselves to intervene in the lives of others.

TREATING PEOPLE AS PERSONS

The great Christian tradition of natural law can assist us in moving in the direction of respecting the full scope of human existence. It is a law written in our hearts and guiding us in acting rightly. It is that broader order of Divine Providence that legal philosopher Russell Hittinger calls "the first grace of God." It is a law that was sewn into the fabric of human existence

[25] See Lawrence E. Read, *I, Pencil* (1958; repr., New York: Foundation for Economic Education, 2008), 11.

[26] Hayek, *Fatal Conceit*, 12.

in advance of the coming of Christ (*in adventum Christi*).[27] Natural law is properly applied to the case of human beings because we have reason and free will. It is our nature as humans to direct ourselves toward our proper ends, which we discover by reasoning about what is best for us and for others to achieve the end to which our nature inclines. Both the giver or helper and the recipient of magnanimity and support are harmed by actions missing the mark of the full scope of our humanity when we let instinct reign over reason.

Are we headed toward a contradiction? After all, this book is in part informed by the belief that every person is an individual with his or her own needs, discernible only in close and meaningful encounters with a few people at a time. If it is only in close encounters with small bands of people that we can find what others truly need, isn't instinct preferable? Could it be that just a sincere and dedicated desire to help suffices, without further discernment of needs?

The avoidance of contradiction comes in the understanding of every individual as *a person*. What is needed is anthropology that transcends extremes. In other words, the enemy is *reductionism*. Reductionism appears at both extremes of the question of what it means to be human: the atomistic and the communistic. The reductionism we see in individualistic social philosophy reduces the person to biological aspects of the self, constrained by the animal needs of the species. Individuals are seen as isolated or self-contained beings, a view leading to amoral approaches to meeting needs, with an emphasis on wants instead of duties and utility instead of ultimate purpose.[28] This simplistic reductionism is associated with Thomas Hobbes and eliminates morality from human life by seeing individuals as prisoners of impersonal forces in nature outside their control. Nothing is

---

[27] See Russell Hittinger, *The First Grace: Rediscovering the Natural Law in a Post-Christian World* (Wilmington, DE: ISI, 2003), xi–xii. The phrase "first grace of God" originates in a letter of recantation by a presbyter named Lucidus in the fifth century. Lucidus rejected some of his previous views concerning the condition of human existence after the fall, which had been condemned by the Council of Arles in 473. Arles was trying the defend a synthesis between human freedom and total predestination. Freedom was not totally extinguished but wounded and God had not completely removed his providence from humanity. God had written his law in every human heart, thus providing for the whole human race a way to himself.

[28] Patricia Donohue-White et. al., *Human Nature and the Discipline of Economics* (Lanham, MD: Lexington Books, 2002), 72–73.

up to us, but the isolated individual reigns, nonetheless. Atomism offers a type of naturalistic immanentism that sees the individual as merely an epiphenomenon of nature itself.

If we cannot reason toward moral norms, we cannot be directed toward human flourishing by acquiring and developing virtue, as we cannot acquire a knowledge of the proper ends of man to be actualized by free acts of choosing what is truly good. All that lies before us is passion. The Scottish Enlightenment thinker David Hume is probably the one who best articulated a disconnect between reason and free will, leaving the passions at the helm, when he stated, "Reason is and ought to be the slave of the passions and may never pretend to any other than to serve and obey them."[29] We will see how every reductionist theory impedes the rational discernment of moral norms and principles of human action that can assist us in discovering how to help people beyond the mere satisfaction of biological needs. In the case of Hume, our reason only has instrumental or utilitarian power to help us get what our appetites desire.

Is this applicable to the care of the poor? Yes. Emotions are predominant in many actions we undertake on behalf of the poor. How many people speak of helping others—but not in their own neighborhood? Emotionally, we retreat from the scenario of suffering humanity. We do not want the poor to come too close; closeness is scary, threatening. We want the facile institutionalization of care that comforts our consciences and avoids the smells. Often, we place a Christmas tree in the back of our churches and there are names and items written on hanging pieces of paper. Bureaucracies are created, labeled "ministries," and commissioned to grab the shiny bike we brought on Sunday and bring it to a poor child who remains a stranger, a member of a family we never met or want to meet. A sincere and necessary desire to help remains, but the passions win.

What does loving our neighbor require? What is it supposed to look like? Is the message of service an interruption in our daily lives, or is it integral to it? If it is integral to our lives, we will go beyond what happens at church and look deeply at our very lives, at home and in the marketplace. Emotive reductionism sees charity as our obligation in one corner of our lives, on Sundays, volunteering in ministry, going on a mission trip, donating to some campaign our church initiated. Christian giving of this kind is atomistic in the sense that it segregates us into isolated compartments of social existence.

[29] David Hume, *A Treatise of Human Nature*, ed. L. A. Selby Bigge (Oxford: Oxford University Press, 1946), bk. 2, pt. 3, sec. 3.

Yet, living a life of service must transcend and imbue all our lives and the intersecting circles of exchange that inform it.

Such an integrated view of service and love will help us discover which activities are not consistent with authentic flourishing, as we develop habits of being within all those circles. Reflecting on how we love at home will assist us in detecting when the practices of our ministries are not fully consistent with authentic compassion. When we reflect on how we act in the marketplace, we also discover that the best engagement there is personal, relational, and focused on being productive. Have you thought about how it was possible for the members of the church in Jerusalem to bring anything and place it at the feet of the apostles? Were they good at making profit or careless about it? (Acts 2:44; 4:42–47)[30] Have you noticed that the Samaritan was able to pay for the stranger's care in abundance? Having the economic capacity to assist others must motivate us to engage in productive activity in an economic system that encourages enterprise (Luke 10:25–37).[31] It should stress our subsidiary role as we collaborate with those within poor communities who also want to put their economic subjectivity in motion.

There is one crucial reason for the greatness of enterprise, especially as a solution to poverty. That reason lies in what George Gilder calls the main virtue of enterprise, *the virtue of surprise*. He says, "Entrepreneurship is the launching of surprises. The process of wealth creation is offensive to levelers and planners because it yields mountains of new wealth in ways that could not possibly be planned. But unpredictability is fundamental to free human enterprise."[32] Human agency is about expectations, visions, risk, unpredictability, opportunity, insight, the angst of expectation, and creativity. Philosopher Michael Novak put it like this:

> What is the virtue of enterprise? Like any other virtue, it is a habit or disposition—in this case, a disposition of both the intellect and the will. It is a disposition, first, to notice, to gain insight into, to discover something that others unseeingly pass by. It is a disposition, second,

[30] For an insightful examination of these passages, see Art Lindsley, "Does Acts 2–5 Teach Socialism?" *Institute for Faith, Work & and Economics*, July 17, 2012, https://tifwe.org/does-acts-2-5-teach-socialism/.

[31] See Tom Nelson, *Economics of Brotherly Love*, 13–16.

[32] See George Gilder, "Unleash the Mind," Discovery Institute, August 13, 2012, https://www.discovery.org/a/19401/.

> to take risks … and to begin making happen what the agent sees as at least a possibility.[33]

In contrast, the dependency induced by interventionism tends to be safe, stale, predictable, boredom-inducing, and ends up becoming self-focused instead of thriving in authentic community. I will never forget the day I was sitting at my ministry desk seeing the same lines of people coming for the crumbs I had for them. It dawned on me that the younger families in line consisted of the children of the families that for a long time had come for food. I was a poverty manager, helping people remain fed but still in the atrophied anomie of dependency. If we inject the element of surprise into the systems we create to attend to the needs of the poor, people will prosper. But it seems more appealing to discuss income inequality and structures and systems. Not that such discussion ought to be avoided, but we must first see the poor in a new light and see human beings as capable of applying intelligence and effort in the natural state of nature and recreate it in view of satisfying their needs and the needs of others. Human beings were made to interact and exchange, and they are situated in spontaneous orders we call markets.

PROMOTING ENTERPRISE

This is why societies that protect elements such as property rights and facilitate enterprise elevate the living standards of the poor. As economists Victor Claar and Robin Klay explain in *Economics in Christian Perspective*, "Societies built on a foundation of political democracy, free markets, and strong moral and cultural institutions respect the freedom of human agency and provide an especially fertile environment for human flourishing under God's care."[34] In a world of limited resources, a world of scarcity, the unleashing of the full scope of the capacities of the poor is what matters most. Because all resources are scarce, the world of invention is crucial, and that impregnates society with *dynamism*. As Father Robert Sirico puts it, if you want to help the poor, start a business, engage in free market activity. "There will always be a need for charity," he writes. "But the one thing that is absolutely proven to raise people out of poverty isn't charity or foreign

---

[33] Novak, *Business as a Calling*, 82.

[34] See Victor V. Claar and Robin J. Klay, *Economics in Christian Perspective: Theory, Policy and Life Choices* (Downers Grove, IL: IVP Academic, 2007), 24.

aid; it's the free market, and especially business that calls on the capacity of the poor to create wealth, instead of only addressing their needs."[35]

Obviating the capacities of the poor incentivizes a static existence and the need to hoard in search of security. This type of risk aversion promotes activism more than activity. That is, politics triumphs over a moral vision of the person as an engine of economic prosperity. There isn't a conspiracy of forces at the root of one's poverty that must be fixed by intervention. Human systems will always need to be revised, because our imperfection often translates into the frameworks we create. However, in America, there is enough space for human agency to prevent the victim-victimizer outlook from creating the narrative that some culprits have a hold on the destiny of the poor. We must defend the free market, engage it, and assist those trying to do the same in poor communities. Instead of stewards of their safety hammock, let's become supporters of their enterprising spirit. *We must recapture our subjectivity, our individuality amid loving communities, from the clutches of collectivism.*

As the suppression of enterprise takes a hold, attention shifts toward equalizing via confiscatory policy instead of human activity in a dynamic environment of risk and possibilities. Yes, there are structures and institutions that must at times be challenged. What is often challenged, however, is any policy questioning the preeminence of interventionism. We fight "the power" in the cause of expanding the power of the state, in the name of justice and compassion. Established structures often impede the dynamism embedded in the market economy. It is not uncommon to see a three-headed monster embracing the activism that stifles market dynamism: the bureaucracies of the state, big corporations that benefit from big government, and big charities that receive a good slice of the loot.

As Father Sirico states, it is often difficult to make a case for the morality of the market and for the dynamism and surprise of risk, considering the seemingly obvious good we often accomplish through our interventions.[36] The task seems heretical to those invested in the present system. However, the poor themselves often respond positively to the challenge, even though their quest for subjectivity is quenched by our *interventionism of despair*, giving comfort to a *politics of despair*. Interventionism uses the despair those in charity work perceive and amplifies the message, telling people to

[35] Robert Sirico, *Defending the Free Market: The Moral Case for a Free Economy* (Washington, DC: Regnery, 2012), 45.

[36] Sirico, *Defending the Free Market*, 46–47.

stay put and fight against the very dynamism that can become their greatest resource. *Do not blame the poor for their poverty.* Blame these systems of despair.

The poor, again, are the first to agree with these words from economist Anne Bradley: "If I work harder, become more innovative, and earn a greater income through hard work and discipline, I benefit without harming anyone."[37] A call to responsibility is more often than not perceived as an affront to the poor, as if we are saying the poor are irresponsible. It is in reality an affirmation of the voice of the poor and a determination to protect or create dynamic systems where the poor have a space for personal engagement. That call might involve removing legal impediments to enterprise, easing onerous regulations, or investing in their enterprising ideas. Whatever the practical application is, the commitment must be to create dynamic environments for dynamic beings.

[37] See Anne R. Bradley, "Why Does Income Inequality Exist? An Economic and Biblical Explanation," in *For the Least of These*, 160.

4

Avoiding False Ideas

We cannot escape the fact that all action is individual action, and economists accept a sort of methodological individualism in their examination of human action.[1] Yet, the idea that we are islands unto ourselves—ontological individualism—is false. As the authors of *The Free Person and the Free Economy* tell us, "Membership in a community of persons … remains as essential to the nature of a healthy human being as does the

[1] Karl Popper defined methodological individualism as "the doctrine that all social phenomena, and especially the functioning of all social institutions, should always be understood as resulting from the decisions, actions, attitudes, etc., of human individuals, and that we should never be satisfied by an explanation in terms of so-called 'collectives.'" Karl Popper, *The Open Society and Its Enemies*, vol. 2 (London: Routledge and Kegan Paul, 1945), 91. Ludwig von Mises, according to Geoffrey Hodgson, "provides no clear definition of the term and includes statements such as: 'The hangman, not the state, executes a criminal.… For a social collective has no existence and reality outside of the individual members' actions. The life of a collective is lived in the actions of individuals constituting its body.… There is no substratum of society other than the actions of individuals.'" Geoffrey M. Hodgson, "Meanings of Methodological Individualism,'" *Journal of Economic Methodology* 14, no. 2 (June 2007): 211–26 (quote at p. 3 of pdf version), https://uhra.herts.ac.uk/bitstream/handle/2299/2795/900694.pdf%3Bjsessionid%3D7BCF17A9DC8940C0D41DE875171261E2?sequence%3D1.

capacity to take appropriate individual action."[2] It is important to note that serious defenders of free-market economics reject atomism.[3] Ludwig von Mises contends that free markets are communities of social cooperation:

> The market economy is the social system of the division of labor under private ownership of the means of production. Everybody acts on his own behalf; but everybody's actions aim at the satisfaction of other people's needs as well as at the satisfaction of his own. Everybody in acting serves his fellow citizens. Everybody, on the other hand, is served by his fellow citizens. Everybody is both a means and an end in himself, an ultimate end for himself and a means to other people in their endeavors to attain their own ends.[4]

If we reduce our attention to a narrow set of people to avoid the difficulties of attending to the needs of too many but still misunderstand the social nature of the person, we end up reducing the person to a specimen of some very general category. A specimen is an example of a larger type, a product or commodity, a sample for testing the substance of the whole. This often happens when we intervene in the lives of people without regard to their existential reality, seeing only that "they are human beings." That is, they possess certain general characteristics or potentialities intrinsic to every human being. Limiting our attention to intrinsic aspects of the self allows us to find easier ways to serve, as we can ascertain needs across the board of the general designation "human." Don't tell me about your existential needs, which are too complex. But I do know you need food, because all humans need food.

---

[2] Anthony Santelli Jr. et el., *The Free Economy and the Free Person: A Personalist View of Market Economics* (Lanham, MD: Lexington Books, 2002), 68.

[3] See for example, Friedrich von Hayek, *Individualism and Economic Order* (London: Routledge & Kagan Paul, 1949), 6; Adam Smith said, "In civilized society, man stands at all times in need of the cooperation and assistance of great multitudes, while his whole life is scarce sufficient to gain the friendship of a few persons." See Adam Smith, *The Wealth of Nations*, 1.2.2. James Buchanan also is on the side of the importance of community in free-market economics. He even proposed to change the name of economics or political economy to "symbiosis" to emphasize the importance of cooperation and exchange. See James Buchanan "What Should Economists Do?" S*outhern Economic Journal* 30 (1964): 213–222.

[4] Ludwig von Mises, *Human Action: A Treatise on Economics* (1949; repr. Auburn, AL: Mises Institute, 2008), 258.

Intrinsic dignity is a necessary component of our approach to every person we encounter. But the potentialities built into that dignity call for actualization. My intrinsic capacity to reason leads me to know and believe and accept certain things as true or false. It can lead people to ponder and envision, to be creative and act upon what they discern. That completes their dignity. Our volitional capacity to choose is actualized by acts of choice, for ill or good. The existential dignity of the person must not be avoided because it is easier to discern general needs.

Holism and Historicism

Reducing the person to a certain element is a theme explored carefully by the philosopher Karl Popper. His political philosophy showed how we frequently find ourselves between two great errors, *holism* and *historicism*.[5] What Popper means by holism is the tendency in social science to study society as a whole, as if it were an organism that transcends the individual members of society. When we attempt to explain social processes as wholes, we might be tempted to regulate the whole of social life through large-scale social planning. Planners imagine that they can lay bare the whole of human history and the segments of epochs through an evolutionary analysis of the whole.[6] What happens to the individual person? The person is obscured, his uniqueness questioned or merely ignored as unimportant to the analysis. This type of holism does not refer to taking into consideration all aspects of the self but to ignoring the self and focusing on the general category. In charity work, holism is depersonalizing, and depersonalization is a terrible error often committed in the name of benefiting those falling under a given social class, region, ethnicity, or race.

In a sense, holism is an attempt at creating "*neatness*," a system where everything runs smoothly because we have found the key to the whole. Our technocratic society is always looking for it. All we get with holism is a quest for institutional efficiency. Our bureaucracies of compassion must run like clockwork, even if they accomplish little. Popper's "open society," in contrast, is characterized by the exercise of the virtues of inventiveness

[5] For a thorough account of Popper's views on holism and historicism, see Karl Popper, *The Poverty of Historicism* (1957; repr., New York: Routledge, 1972).

[6] See Anthony O'Hare, *Karl Popper: Philosophy and Problems* (Cambridge: Cambridge University Press, 2010), 121–48.

and creativity in the pursuit of pragmatic solutions to social problems. There can be no "rational state" that runs like a well-oiled machine, with every individual part (people) functioning within some preordained sphere.[7]

The way we often approach poverty-alleviation processes is holistic. We focus on the problem, then the program, and at the end, possibly, the person. This hierarchization of service insists on process, data, quantifiable elements, "clients," and numbers. The individual person is seen through the assumptions filtered by a prism that illuminates the whole, and that whole is the general concept of poverty.

History, however, is like every life lived, mostly consisting of a series of unplanned events. It is utopian to dream of the possibility of total control of social situations, which often leads to totalitarianism.[8] This idea of the expanded capacity of the human mind and the macrosystems of society to impose solutions is a perennial temptation in poverty-alleviation efforts. When we say "the poor," we might think we are saying much and that the entire schema of poverty is one solved as a whole, via impersonal intervention. It misses the person with a name and a history and the individual capacity for self-realization.

A similar threat comes from historicism.[9] Historicism is the belief in an inevitable thrust of history, independent of human volition. This development follows certain principles embedded in the fabric of social existence, making history inexorable and necessary. The end of history and its various stages are determined by processes and informed by determined and inescapable elements. The best modern example of historicism is the dialectical materialism of Karl Marx. The link between holism and historicism is that holism holds that individuals are formed exhaustibly by the social groupings to which they belong, while historicism suggests that we can understand such a social grouping only in terms of the internal principles that determine its development.

[7] See Alan Haworth, "The Open Society Revisited," *Philosophy Now*, 2002, https://philosophynow.org/issues/38/The_Open_Society_Revisited.

[8] See Oseni Taiwo Afisi, "Karl Popper's Critical Rationalism and the Politics of Liberal Communitarianism" (PhD diss., University of Canterbury, 2015).

[9] See Karl Popper, *The Open Society and Its Enemies*, 5th ed., vol. 1 (Princeton: Princeton University Press, 1966); Karl Popper, *Conjectures and Refutations*, 5th ed. (London: Routledge and Kegan, 1989); William Gorton, "Karl Popper: Political Philosophy," Internet Encyclopedia of Philosophy, https://iep.utm.edu/popp-pol/.

Popper saw this view of history and historical examination as both theoretically problematic and socially dangerous. It ought to be clear that holism and historicism are linked. Holism reduces the person to the internal workings of general processes and the grouping of conditions and of people (poverty, the poor), and historicism posits the inevitability of what eventuates for these groups. The individual is a problem for both paradigms. When we see the poor through this two-headed, deterministic monster, controlling the poor can be justified both because we see them as indelibly marked by the label and because there is nothing else that we can expect from the merciless lottery of history. Their poverty is destiny, and our totalistic view of their treatment is the correct way to address it. The subjectivity of the poor is, after all, a mirage. For Popper, totalistic answers concerning the life of humans in history are "typically based upon historicist and holist presuppositions," even though "these presuppositions are fundamentally incoherent."[10]

Atomism

But there are other atomistic extremes that seem more frightening. These reject any general category (even that of human) as capable of telling us anything about authentic human needs. The reason is that these theories affirm that there is no such thing as human nature. As there is no essence or quiddity, there are no goods pertaining to the species in need of actualization. In such a case, it becomes impossible to speak of moral norms or actions toward developing the character of the person in a certain way, as there are no objective moral norms. All lifestyles and choices must be treated with *equal regard or respect*. In the case of those in need the gravitation shifts toward meeting certain human needs or providing certain services that appeal to any lifestyle. We must ask nothing from the poor, expect nothing, demand nothing—and provide everything. Under this type of reductionism, making moral choices concerning human behavior constitutes a form of oppression, because by definition they are impositions of a narrative by those with power over the poor.

A good example of this radical form of atomism can be found in the German idealist tradition of thinkers such as J. G. Fichte, F. W. J. Schelling, and Romantics such as Friedrich Schlegel and Friedrich Hölderlin, as they

[10] Stephen Horton, "Karl Popper," *Stanford Encyclopedia of Philosophy* (Winter 2023 Edition), ed. Edward N. Zalta and Uri Nodelman, https://plato.stanford.edu/archives/win2023/entries/popper/.

interpreted the transcendental idealism of Immanuel Kant.[11] Idealism confines "the real" to the mind and the world to the categories we create in our minds. We create both the meaning and the content of our experience. Things in themselves (*neumenon* in Greek and *Ding an sich* in German) are the creation of our minds; there is no content "out there," so to speak. Space, matter, and time are only subjective forms of human intuition that would not subsist in themselves without our intuition. Thus, human nature does not exist, as all that exists is the *geist*, or the ideas in our minds.

Idealism arises out of the Kantian synthesis. In his *Critique of Pure Reason* Kant tried to avoid the problems posited by the denial of the existence of a material world outside our minds. He believed that we only experience the appearance of the things outside of ourselves, but space, matter, and time are, at the same time, empirically real. Our experience of things is an experience of phenomena formed through deciphering images mediated through our senses. We do not have access to things in themselves but only to images. These images are then articulated and made intelligible by way of a sort of interpretive grid we possess, which Kant called *a priori forms of cognition*. This grid is made of concepts such as number, color, being, nonbeing, negation, causality, and others from which we generate an idea. Taking Kant's belief that we only have mediated knowledge of the world "out there," idealist thinkers took a step further. As the only direct and intuitive knowledge of reality we possess is that of our own ideas, they doubted the existence of a world outside our minds. This becomes the ultimate form of atomism, the problem of other minds, the aloneness of solipsism.[12]

We have very few ontological solipsists in the world, as the philosophical conclusions the theory provides are quite counterintuitive. Nonetheless, there are many *practical solipsists*, living as if they are the world's only inhabitants, caring only about their own affairs and their own satisfactions. People who truly do not care about the fate of the poor abound. They often

---

[11] For a thorough discussion of German idealism, see Robert Solomon and Kathleen Higgins, eds., *The Age of German Idealism* (New York: Routledge, 2003).

[12] See Anita Avramides, "Other Minds," *Stanford Encyclopedia of Philosophy* (Winter 2020 Edition), ed. Edward N. Zalta, https://plato.stanford.edu/archives/win2020/entries/other-minds/. In *Appearance and Reality* (1893) British idealist F. H. Bradley defines solipsism as follows: "I cannot transcend experience, and experience must be my experience. From this it follows that nothing beyond my self exists; for what is experience is its [the self's] states." See Editors, "Solipsism," *Britannica*, August 28, 2023, https://www.britannica.com/topic/solipsism.

instrumentalize the language of compassion if there is an advantage for them in the performance. Even in the church there are those so concerned with the life of heaven that they find the lives of those in need now to be a distraction from the only important thing.

There is also the practical solipsism of some large organizations that bypass the basic communities and intervene in the lives of people in poor communities from afar, as foreigners or invaders, because they have the resources. Ignoring the principle of affiliation, which calls for action through existing basic communities to which the poor already belong, they isolate the poor from their context and absolve those who ought to be the ones with the primary task of supporting those in need. Why mend fences with those closer to the person in need if surrendered relationships can remain broken?

There are churches and organizations not interested in getting to know others also serving in these communities or afraid of the positive outcomes resulting from the work of others, afraid of losing support or losing church members. So they isolate themselves as if they are the only game in town. Then there is the practical solipsism of government interventionism, tying the individual in his community directly to a federal agency far away in Washington. Why bother listening to my pastor or my family members when a government check or benefit can become a reward for my poverty?

The Postmodern Delusion

Yet another reductionist philosophy appears to be taking hold of the collective consciousness. Since the 1960s a fundamental transformation in anthropology comes from the ruminations of *postmodernism*, which ironically offers a radical individualism in the social and sexual realm, mixed with a suffocating collectivism in the economic and political sphere.[13] Disillusionment about modernity and the prevalent alternatives to modern technological life brought about a nihilistic, pessimistic, and deeply skeptical response that questions everything. Postmodern theory affirms that there are no unifying narratives, objective truths, or the possibility of progress in human life. As Helen Pluckrose and James Lindsay put it, "Postmodernism raised such doubts about the structure of thought and society that it is ultimately a form of cynicism."[14] Cynicism is the destroyer of hope,

[13] For an excellent description of postmodernism, see Pluckrose and Lindsay, *Cynical Theories*, chaps. 1–2.

[14] Pluckrose and Lindsay, *Cynical Theories*, 22.

and hope is the sister of purpose. Cynical activity among those in poverty abounds, as if only a radical change of our entire society can lead to the great Valhalla of utopian "justice."

Today we have an urgent challenge to oppose this destructive, reductionist paradigm as it radically alters the foundations of our society in virtually every area of life. Cynicism about the possibility of reform gives rein to a very negative attitude toward service to the poor that has as its center *political activism*. If the whole social system is a false impression hiding an agenda to control and oppress, activities such as protesting in a way that destroys small businesses owned by people in the same poor neighborhoods the protestors claim to defend becomes an instance of courage and authentic support for those in poverty. Charity work of any kind becomes a distraction, a clever ploy to keep the oppressed away from developing the necessary consciousness for liberation. Many organizations join movements to gain a sense of being aware and possessing the right consciousness about "systemic oppression." They want to ally themselves with destructive forces in a quest for relevance.

How is it that postmodernism sends many into the realm of political activism? The two main areas of concern in postmodernism's paradigm are *knowledge* and *power*. Knowledge is questioned, even scientific knowledge. Everything in modern society is a simulation of the "real." French postmodernist Jean Baudrillard presented such skepticism as the despair of a society that lost the *original of existence* and only moves forward with *copies* or "simulacra" of things.[15] The postmodern analysis of society depicts our present order as incapable of offering any answers, promoting a loss of authenticity and fashioning an unstable self, wandering through a fog of false images while we entertain ourselves with technology and consumer society. The whole of the social arrangement is a subtle conspiracy of power affirmed by the control of narratives. We cannot identify the conspirators, but they are there. We know they exist because the results of cultural and institutional processes are the crumbs leading to their hiding place.[16]

---

[15] See Jean Baudrillard, *Simulacra and Simulation*, trans. Sheila Glaser (Ann Arbor: University of Michigan Press, 1994).

[16] This idea is now part of the federal government's policies. The Title VI Legal Manual of the Civil Rights Division of the US Justice Department addresses the use of disparate impact to "seek to ensure that programs accepting federal money are not administered in a way that perpetuates the repercussions of past discrimination." The way to ascertain discrimination is by investigating the outcomes of processes:

A *waning of affect* results from a social system that produces despondency. That is, there is a loss of interest and meaning in everything that exists and a need to launch at everything that we have been told is true. Nihilistic despair for the sake of nihilistic despair seems an appropriate response. In response to the purported conditions of modernity, the postmodern paradigm offered the following answers: (1) individual identity is a social construct; (2) morality is also a social construct and cannot be deduced from anything in the world itself; (3) everything in society must be "deconstructed"; (4) these views must be globalized, and everyone must conform to the new paradigm.[17] In a word, postmodernism offered revolutionary madness.

In postmodern theory, since moral norms are impositions of power through the control of the knowledge-validation process, any critique of a given culture or value is seen as a biased impossibility, as the one critiquing it cannot escape the strictures of his own culture. No moral view is superior, and ascertaining that a given value or action is reprehensible or avoidable is suspect. Those who belong to oppressive groups are prisoners of the worldview informing their group, and their assessments are to be judged through a political determination made by the oppressed. For example, a white, heterosexual, Christian male will reflect in his critique the bias of his identifying group, and at best he could become an ally or fellow traveler if he embraces the narrative of the oppressed. Postmodernism has no space for Christian compassion or even secular magnanimity, because both entail a narrative about man and society contrary to what it sees as real—there isn't a God whose commands we follow or knowledge of the good we can acquire by experiencing human action, following the wisdom of the past, or reasoning about *basic human goods*.[18]

"In a disparate impact case, the investigation focuses on the consequences of the recipient's practices, rather than the recipient's intent." If the outcome is unequal, then the process is discriminatory. See Section VII, Proving Discrimination-Disparate Impact, Civil Rights Division of the US Justice Department. https://www.justice.gov/crt/fcs/T6Manual7.

[17] Pluckrose and Lindsay, *Cynical Theories*, 26–29.

[18] Basic human goods are aspects of human well-being and flourishing whose pursuit is worthwhile. Pursuing them is the first principle of practical reason. We are reasonable, and human choices are rendered intelligible, when we pursue these goods. Philosopher John Finnis lists these goods as life itself, health, knowledge, play, beauty, friendship, reasonableness, and religion. See John Finnis, *Natural Law and Natural Rights*, cited in George, *In Defense of Natural Law*, 45.

If we accept the neo-Marxist/postmodern paradigm[19] contending that it is impossible to render judgements about various behaviors, the entire process of assisting those in need is rendered impossible, beyond the transfer of resources to certain classes or joining a political movement whose judgments must be embraced without complaint. In effect, the cynicism of postmodernism sees the entire process of affiliation, bonding, categorization, and discernment as oppressive. Any decision concerning helping those in need after a process of determination must be an imposition of power. These decisions and principles are "assumed either to be ignorant (or dismissive) of the realities of oppression, by definition, or a cynical attempt to serve the critic's own interests." [20] The one on the side of the road needing my help is not my neighbor, unless he is of my own identity group. If not, my attempt at helping him is in itself an assertion of power and the recognition that I cooperated with his injurious state but am unwilling to surrender my privileges. After all, individuals are "vehicles of discourses of power," and we do not belong to the same type of being as others, if others stand differentially in relation to power.

Private charity becomes evil. Only an equal distribution of resources through the powers of the state controlled by the "oppressed" could be a justifiable action on behalf of the poor. Postmodernism has fractured society in such a way that we no longer share a common vocabulary nor embrace common definitions of virtue and vice. Alasdair MacIntyre was prescient in *After Virtue* when he described present moral debates as "shrill" in tone due to the fact that "the language and the appearances of morality persist even though the integral substance of morality has to a large degree been fragmented and then in part destroyed."[21]

---

[19] Neo-Marxism is also known as Marxist revisionism. This process encompasses various currents brewing in Marxism that began to arise after the death of Marx and that tried to explain why a number of Marxist predictions failed to materialize. We can say that the first prominent revisionist was Eduard Bernstein, who rejected dialectical materialism. The best known is Vladimir Illich Ulyanov (Lenin), who tried to understand why the progressive pauperization of the proletariat did not effect world revolution. Lenin developed the theory of imperialism as the final stage of capitalism to explain the failure. The Frankfurt School of Critical Theory and Antonio Gramsci's cultural Marxism are other revisionisms.

[20] Pluckrose and Lindsay, *Cynical Theories*, 41.

[21] Alasdair MacIntyre, *After Virtue* (Notre Dame, IN: University of Notre Dame Press, 1984), 11–12, 19.

Take the thought of Marxist scholar Peter McLaren:

> Liberation theology, which was born out of the self-theologizing of radical Catholic Action communities in America Latina, is systematically opposed to the trenchant conservative politics of white evangelical America in the U.S. who encourage individual charity over economic transformation and distributive social justice so familiar to many living in the richest country in the world.[22]

McLaren sees private charity as opposed to transformation and distributive justice because these latter two exist only within his socialist framework. It is either revolutionary activism in favor of the revolutionary destruction of market economies or it is private and voluntary charity. The type of transformation offered by Christian principles does not enter into the picture.

The neo-Marxist paradigm presents false alternatives. Unfortunately, academia and the education of social workers are impregnated with alternatives that give no space for better insight. A good example comes from one of the main textbooks in the field, *Social Problems* by Stanley Eitzen, Maxine Baca Zinn, and Kelly Eitzen Smith, now on its thirteenth edition. Responding to the question of what causes poverty, they tell us that "there are two very different answers to the question." One answer is that the poor are innately deficient biologically and culturally, and the other is that society is structurally and institutionally against the poor. In short, the institutional answer blames capitalism, where "who gets what is determined by profit rather than collective need."[23]

But are these our only alternatives: either the poor are inferior, or capitalism creates poverty? Which one do you think is chosen by those who are prepared academically to work with the poor? In effect, social workers are often called to become political activists of the Left. In *The Practice of Macro Social Work*, William G. Brueggemann says that "social work is called to transform society to create a more just social order." Social workers are called to join "social movements" because the problem of poverty is solved by radically altering the social order. In which political direction is

[22] Peter McLaren and Peter Jandrić, "Karl Marx and Liberation Theology: Dialectical Materialism and Christian Spirituality in, against, and beyond Contemporary Capitalism," *Triple C* 16, no. 2 (2018): 598–607, https://www.triple-c.at/index.php/tripleC/article/view/965.

[23] Stanley Eitzen, Maxine Baca Zinn, and Kelly Eitzen Smith, *Social Problems*, 12th edition (Boston: Allyn & Bacon, 2012), 189–97.

the discipline supposed to accomplish such a daunting task? Brueggeman answers by citing a major liberation theology activist-scholar, Gustavo Gutierrez: "To do nothing in favor of those who are oppressed is to act against them." Social work is for anti-capitalist activism and for the utopian dreams of revolution, for building the perfect society where a "fully human life" without violence and human misery is finally attained.[24]

Critical Theory

The knowledge-power linkage is essential to "solving" everything. If powerful and oppressive forces in society arrange everything in hierarchies that preserve their advantage, only a contrary exertion of power can break that system. The first linkage in the chain of power is discourse; that is, language and social rules are the tool of oppressors to legitimize their advantage, and these must be deconstructed. We cannot miss how the meaning of things is now being challenged everywhere. The Marxist paradigm of dialectical oppression is embraced but only as a skeletal construct with activist instrumental value. In Marx, the key to historical change was action and revolution.

If that is what lies at the base of social reality, poverty alleviation within the oppressive system is but a manifestation or epiphenomenon of oppression. When you hand out a bag of food, welcome a homeless person to a home, or positively challenge someone you befriended to make certain changes in lifestyle, you are cooperating with the perpetuation of poverty, not addressing it. You are an agent of the devilish capitalist system puffing smoke to create the smokescreen of false consciousness. If you open a Bible to study it with a group of neighbors to seek God's wisdom, you are wasting valuable time that could be dedicated to "fighting the power." Your main tasks must be political activism to bring about radical change.

In effect, critical theorists such as Herbert Marcuse believed that any action within the capitalist system that was not actively fighting it was conforming to oppression and being used by the capitalist apparatus, which he termed the *performance principle*.[25] We are manipulated by the system in such a way that it affects our libido and rationality, and we rationalize our conformity. As Marcuse put it concerning those who do not rebel,

[24] Brueggemann, *Macro Social Work*, 377.

[25] See Arnold Farr, "Herbert Marcuse," *Stanford Encyclopedia of Philosophy* (Summer 2021 Edition), ed. Edward N. Zalta, https://plato.stanford.edu/archives/sum2021/entries/marcuse/.

"He desires what he is supposed to desire."[26] Your engagement with the poor, absent revolutionary conscience and activism, is an aspect of what Marcuse, deriving this concept from Marx's surplus value, called "surplus repression." As Stephen Eric Bronner puts it, this repression "will also take institutional form in the patriarchal-monogamous family, the church, the hierarchical division of labor, the bureaucratic state, and a mass media ... through which 'surplus repression' is extracted and maintained for the benefit of the given order."[27]

According to Marx, for revolution to come a social class, seen as a being with an objective identity, had to move from being a class *in* itself to becoming a class *for* itself. It had to develop a class consciousness that mobilized the group against its own false consciousness and against its oppressor. Everything else in social reality was reducible to the identity of class.[28] That element of Marxian orthodoxy is virtually extinct today. In neo-Marxism, oppression does not come from a single and identifiable matrix at the top but is infused into and permeates all levels of society within a maze of intersectional matrixes whose dynamics exist within the social system itself, apart from the will of individuals. Intersectional oppression is manifested in individuals as members of identity groups and through institutions and language. These self-perpetuating systems of oppression must be opposed by challenging everything, problematizing the menial, and seeking political power through direct action against patriarchy, whiteness, heteronormativity, and a whole host of other systems of oppression.[29] The various critical theories in existence are "critical" because they attempt to identify problems and mobilize toward political change. This activism and will to power are in great measure all that is left of Marx's ideas on class consciousness.

---

[26] Herbert Marcuse, *Eros and Civilization: A Philosophical Inquiry into Freud* (Boston: Beacon Press, 1955), 46.

[27] Stephen Eric Bronner, *Of Critical Theory and Its Theorists* (Oxford: Blackwell, 1994), 241; See Marcuse, *Eros and Civilization*, 34.

[28] Karl Marx and Friedrich Engels, *The Communist Manifesto*, 2nd revised ed. (Moscow: Progress, 1977), 35: "The history of all hitherto existing society is the history of class struggle."

[29] See Abigail Favale, *The Genesis of Gender: A Christian Theory* (San Francisco: Ignatius Press, 2022).

If there is one critical theory that can be called American, it is *critical race theory*. This type of critical theory has two different manifestations: a "materialist" strain, with emphasis on political and economic systems; and a "postmodern," focusing on social identity, culture, and language.[30] Its purported founder, Derrick Bell, was a materialist and historical revisionist who rejected the possibility of any moral progress in American life when it comes to race. Any progress is but a phase in a plot to perpetuate the system and "largely a mirage obscuring the fact that whites continue, consciously or unconsciously, to do all in their power to ensure their dominion and maintain their control."[31]

The concept of justice within such a framework is meaningless. *Everything* is unjust within the system. Reform is impossible and if embraced must be so only instrumentally, as a way to destroy the entire system. Every person working in poor and minority populations must become an anti-capitalist revolutionary and form a "*united front*" with other activists as they inflict a thousand cuts on the body politic.[32]

Many of those serving the poor are being exposed to or even led by ideas consistent with the foundational premises of critical race theory. As the concept has been so politicized in the media, we must be cognizant of the elements informing action more than the labels used. Critical race thinkers Richard Delgado and Jean Stefancic are explicit that the theory is a rejection of the very foundational premises informing western civilization, the founding and traditional American ethos, and the early civil rights movement: "Unlike traditional civil rights discourse, which stresses incrementalism and step-by-step progress, critical race theory questions the very foundations of

---

[30] See Pluckrose and Lindsay, *Cynical Theories*, 114.

[31] See Derrick Bell, "*Brown v. Board of Education* and the Interest-Convergence Dilemma," *Harvard Law Review* 93, no. 3 (1980); Pluckrose and Lindsay, *Cynical Theories*, 115–16.

[32] United Front Theory was developed by Vladimir Lenin, especially in his book *Two Tactics*. The theory admits activism in areas that are not overtly revolutionary within capitalist societies if the activism hurts the system, thus indirectly advancing revolution. For a fuller explanation, see Ismael Hernandez, "Is Black Lives Matter the Solution?" in *Race & Justice in America: The Civil Rights Movement, Black Lives Matter, and the Way Forward*, ed. Kevin Schmiesing (Fort Myers, FL: Freedom & Virtue Institute, 2021), 73n5.

the liberal order, including equality theory, legal reasoning, Enlightenment rationalism, and neutral principles of constitutional law."[33]

Critical race theory is postmodernism painted all over with Marxist revolutionary activism, or as Pluckrose and Lindsay describe it, "applied postmodernism."[34] It defies the very concept of poverty alleviation and human flourishing that those looking for better ways to serve the poor want to engage. It rejects virtually everything in our society that is presented as a way forward, because things cannot get better. Conventional processes of social interaction and intellectual inquiry are attacked. There is no truth as such, because truth, as the philosopher Samuel Gregg points out, "has been relegated to cultural perspective." There is "my truth" and "your truth," "black truth" and "white truth."[35] Traditional research is seen as a standpoint that cannot fit black reality as filtered by the black group narrative. This narrative is political, and some within the group determine it. Traditional ways of inquiry are, in the thought of radical feminist scholar Patricia Hill-Collins, a "Eurocentric masculinist knowledge-validation process."[36] The poverty of non-minorities might need deeper explanation but not that of minorities. We live in a culture that cannot escape racism, because it is in every fabric of its constitution; whites are racist because they are whites in a society dominated by an oppression called "whiteness"; and racism is redefined as "prejudice plus power," which means that nonwhites (those without power) by definition cannot exhibit it.

---

[33] See Richard Delgado and Jean Stefancic, *Critical Race Theory: An Introduction* (New York: New York University Press, 2017), 3.

[34] Pluckrose and Lindsay, *Cynical Theories*, 122–23.

[35] See Samuel Gregg, *Morality, Law, and Public Policy* (Sydney: St. Thomas More Society, 2001), 81.

[36] See Patricia Hill-Collins, "The Social Construction of Black Feminist Thought," in *Black Women in America: Social Science Perspectives*, ed. Micheline Malson et al. (Chicago: University of Chicago Press, 1988), 303.

5

Getting Justice Right

The concept of justice was not always seen through the lenses of these modern and postmodern understandings. According to one of the earliest senses of justice in Aristotle, justice was conformity with an authoritative rule or law of conduct. It was a "moral disposition which renders men apt to do just things and which causes them to act justly and to wish what is just."[1] In that sense, justice is considered a universal virtue in human nature as man pursues happiness.[2] This was similar to the view of his teacher Plato, who saw justice as the inner nature of the human spirit.[3] Aristotle distinguished two areas of justice, corrective and distributive. Corrective justice included economic exchange and criminal punishment. Distributive justice focused on the outcomes of meritorious living, as people get what they deserve.[4]

---

[1] Aristotle, *Nicomachean Ethics*, bk. 5, trans. H. Rackham, Perseus Digital Library, http://www.perseus.tufts.edu/hopper/text?doc=Perseus%3Atext%3A1999.01.0054%3Abekker+page%3D1129a

[2] Anton-Hermann Chroust and David L. Osborn, "Aristotle's Conception of Justice," *Notre Dame Law Review* 17 (1942): 129–30, http://scholarship.law.nd.edu/ndlr/vol17/iss2/2.

[3] Mark LeBar, "Justice as a Virtue," *Stanford Encyclopedia of Philosophy* (Fall 2020 Edition), ed. Edward N. Zalta, https://plato.stanford.edu/archives/fall2020/entries/justice-virtue/.

[4] See John Addison Teevan, *Integrated Justice and Equality: Biblical Wisdom for Those Who Do Good Works* (Grand Rapids, MI: Christian's Library Press, 2014), 22–23.

Closer to the Christian era we find the ideas of Cicero, who defined justice as a virtue for social cohesion. Justice is the glue that keeps the city together and allows social harmony. Cicero saw justice as integral to the hegemonic success of Rome, both internally and externally, marrying justice with power. As political theorist Michael Howley states, "For Cicero, Rome's power derived more than anything else from the justice of its institutions. Rome offers the living example of the best practical regime."[5] For Cicero, moral uprightness is what makes a regime just and successful.

As we get to the Christian period, we notice a definition of justice as righteousness. That righteousness is God's (Romans 3:21–22), and justice is first the honor of God, rendering to him the oblation he deserves. In turn, that vertical relationship turns horizontal, as we treat our neighbor justly. As Jesus said, when you "give to the needy," you are "practicing your righteousness" (Matthew 6:1–2, ESV), where *righteousness* can be translated as *justice*.[6]

As we continue to move through history, we see the legacy of Plato and Aristotle in the early church father Augustine. In book 3 of the *Confessions*, Augustine discusses justice, describing it as following the laws of the nations according to custom, as long as they do not transgress God's law.[7] That is, if a law is stable and enjoys the consent of citizens, it ought not be disobeyed—unless it is contrary to God's law, which would mean it is by definition unjust, and "an unjust law is no law at all."[8] The medieval period continues the Aristotelian mindset, especially in the works of Thomas Aquinas. His understanding of justice is directly linked with his anthropology. Human beings are created by God as social beings. At every instant of human life, men are members of societies, whether these be natural ones like the family, divine institutions such as the church, or human constructs such as a political party. Our lives are interrelated, and our acts are relational. Justice is the virtue that informs right relationship with others. How do we accomplish the task? By rendering to each his due "by a constant and

[5] See Michael Howley, "Cicero on Justice, Empire, and the Exceptional Republic," Classics of Strategy and Diplomacy, April 15, 2021, https://classicsofstrategy.com/2021/04/15/cicero-on-justice-empire-and-the-exceptional-republic/.

[6] For a good summary of biblical justice, see Teevan, *Integrated Justice and Equality*, 30–38.

[7] Augustine, *Confessions* 3.8.15.

[8] Augustine, *De Libero Arbitrio*, 1.5.

perpetual will."[9] That is, giving to others what they deserve is a personal virtue or a habit, which is the effect of repeated voluntary actions that form our character.[10]

Justice Corrupted

A sea of change has occurred since this period, spearheaded by the Protestant Reformation, the secularist and anticlerical Enlightenment, and the later disillusionment with the chief tenets of the Enlightenment. In the seventeenth and eighteenth centuries, continental Enlightenment thinkers such as Francis Bacon and Jeremy Bentham envisioned empirical science and reasoning forming a new world where all our problems would be solved, and where metaphysics was rejected and, with that rejection, any grounding of justice on anything beyond the human mind.[11] Bentham, often considered the father of modern utilitarianism, saw justice and all the virtues not in terms of right and wrong but as connected to pleasure and pain: the only good was pleasure and the only evil was pain.[12] Not much earlier, in the seventeenth century, Thomas Hobbes had denied the objective value of justice as a virtue. Hobbes rejected metaphysics, opting for a radical empiricism of experience. Man is another beast with a body that exhausts his existence and is driven by appetite and instinct. The natural state of "man against man" sees him in the despair of a life that is "solitary, poor, nasty, brutish, and short."[13] Men create the state through the conventions of a covenant whose dictates become by definition just. Men trade personal freedom for security, and in the security of the covenant their freedom is limited by whatever is

---

[9] See Thomas Aquinas, *Summa Theologica*, II-II, q. 58, https://www.newadvent.org/summa/3058.htm.

[10] See Stephen Grabill, Kevin Schmiesing, and Gloria Zúñiga, *Doing Justice to Justice* (Grand Rapids, MI: Acton Institute, 2002), 1.

[11] Bacon was a Christian and remained one until his death. He emphasized the separation but complementarity of science and religion and linked virtue to scientific inquiry.

[12] See Philip Schofield, "Bentham, Jeremy: On Justice," in *Encyclopedia of the Philosophy of Law and Social Philosophy*, ed. M. Sellers and S. Kirste (Dordrecht, Netherlands: Springer, 2023), https://doi.org/10.1007/978-94-007-6519-1_931.

[13] Thomas Hobbes, *Leviathan*, pt. 1, chap. 13.

not specified in it. Hobbes's theory of justice is reductionism at its worst, reduced to the arbitrariness of conventions. Similarly, David Hume offered skepticism and arbitrariness as the basis for justice. As reason cannot tell us anything about the proper ends of human choice, it is "as Scouts and Spies to range abroad and find a way to the things desired."[14] Hume added that "public utility is the sole origin of justice."[15] In other words, justice is an instrumental social construct to help us get what we want.[16]

The concept of justice in modernity has been deeply affected by the utilitarian calculus of pleasure and pain. In the centuries since medieval times the locus of reality and the source of morality have shifted from God to nature to the state, and finally, to man himself as the "measure of all things." This is radically different from what Christian revelation and natural-law thinking tell us about the virtues. In the Christian tradition, the knowledge of the good is wisdom, and that human wisdom recognizes the nature of the created order as God imparted it with meaning and purpose. Ancient Greek philosophy heavily influenced the development of Christian moral theology, which sees the virtues as incommensurable characteristics or traits leading to the fulfillment or completeness of our nature. That is, we were made by God with a given nature and with purpose and with the capacity to develop and acquire a fulfillment that is integral. Justice is a key virtue. We can live it in our daily lives, and we can grow in virtue by continually practicing it. Justice has its locus in God. Utilitarian morality rejects this in favor of justice being a human construct, instrumentally valuable only insofar as it assists us in getting what our appetites discern as pleasurable, satisfying, or useful.

However, some prominent liberals have tried to find an alternative between utilitarianism and traditional notions of natural law. Probably the most prominent liberal modern thinker on justice is John Rawls. Much has been written as a critique of Rawls's view of social justice, and it remains

---

[14] Thomas Hobbes, *Leviathan*, pt. 1, chap. 8.

[15] David Hume, *An Enquiry Concerning the Principles of Morals*, ed. Tom Beauchamp (Oxford: Basil Blackwell, 1998), 145. Hume and Hobbes are simply samples of many other utilitarian and skeptic renditions of justice, such as those of Jeremy Bentham and John Stuart Mill. See Samuel Gregg, *On Ordered Liberty: A Treatise on the Free Society* (Lanham, MD: Lexington Books, 2003), 13–17.

[16] For an account of further steps on the historical account of justice, see Teevan, *Integrated Justice and Equality*, chap. 2.

a source of contention.[17] While recognizing the problems with utilitarianism, Rawls criticized those challenging the principle of utility for having "failed to construct a workable and systematic moral concept to oppose it."[18] For Rawls, that workable and systematic concept is *social justice*. His philosophical quest was to determine the set of conditions under which we can organize a just society. His thought experiment in the end excludes the worldviews of traditional believers from the public square. He argued that in a supposedly unbiased "original position" we could identify principles of justice that end up affirming a kind of comprehensive liberal-progressive worldview as the one offering terms of social engagement that all reasonable people can accept.[19] Political power is dependent on this acceptance by reasonable people, which he calls the "criterion of reciprocity." Rawls's goal was not overtly exclusionary of religious believers; he tried to identify principles of civil engagement acceptable to believers and unbelievers alike yet ended up excluding the former. What is most startling about his quest is that he tried to accomplish it by bracketing important questions about human nature and our destiny.[20]

In 1993, Rawls published a new book, *Political Liberalism*, where he offered amendments to his positions in *A Theory of Justice*. He realized that his views could suffer from being self-referentially incoherent, as he seemed to propose a secularist comprehensive view of society while excluding other comprehensive views precisely because they were comprehensive. Moreover, his comprehensive liberalism was still a minority view in many parts of the world. Why exclude the views of large portions of humanity? As Princeton philosopher Robert P. George puts it, "To appeal to comprehensive

[17] It is difficult to present a comprehensive list of responses to Rawls's views. For a limited anthology see Norman Daniels, ed., *Reading Rawls: Critical Studies on Rawls' "A Theory of Justice."* (Stanford, CA: Stanford University Press, 1975); Robert P. George and Christopher Wolfe, eds., *Natural Law and Public Reason* (Washington, DC: Georgetown University Press, 2000); Marc Fleurbaey, Maurice Salles, and John Weymark, eds., *John Rawls's Theory of Justice: Some Critical Comments* (Cambridge: Cambridge University Press, 2010).

[18] John Rawls, *A Theory of Justice* (Cambridge, MA: Harvard University Press, 1971), viii.

[19] The idea of terms of engagement that most reasonable people can accept is called by Rawls the "criterion of reciprocity."

[20] See Robert P. George, "Public Morality, Public Reasons," *First Things*, November 2006, https://www.firstthings.com/article/2006/11/public-morality-public-reason.

liberalism, Rawls concedes, would be no less sectarian than to appeal to Catholicism or Judaism. Some alternative must, therefore, be found or the social stability of such regimes would be in constant jeopardy."[21]

In his second book, he seemed to have a less ambitious goal of vindicating *only* political liberalism, instead of wholesale liberalism. Rawls tried to find a sort of neutral ground in excluding the reasonable comprehensive views of believers in important matters of constitutional law and justice. Only those terms of engagement that citizens embracing all sorts of comprehensive views could accept would be allowed as a basis for law and public debate. In *Political Liberalism*, Rawls called these terms of engagement "public reasons."[22] He thought that liberalism could dispense from moral and metaphysical discussions, and normative terms could be narrowed to politics.[23] For example, a Presbyterian or a Catholic who is prepared to defend his opposition to abortion using strictly non-theological reasons and enact laws protecting the unborn based on those reasons must be prevented from doing so because his reasons come from principles drawn from what Rawls called "comprehensive doctrines." It does not matter if his position is correct, it is excluded as not meeting the criteria of "public reasons."

In the end, Rawls's political liberalism in practice becomes wholesale comprehensive liberalism.[24] How does Rawls try to accomplish bracketing the comprehensive beliefs of non-liberals without affirming his own comprehensive liberalism overtly? By simply denying, in a sort of oracle or decree, without giving reasons or addressing their merits, that the comprehensive views of non-liberals can be "publicly and fully established by reason."

What is left? What is left is the moralizing of progressivism seeing those "at the bottom" as victims of forces arising from the structures of society and from nature itself. It is inevitable that we descend into the realm of politi-

---

[21] George, "Public Morality, Public Reasons."

[22] The idea of public reason can be traced back to Rousseau, Hobbes, and Kant. In contemporary times it has been explored by Jürgen Habermas, Gerald Gaus, and others. John Rawls clarifies in *Justice as Fairness: A Restatement* that issues that "border" on a constitutional essential and are politically divisive ought to be covered under his view of public reasons. See John Rawls, *Justice as Fairness: A Restatement* (Cambridge, MA: Harvard University Press, 2001), 41, 117.

[23] See John Rawls, "Justice as Fairness: Political, Not Metaphysical," *Philosophy and Political Affairs*, 14 (1985): 223–51.

[24] See George, *In Defense of Natural Law*, 316–18.

cal vying for benefits and fair shares under political liberalism. The moral task of those serving the poor is necessarily jeopardized. The concept of political *redress* becomes essential as the remedy to an unjust society. Not only should citizens have equal basic rights under the law—Rawls's first principle of justice—but every citizen has a right to equal outcomes—his second principle, encapsulated in what he called "the difference principle."[25] The difference principle governs the distribution of income, wealth, positions of responsibility and power, and the foundations for self-respect. Inequalities in the distribution of these goods are reasonable only if they benefit the least well-off positions of society. The concept of merit is no longer the basis for deserts. His system upends the principle that people with greater talents deserve greater rewards.

Not only are merit and deserts dependent on the claims of those at the bottom as a group, but the moral norms of the society are abolished, as Rawls bracketed moral norms arising from comprehensive systems of thought. This Rawlsian principle is seen in the Supreme Court's reasoning in the *Roe v. Wade* abortion decision of 1973. In the 1992 *Casey* ruling upholding the right to choose, the Court stated, "At the heart of liberty is the right to define one's own concept of existence, of meaning, of the universe, and of the mystery of human life." Every person creates his own moral code, and every belief, behavior, and lifestyle deserve equal regard and respect—except for a few beliefs arising from comprehensive liberalism, which must be accepted universally.

What is justice? Whatever aligns with the Rawlsian difference principle, devoid of any metaphysical understanding of natural law. Social justice is fairness in society along the lines of the difference principle. It is not difficult to see here the merging of radical collectivism in political and economic areas of life and radical individualism in the social and moral realm. If justice is a political exercise and any action within the political and legal system is just only if it benefits those at the bottom, then belonging to a category "at the bottom" brings about benefit and places great power in the hands of whoever purports to speak for them in the political arena. In the moral sphere, if objective morality is bracketed and each individual moral hierarchy is affirmed, radical individualism results. What we have here is the *political reification* of collective identity and individual autonomy.

Justice as a virtue inherent in individuals will tend to fade under the difference principle. In effect, Rawls says virtually nothing about it, except

[25] See the second part of Rawls, *Theory of Justice*.

for the statement that reasonable people ought to support fair institutions. It is reasonable that he ignores the virtues because, if political virtues are the only ones informing public reason and they can be derived independently of comprehensive doctrines, the entire tradition of Christian reflection on the virtues is beside the point. Justice as a political virtue is embedded in institutions, not in people. It is a general idea to be observed in institutions as they transfer resources and avoid any meaningful affirmation of what the good life is. Once you posit justice as strictly concerning redistribution and law, you are placing the concept within a statist framework informed by the notion of fair shares.

Rawls eliminates from the purpose of government and public social life any discussion about what builds a sound character or what are the ultimate ends of existence. In his conception, a polity would be unjust if it highlighted the good life or fostered high moral aspirations in its citizens. Society should not stress moral ideals but remain a mere conduit for individual expression and the transfer of resources from some to others. Yet we must ask, is moral indifference conducive to the best state of affairs in society? More importantly, if the law is a teacher with didactic power, aren't we downplaying the moral meaning of life by refusing to discuss the substance of alternative conceptions of the good?

JUSTICE AND CHARITY

How does this concept of justice affect charity work? If we were to follow the difference principle, any moral expectation would disappear from charity work. More importantly, any attempt at inspiring people and encouraging them toward a moral end would be an intrusion and nothing less than an injustice. Granted, Rawls believes that within private voluntary associations moral criteria could be foundational. But service to the poor is not offered only to members of groups but to everyone. I certainly expect an individual joining my church to assent voluntarily to our theology and principles of moral worth. But what about service to those in need who often do not belong to our church or organization? It is unreasonable to expect that a society whose laws determine that all lifestyles and conceptions of the good deserve equal regard will not have an indifferentist influence on the population and on the basic communities of society. The powerful general social vision of fairness and justice bracketing moral norms is detrimental to the preaching of other conceptions of the good.

Finally, on what objective basis are we to determine who is the least advantaged, once we remove concepts such as merit or effort? In the end, the difference principle is swallowed by the arbitrariness of utilitarianism. As Samuel Gregg states, "We are forced to make an arbitrary judgment about when to assess the validity of the precise distribution of goods at any point in time in the future."[26] How can we determine advantage in every individual instance with every individual person? How can we measure objectively one life lived against another? Our calculus eventually becomes dependent on group identity. It becomes parasitic to the politics of group advantage in the face of the impossibility of an objective calculus of just deserts to determine who is disadvantaged. Inevitably we descend into the identity politics that is consuming the body of the liberalism formed by men like John Rawls.

Deconstructed Social Justice

Although postmodernism decries the loss of the individual and the self, its practical prescriptions are deeply deterministic and collectivist. Postmodernism has ingested the element that consumed Rawlsian liberalism by adopting identity politics. Brueggemann notes how postmodern social movements "encourage us to resist forfeiting our individuality for individualism. Instead of being forced back on us, we fall back into community. Postmodern movements attack everything that separates us from one another, alienates us, or splits up community life."[27] Here we have the full-blown contradictions and confused thinking of postmodernism as it collapses into deterministic anthropology. This is so because the individual is a prisoner of identifying labels that inform his or her identity and destiny. If postmodernism were merely a nihilistic theory confined to eccentric sectors within academic departments and its deconstructions remained word play conducted by academics "nitpicking at words in order to deliberately miss the point,"[28] there would be no need to invest our time examining it. But do not be fooled: it is here. It is in your church, your ministry, your agency, and it will affect your service. Critical theory is applied neo-Marxism with a touch of insanity,

[26] Gregg, *On Ordered Liberty*, 24.

[27] Brueggemann, *Macro Social Work*, 399.

[28] Pluckrose and Lindsay, *Cynical Theories*, 47.

operating under the label of "social justice."[29] Its actionable vehicle is a movement we can call "deconstructed social justice" (DSJ).

DSJ is politically charged to the core and can transform service to the poor by putting the fear of God in charity decision-makers and volunteers who will gravitate more and more toward ineffectual and safe types of service, refusing to make any value judgments. Critical theory moved from a fringe set of ideas coming mostly from French scholars to a more influential academic endeavor to a cultural nihilistic challenge to common cultural discourse to finally becoming a praxis mutated within various leftist endeavors and movements that we can classify as DSJ.

What happened to Hegel's philosophy in the hands of Marx seems to have happened to critical theory in the hands of neo-Marxism. For Hegel, history moved in a directional spiral of "dialectical" patterns, according to which within a given state of affairs in the realm of ideas generated contradictions that were sublated or transcended at the next moment in history. Ideas informed life at one level and conformed the spirit or *geist* of a civilization. Society moved forward toward higher levels of consciousness until a utopian state of full conformity with a universal *geist* was attained.[30] Hegelian dialectics were not a praxis but a totalistic description of human history. Marx's theory of history followed a similar pattern but became a theory of praxis, of social change. Like Hegel, Marx view of history was "directional," but the mystifying spiritual discontinuities that give rise to new stages of consciousness occur objectively in the material world of human economic life. The ideas of an era are not the source of change but the manifestations of changes in the modes of production—elements

[29] Pluckrose and Lindsay, *Cynical Theories*, 46–47. Pluckrose and Lindsay refer to "Social Justice" as a political term that masks neo-Marxist and postmodern elements. It is to be differentiated from social justice per se. In fact, traditional notions of social justice are the ones deconstructed under the rubric of "Social Justice."

[30] For Hegel's view of the *geist* see Michael N. Foster, *Hegel's Philosophy of Spirit: A Critical Guide* (Cambridge: Cambridge University Press, 2019), 29–54; G. W. Hegel, *Phenomenology of Spirit*, trans. A. V. Miller with an analysis of the text by J. N. Findlay (Oxford: Oxford University Press, 1979); Michael Sugrue, "Hegel: *The Phenomenology of Geist*," Lecture 2, Great Minds of the Western Intellectual Tradition, 2nd ed. (Audiotapes, The Teaching Company, 1995).

such as the division of labor and social classes are fundamental. Marxism pretended to change the world not to explain the mind.[31]

Importantly, some Christians have embraced the colonization of Christianity by Marxist thought, preeminently those of the liberation theology camp. I was one of them.[32] While attending Jesuit seminary I often heard the mantra that socialism is the praxis of Christianity. In reality, Christianity was the host for the parasite of Marxism. We do not get Christian praxis by embracing an anthropology that affirms the collapse of the self within the grand utopian plan for the whole.

In analogous fashion, postmodernism was initially a cynical critique of modern industrialized and technological society. After the twentieth century experienced devastating wars and Soviet Stalinism proved to be yet another cruelty of history, some thinkers saw no hope in modernity and found the Enlightenment project to be a failure. Desperation, pessimism, and angst informed a nihilistic expression of despair. So profound was their cry that they saw no direction in history, no meaning at all in the raw facticity of existence, no truth to be salvaged from a world of impressions without meaning in disparate and constant entropic thrust toward nothingness. It was a cry, not a program.

However, starting in the late twentieth century, critical theory began to be embraced and adapted in other fields: sociology, anthropology, social work, legal studies, and ethnic and gender studies. It might have been within academic branches such as postcolonial studies in political science, critical legal studies, and black feminist scholarship that critical theory grew most in importance. The theory also changed, by embracing certain collectivist constructions as worthy of preserving, instead of the earlier wholesale, radical deconstructionism more apt for the classroom than for the streets. At the same time, activists on the ground were growing in influence, advocating leftist political change in areas such as race and gender and attacking globalization. Critical theory became DSJ.

Those who want to embrace authentic service to the poor should view DSJ as an impediment, not an ally. What has transpired in this history of

---

[31] See Patrick Lancaster Gardiner, "History as a Process of Dialectical Change: Hegel and Marx," *Britannica*, https://www.britannica.com/topic/philosophy-of-history/Objectivity-and-evaluation.

[32] For a detailed recount of my journey, see Ismael Hernandez, *Not Tragically Colored: Freedom, Personhood, and the Renewal of Black America* (Grand Rapids, MI: Acton Institute, 2016), chap. 1.

reductionism is the creation of a monstrous ideology reducing the person to a specimen, totally defined within the boundaries of identity groups such as race, gender, and sexuality. A critique of the fractured self in modernity became a movement to fracture society in postmodernist neo-Marxism. In the new universe there is no place for true compassion because we only suffer with the clan, with our identity posse. There are only victims and victimizers, divided by a strict political delineation. As there is no human nature nor human goods to be advanced, we get only a contest for power. Activism is the new sacrament, and charity is yet another epiphenomenon arising from a complex web of oppressive systems.

All that remains in us is raw desire and the power needed to satisfy it. As existential needs tend to be very complex and grounding human action on transcendent moral norms that place demands on the individual is illusory and oppressive, we gravitate toward the facile, meeting biological or psychological needs without any grounding on a common essence.

On the other extreme, the individual person is denied as unique, unrepeatable, and necessary. The individual collapses within the affairs, institutions, and needs of the group. The group is often a restricted category such as social class, race, ethnicity, gender, or nation. This kind of collectivism is manifested both in academic inquiry and in social activism, where individuals become mere drops within the great wave of a cause. Purpose and meaning exist only within the wave of the movement. Apart from the wave humans are merely a curious accumulation of atoms destined to nothingness.

The liberal consensus—which saw progress in the weakening of racial identity markers as a basis for opening opportunities and granting rights because these markers were the source of racist white oppression in our history—is rejected. Every person is but a speck of race and a multitude of other oppressed identities within a "matrix of domination."[33] Under *intersectionality*, a concept coined by black feminist scholar Kimberlé W. Crenshaw, we must embrace our identities and identity politics has been "a source of strength, community, and intellectual development"[34] for African Americans.

---

[33] See Patricia Hill-Collins, *Black Feminist Thought: Knowledge, Consciousness, and the Politics of Empowerment* (Boston: Unwin Hyman, 1990), 221–38.

[34] Kimberlé Crenshaw, "Mapping the Margins: Intersectionality, Identity Politics, and Violence against Women of Color," *Stanford Law Review* 43, no. 6 (1991), 1242. https://doi.org/10.2307/1229039. 1242.

Crenshaw introduced a change in postmodern thought. Postmodern thought saw gender, race, and other labels as social constructs imposed through social law—they lacked substantial or objective essence. They were a subjective and false sort of identity, a performance. Judith Butler, probably the most influential postmodernist gender theorist, argued that identity is performatively constituted. Identity is given in discourse through linguistic structures that build the self. There is no stable and coherent human identity.[35] Crenshaw affirmed that, as there was real discrimination, categories of people really exist in spite of being social constructs. As Pluckrose and Lindsay write, "This is intersectionality. It explicitly embraces the postmodern political principle and accepts a variant on the postmodern knowledge principle."[36] Group identity was made to be a political weapon in the struggle against oppression.

It is truly sad that the concept of social justice has been rendered virtually useless to those whose desires do not conform to its deconstructions. Its genus, justice, is treated by Aristotle where he discusses virtue and tells us that justice is always a habit in relation to others. It looks *ad allium*, that is, toward the other, and as such deals with duties and responsibilities.[37] Since it relates to others, it also relates to transactions or exchanges. All other virtues, having effects on other people, have a justice component. As Fr. James Schall notes, "To live in a world in which we owe nothing to anyone, or no one owes anything to us can be a kind of isolated hell."[38] A world without the commutative relationships of justice is inflamed with the tortures of Hades.

[35] See Judith Butler, "Performative Acts and Gender Constitution: An Essay in Phenomenology and Feminist Theory," *Theatre Journal* 40, no. 4 (1988: 519–31); and Judith Butler, *Gender Trouble: Feminism and the Subversion of Identity* (New York: Routledge, 1990).

[36] Pluckrose and Lindsay, *Cynical Theories*, 126.

[37] See James V. Schall, "Justice: The Most Terrible of the Virtues" *Journal of Markets & Morality* 7, no. 2 (Fall 2004): 410.

[38] Schall, "Justice," 412.

TABLE 1: DEFINITIONS OF JUSTICE[39]

Scholastic Term	Modern Term	Definition
Justice	*Justice*	To give what is owed
Commutative Justice	*Commutative Justice*	What is owed beween two persons in exchange
Distributive Justice	*None*	Obligations between a community and its members, divided into general and particular justice
General Justice or Legal Justice	*Social Justice*	What the members of a community owe to that community
Particular Justice	*Distributive Justice*	What a community owes to its members

In traditional Christian thought today, social justice refers to what used to be distributive justice. Table 1 illustrates that the scholastics understood distributive justice as referring to the obligations between a community and its members, both what the community owes to the members (particular justice) and what members owe to the community (general or legal justice). Under DSJ, however, social justice is synonymous with socialism and with what the oppressive capitalist system owes to "the People." Now, the People is a being, a category, that is not synonymous with the citizen but instead with the maze of categories of oppressed people.

This reductionism of individual lives to proximate categories is also seen in the prevalence of transactional systems of care that determine individual human needs on account of the needs of the group. Blacks need inclusion and liberation, whites need repentance, gays need rights, the poor need "stuff," and all "oppressed" groups need revolution. If I have seen a poor person or a black person or a white person, it is as if I already know everything

[39] Source: Joseph Burke, "Distributive Justice and Subsidiarity: The Firm and the State in the Social Order," *Journal of Markets & Morality* 13, no. 2 (2010): 299.

relevant about you, about your life, your hopes, your aspirations, what you need or aspire for. And I don't even know your name yet.

Only that which is worthwhile can constitute a reason for human action. To know what is worthwhile we must understand what makes *individuals* flourish and move forward on the path of integral human fulfillment.[40] It seems imperative that we first understand what it means to be a human being. The *fatal conceit* of the activity often called "poverty alleviation" is the belief that we already know the answer to this question. Our haughtiness commoditizes the person as a product of forces and impulses within the category we assign to them. The priority of individual integral fulfillment is a demanding task positing two foci of action: *the whole person* and *every person*. Social progress as a whole is not realizable if we don't first engage each person in the work of self-fulfillment in various aspects of self. In his encyclical *Caritas in Veritate*, Pope Benedict XVI told us that "authentic human development concerns the whole of the person in every single dimension" and that "progress of a merely economic and technological kind is insufficient."[41] Reverberations of the same idea of wholistic development within various spheres of life are found in Dutch theologian Abraham Kuyper's idea of sphere sovereignty. According to Kuyper, God ordered distinct spheres of life, each having its own tasks, internal order, and dynamism as an expression of God's sovereign reign over the affairs of men. We cannot collapse all the affairs of men within singular constructed categories. God *alone* is absolutely sovereign, the *summum bonum*, over every sphere of life, and no human institution or category can claim this absolute sovereignty.[42]

[40] See George, *In Defense of Natural Law*, 85–87.

[41] Benedict XVI, encyclical letter *Caritas in Veritate* (June 29, 2009), §11 and §23.

[42] See Abraham Cho, "Abraham Kuyper," The Gospel Coalition, November 18, 2013, https://www.thegospelcoalition.org/reviews/abraham-kuyper/.

6

The Human Condition

In the recent past there have been voices challenging the common ways of assisting the poor that seem not to work. Minister John M. Perkins speaks of "acts of charity" that can be "dangerous because givers can feel good about actions that actually accomplish very little, or even create dependency." Robert D. Lupton reminds us how we "have failed to adequately calculate the effects of our service on the lives of those reduced to objects of our pity and patronage." There is also Peter Greer's insight in calling some efforts "the ministry of the big deal," where we instrumentalize the poor, and even Jesus himself, for the sake of growth, expansion, and recognition. And in *The Economics of Neighborly Love*, Tom Nelson stresses the importance of our vision of the human person, a vision often ignored in ways of serving that are utilitarian and transactional: "How we understand the human condition will determine what solutions are offered for greater human flourishing."[1]

The Evolution of Charity

In his seminal work *The Tragedy of American Compassion*, Marvin Olasky traces the history of how a distorted view of the care of the poor evolved,

[1] John M. Perkins, *Beyond Charity: The Call to Christian Community Development* (Grand Rapids, MI: Baker Books, 1993), 23; Lupton, *Toxic Charity*, 5; Peter Greer, *The Spiritual Danger of Doing Good* (Minneapolis: Bethany House, 2013), 76–77; Nelson, *Economics of Neighborly Love*, 130.

ignoring an earlier civic and religious tradition of voluntary service more consistent with the full scope of human dignity. He tells us that "many lives can be saved if we recapture the vision that changed lives up to a century ago, when our concept of compassion was not so corrupt."[2] In early America the dislike for government welfare was widespread, as it was seen as contributing to a degradation of character whose result would be "generation after generation of hereditary paupers."[3] With the passing of time there was a transformation in the way we treated poverty. Voices cried against the threat of intergenerational poverty found in "outdoor relief"[4] to families that continued to receive a daily dole year after year.[5] A change in how we treated the poor was accompanied with a new and nefarious anthropology.

Governmental institutionalized relief programs continued to emerge in the late 1800s and early 1900s. Everyone seemed to express concern for a system that seemed impersonal, but the system endured and grew. Critics lambasted the depersonalization in outdoor relief efforts, often cynically: "Bread, more bread. Soup, more soup. One beggar, one loaf. If two beggars, two loaves. A thousand poor, one soup-house; two thousand, two soup houses."[6] With these new trends came a sort of "compassion fatigue," and the segregation of empathy for the poor accompanied population growth and the segregation of rapid urbanization.

As economic classes separated, it was easier to render the poor invisible and prefer the depersonalization that comes with institutionalized care. Discriminate giving, that type of giving that necessitates encounter, waned in favor of the indiscriminate type based exclusively on the fact of need. Disgust for the new way of doing charity easily transferred to disgust with those receiving relief. As those who could help gave less, the paupers received less. Inevitably, government intervention grew. This was a vicious

[2] Marvin Olasky, *The Tragedy of American Compassion* (Washington, DC: Regnery, 1992), 5.

[3] *American Quarterly Review* 14 (1855): 78, quoted in Olasky, *Tragedy of American Compassion*, 44.

[4] "Outdoor relief" was assistance given in the form of money, food, clothing, or goods without requirement of institutionalization in an almshouse, orphanage, or workhouse which were forms of "indoor relief."

[5] For multiple quotes from the era, see Olasky, *Tragedy of American Compassion*, chap. 4.

[6] Olasky, *Tragedy of American Compassion*, 64.

cycle that repeated itself and continues today. As governmental relief had to be indiscriminate by definition, the chasm between various sectors of society grew wider and the idea that there was no other way but to let the state take control seemed inevitable.

To complicate things, and in no way coincidentally, the tentacles of a destructive ideology grabbed the collective consciousness as Social Darwinism spread in America as a respectable notion embraced by purportedly respectable people. It did not take long for Darwin's conclusions about the natural world and the survival of certain species in savage competition with others to go well beyond the natural sciences within which it initially emerged. The effects of Social Darwinism on the question of relief took various forms. One form challenged the very concept of relief of any kind. As idleness and all sorts of aberrant behaviors could be attributed to heredity, charity toward the poor came to be seen as funding deviancy. Social Darwinian sociologists posited that as humans are prisoners of genes which inexorably determine our behavior, chastising the poor was a way to protect the fit and improve society. Systematic efforts to help the poor caused beggars, paupers, and vagrants—a needy crowd of undesirables—to overflow almshouses, fill the public space with street-begging, and threaten neighborhoods with criminal activity.[7] Intellectuals such as Herbert Spencer sought to explain trends in social and economic life by using Social Darwinism. Poor women gave birth to "gutter children" and "proved to be the prolific mother[s]" of "idiots, imbeciles, drunkards, lunatics, paupers, and prostitutes." Spencer then asked, "Was it kindness or cruelty which, generation after generation, enabled these to multiply and become an increasing curse to the society around them?"[8]

Another form was as condescending and depersonalized as the first. Relief was beneficence arising from the superiority of the giver who paternalistically condescended to the inferior classes. The eugenics movement of the nineteenth and twentieth centuries had a flavor of paternalism, as it was seen as compassionate to prevent the inferior from breeding and dealing with

[7] This was the scenario depicted in a paper presented at a public charities conference held in New York in 1874. See Peter Dobkin Hall, "Social Darwinism and the Poor," Disability History Museum, https://www.disabilitymuseum.org/dhm/edu/essay.html?id=61.

[8] Herbert Spencer, *The Man Versus the State* (Indianapolis: Liberty Classics, 1981), 110.

feeble offspring. The movement sought to improve the health and intelligence of the human race by sterilizing the "unfit" as a service to mankind.[9]

Social Darwinism became a totalistic ideology that viewed the whole of humanity as an organism hierarchically divided. Those who were poor or exhibited bad character were predetermined to fail by an implacable lottery of genes. Yale professor William Graham Sumner dehumanized the poor and doubted that helping them was a good thing. In his worldview, "nature has set up on [the inferior] the process of decline and dissolution" to clean society of elements no longer useful by a terrible but necessary process of elimination.[10] Intervening to prevent the process was wrong.

The oracles of genetic fate were breeders of hopelessness and as such were opposed by Christians who challenged their deterministic impulses. Marvin Olasky tells in detail of the work of evangelical ministries such as the Brooklyn Christian Union, the Buffalo Charity Organization Society, the Charity Organization Society of New York, the Association for the Improvement of the Conditions of the Poor in Baltimore, the Chicago Erring Woman's Refuge for Reform, and many others.[11] The typical narrative of poverty alleviation in America focuses on the New Deal and other government initiatives and historic catalytic events but often neglects to mention the major role of these Christian efforts.

The common thread of the narrative of improvement in the condition of the poor has President Roosevelt's New Deal as the culmination of the emergent primacy of the state in the care of the poor. The economic crisis was real. The unprecedented nature of displacement and unemployment during the 1930s depression bolstered the idea that massive intervention by the federal government was the key to attend poverty. From 1.55 million unemployed in 1929, the number grew to 12.83 million in 1933 and remained at over 5.5 million until 1941.[12] Since then, the fear of a crisis of

[9] See Paul A. Lombardo, *A Century of Eugenics in America: From the Indiana Experiment to the Human Genome Era* (Bloomington: Indiana University Press, 2011).

[10] See William Graham Sumner, *What Social Classes Owe to Each Other* (1883; repr., Caldwell, Idaho: Caxton, 1974), 20.

[11] Olasky, *Tragedy of American Compassion*, 71, 73, 77, 80, and 81. See chaps. 5 and 6 for a thorough list.

[12] See U.S. Bureau of the Census, *Historical Statistics of the United States, Colonial Times to 1957* (Washington, DC, 1960), 70.

poverty has endured as a spur to interventionism. There is no doubt that some people suffer deprivation in our country, but exaggeration of the conditions of the poor has continued to be used as a tool for political purposes.[13]

Even so, an aversion to going "on the dole" remained a strong mark of the culture.[14] Despite the economic crisis of unprecedented heights, support for unemployment relief remained low. It was not until the introduction of New Deal proposals in 1933 that support for relief increased. There remained a stigma to government relief within a culture that saw work as a virtue and receiving help without earning it as shameful. Although a rejection of dependency remained strong in the national ethos, by enlarging the federal role in awarding relief there was a gradual transfer of political allegiance of America's unemployed from local officials and local political machines to Washington, DC.[15]

Failure lurks around the corner of many of our efforts, as they embrace an illusory vision of the human person. We seem to be under the illusion of

---

[13] Certain reports on US poverty have tended to exaggerate conditions. A good example is Kathryn J. Edin and H. Luke Schaefer, *$2.00 a Day: Living on Almost Nothing in America* (Boston: Houghton Mifflin Harcourt, 2015). Their claim of three million children living in conditions we associate with the Third World was stunning. Another example is the 2018 report for the United Nations Human Rights Council stating that "5.3 million [Americans] live in Third Word conditions of absolute poverty." If that were the case, massive direct intervention by many actors would be justified. However, the reports were incorrect. The Comprehensive Income Dataset (CID) Project has shown otherwise. Its detailed examinations using a variety of data sources shows that not a single child in the linked dataset lives on less than $2 per day. For a detailed examination of the CID, see Kevin Corinth and Bruce Meyer, *How to Better Measure Poverty: The Comprehensive Income Dataset*, American Enterprise Institute, December 19, 2023, https://cosm.aei.org/how-to-better-measure-poverty/.

[14] Probably the best contemporary study of attitudes toward relief was conducted by Yale sociologist and economist E. W. Bakke. The 2004 *Encyclopedia of the Great Depression* highlights his New Haven study on attitudes toward receiving relief, which stands "as a powerful statement of the importance of stable, adequately paying work opportunities for individual well-being, as well as broader social well-being." See Robert S. *McElvaine, ed., Encyclopedia of the Great Depression: A–K, vol. 1.* (New York: Macmillan Reference USA, 2004), 86–87.

[15] Wendy L. Wall, "The New Deal," *Oxford Research Encyclopedia of American History*, December 22, 2016, https://doi.org/10.1093/acrefore/9780199329175.013.87

greater insight, an expanded capacity growing on top of what Wilhelm Röpke called "enmassment." The concept refers to the belief that the technological and material progress that surrounds us is an indication that we are heading toward Valhalla, that the intelligentsia has the magic wand to cure all ills, and that "paradise is just around the corner: the paradise of a society whose idea of bliss is leisure, gadgets, and continuous fast displacement on concrete highways."[16]

To put it simply, the hubris of modern man penetrates every corner of civil society and is there at the heart of many efforts to care for the poor. Modern mass society is said to be so complex as to necessitate design and planning by those whose expertise places them on higher ground. The endeavor would be too overwhelming without bureaucracy, and bureaucracy reflects the normative human desire to simplify complexity. We believe that, with the assistance of technological prowess and a good amount of money, we can beat the poverty problem. What is needed is willingness, resources, and conformity to the grand plan. The quantification of solutions showcases this success.

Quantification is heavily assisted by dependency on the hand that rocks the cradle of funding. Basic communities have become appendages of the state. In the case of "faith-based" ministry to the poor, the merging of state funding with Christian service impinges on the most important right, religious liberty. The world of economics is closely aligned with religious freedom. If we come to see freedom merely as the removal of all constraints on human action so that "I can do whatever I want," as historian Kevin Schmiesing observes, "then the political and economic spheres will inevitably become battlegrounds where interest groups engage in power struggles so as to gain the upper hand and thereby claim the spoils of victory—financial and otherwise."[17] It follows that the collapse of basic communities within the institutions and activities of the state ends up connecting the individual directly with the macrosystems of governmental agencies, bypassing the necessary communities closer to the individual as he lives his life. An important institution, the church, is neglected, and worse, the church itself is linked to the same macrosystems threatening religious freedom by depending heavily on public funding.

---

[16] Röpke, *Humane Economy*, 37.

[17] See Kevin Schmiesing, ed., *One and Indivisible: The Relationship Between Religious and Economic Freedom* (Grand Rapids, MI: Acton Institute, 2016), ix.

Our church ministries and nonprofit poverty-alleviation (or poverty-breeding?) centers become part of that grand plan, and the poor become, to use Röpke's apt description of people in the state of enmassment, "mere passively activated mass particles or social molecules"[18]—scenery in the drama of our good intentions, ensnared in the tentacles of transactional systems of care. The problem is that human beings are not merely elements in a collection or social molecules. The individual is not a social construct whose contours are determined by way of "social law."[19] We are *persons*.

A Christian View of the Person

Pondering the human condition in history might help us to understand what a person is. Many disciplines attempt to gain from such experiential insight. However, I speak as a Christian; thus I ground whatever insights we acquire in man's relation to God. In effect, we cannot escape mere instinct in explaining man in historical context unless we understand that the person is irreducible to biology. Reductionism is attractive because we live in a scientific era where we can take things apart to understand them. Organic life, for example, can be broken apart into organs, cells, and parts of cells. These in turn can be dissected into molecules and even further into energy fields. We can come to believe that we have accounted for all of existence by breaking their material components apart. Biology itself is often seen as reducible to fundamental physics.

The scientific progress we have experienced seems to contradict the Aristotelian and Thomistic view of things having a purpose built into themselves, an essence that gives us valuable information. The classification and ultimate explanation of entities, their ontology, is seen to be discovered exclusively

---

[18] Röpke, *Humane Economy*, 41.

[19] In existentialist philosophy there is not a given human nature. By acting in the world, you must invent yourself, transcending the immediacy of your circumstances. Such a task is not easy, this thinking goes, so we invent the idea of a telos or purpose, and we invent the idea of a preordained blueprint that we call nature. Without a given nature, there is an open-ended realm of possibilities; in this pursuit exists freedom. Social laws—the cultural, political, and legal expectations—are therefore merely attempts by some to define others so as to control them. Oppression occurs when one group sets itself up as the "Subject," while others remain as "Objects." See Jennifer McWeeny, "Origins of Otherness: Non-Conceptual Ethical Encounters in Beauvoir and Levinas," *Simone de Beauvoir Studies* 26 (2009–2010): 5–17.

by way of reducing them to their smaller material parts. Interestingly, even in the sciences there is great skepticism about the reductionist movement. Trends emerging within the philosophy of science have engaged reductionism within specialized sciences and the relationship between contemporary science and fundamental Aristotelian concepts such as "hylomorphism," "substance," and "faculties." [20]

Although there are many schools of thought purporting to ground human existence subjectively in the products of the human mind, they share in the error of Sartre's dictum: *existence precedes essence*.[21] As there is no God to infuse meaning into his creation, we exist as meaningless raw matter, trapped in the "facticity" of existence before we create ourselves.[22] If we think a little about this anthropology, we notice that there is nothing intrinsically good about the human person and we cannot discover the human goods or perfections that constitute a person.

---

[20] Atheist philosophers such as Thomas Nagel question reductionism. See Nagel, *Mind and Cosmos: Why the Materialist Neo-Darwinian Conception of Nature is Almost Certainly False* (Oxford: Oxford University Press, 2012), 4–5. Another example of a scientist rejecting the ontological reductionism of scientism is Michael Polanyi, a twentieth-century polymath and philosopher. As a practicing scientist, he challenged misconceptions and distortions surrounding the understanding of how we know reality prevalent among some scientists. In *Science, Faith and Society* (1946), Polanyi rejects a positivist account of science that ignores the role personal commitments play in scientific endeavors. Contemporary philosophers of science also cast doubt on scientism: see *Neo-Aristotelian Perspectives on Contemporary Science*, ed. William M. R. Simpson, Robert C. Koons, and Nicholas J. Teh (New York: Routledge, 2017).

[21] Jean-Paul Sartre, "Existentialism Is a Humanism," in *Existentialism from Dostoyevsky to Sartre*, ed. Walter Kaufmann (New York: Meridian, 1989). This text is a lecture delivered in 1946.

[22] *Facticity* was probably first used by the German idealist Fichte. However, it is most associated with the thought of Heidegger. It has various meanings, from the positivist and empirical understanding as facts that can be explained to the opposite view of those things that resist explanation. My usage here is aligned with that of the existentialists Sartre and Beauvoir. Facticity refers to any pre-discursive factors against which human identity is created and against which our freedom contends. In this view, for example, the sexual organs given at birth are elements that constrain our pursuit of freedom, and they are not considered sexual organs until the human mind attributes to them this category.

What to say about these false alternatives? What do we have to offer? The great Christian tradition and the Scriptures are a good guide for how to face the onslaught of false anthropology that forms the basis of many of the systems we have engaged. It is in the Scriptures that we find a narrative of origins with the right vision of the human person (anthropology), the right meaning of existence (ontology), and the right understanding of our ultimate ends (teleology). In the deterministic paradigm the creator is either humanity itself or impersonal forces outside our control. As they are impersonal, they are merciless and do not care about our ultimate destiny. Compulsion moves that narrative further. We are the demigods who instantiate reality with our words. Nothing is given, so man intervenes to create reality and impose it in discourse through the acquisition of power. The individual is subsumed within identity groups: class, race, ethnicity, gender, or a myriad of identifiers denying that every person is unique and unrepeatable.

The narrative we offer begins "in the beginning" (Gen. 1:1). We counter the deterministic paradigm with the *Genesis paradigm*.[23] In Genesis, we are shown to be creatures of a loving God who not only reveals himself but wants to be in intimate union with his creatures. He holds us in existence from the moment that his word speaks the cosmos into existence. We do not instantiate our existence and our identity through acts of the undeterred will or through power over a social narrative, only to one day die and disappear into cosmic nothingness. We come from someone and are called to return to him. Moreover, it is a creative act, the one that instantiates the material world. Creativity is at the beginning of material existence; we cannot avoid it or ignore it.

The first chapter in Genesis is a cosmic narration, with stages offering increasing complexity. Every stage of creation is pronounced as good by the Word (Greek: *Logos*; Latin: *Verbum*). The power of his words instantiates goodness. "Then God said: Let there be light, and there was light. God saw that the light was good" (Gen. 1:3). At every step of his creative endeavor there is a progression, from grace to grace. An act of *creative intelligence* is what is at the foundation of the cosmos.

Entrepreneurship is consistent with this narrative of beginnings, because it is an activity that points to the very constitution of existence, as it pursues economic and social good through the radical capacity of thought and action. Karl Marx and the early economists offered a truncated view of

[23] Here I am indebted to the thought of the great scholar Abigail Favale, especially in her previously cited *Genesis of Gender*.

economic life, because they infused their theories with a limited anthropological reasoning—they missed the mind as the creator of wealth. Hegelian and postmodernist neo-Gnostic alternative anthropologies entail a similar reductionist error; they miss the body in favor of mind.[24]

Cogito, ergo sum, "I think, therefore I am," is the principle, because existence precedes essence and mind instantiates existence by an act of human will. The body is but an addendum. This "first principle" of René Descartes's philosophy is the famous maxim that summarizes the reductionism.[25] His philosophy also presents a mind-body dualism, which he offers in his *Meditations on First Philosophy*.[26] Body is extended substance, while mind is thinking substance and true self is only thinking substance. He posits that "it is therefore certain that I am truly distinct from my body, and that I can exist without it."[27]

That all things are good speaks of meaning and purpose, embedded as it were in the very fabric of their existence—goodness is intrinsic to the created universe and so are intelligence and action. Meaning and purpose are not created by us. Instead, they are given to us as a gift. Everything surrounding us has a truth about it, a meaning, a purpose, and a destiny. The apex of this unfolding story is reached with the creation of man as the embodiment of intelligence, creativity, and goodness, all in God's image: "Then God said: Let us make human beings in our image, after our likeness. Let them have dominion over the fish of the sea, the birds of the air, the tame animals, all the wild animals, and all the creatures that crawl on the earth" (Gen. 1:26).

Human beings are to be stewards of a created order that is good because they are image-bearers, resembling God himself. This image of God is given only to humans, and among the potentialities it includes are reason—

[24] Neo-Gnosticism is a modern version of the old heresy.

[25] The phrase appeared in French in Descartes's 1637 *Discourse on the Method* in the first paragraph of its fourth part. In 1641, it appeared in Latin in his *Meditations on First Philosophy*, though not explicitly as "cogito, ergo sum."

[26] For a discussion of mind-body dualism and other types of dualism, see Robert P. George and Christopher Tollefsen, *Embryo: A Defense of Human Life* (New York: Doubleday, 2008), chap. 3.

[27] Rene Descartes, *Meditations on First Philosophy*, 3.4: Meditations 5 and 6, LibreTexts Humanities, https://human.libretexts.org/Bookshelves/Philosophy/Rene_Descartes_-_Meditations_on_First_Philosophy_(Bennett)/03%3A_Meditations_on_First_Philosophy_1641/3.04%3A_Meditations_5_and_6.

to discover the truths of existence—and volition—the capacity of freely choosing, with its creative power to transform the earth. We are called to discover the mysteries of the universe and recreate them to produce more goodness. Everything exudes meaning, purpose, and, especially, love. The very act of creation is a disinterested gift of self, as God could gain nothing from creating it. In the words of Pope John Paul II, "The human person becomes a gift in the freedom of love."[28] Why does he create? Because he is love. Love created us.

BODY AND SOUL

Not only that, but God made man, male and female, which reflects the goodness of creation (Gen. 1:27). That dual existence is good—that is, it has meaning and purpose embedded in it. It is not a social construct of power but a reality of our existence from the beginning. Both man and woman share fully in the commission of tending the earth, because both share fully in the same image of God. In the deterministic paradigm reality is a linguistic trick of power. There might be a facticity to the raw matter in the male and the female, but it is just there, mute and void of meaning; we become the gods who instantiate meaning. In the Genesis paradigm God infused meaning into *every* particle of matter. That world of love, purpose, and meaning is a gift to us, not a wordplay invented by power. We have been entrusted with that reality; we are not its progenitors.

The story continues to unfold in Genesis 2 from a different vantage point. Genesis 1 is a macro view of the unfolding cosmos. We can see it revealed from the vantage point of God, the giver of life. In Genesis 2 we are sent into an earthly vantage point, a horizontal understanding of creation. It is a history in a garden between rivers, and God is seen as intimately united with his creation, walking in the garden side by side with man. God is not a foreigner, He is not the uninterested god of deism, speaking existence from afar and retreating. As Abigail Favale states, Genesis 1 emphasizes God's transcendence, while Genesis 2 emphasizes his immanence and intimacy.[29]

---

[28] Pope John Paul II, General Audience, January 16, 1980, https://www.vatican.va/content/john-paul-ii/en/audiences/1980/documents/hf_jp-ii_aud_19800116.html.

[29] Abigail Favale, "The Genesis of Gender," Lecture, St. Benedict Institute, Hope College, October 4, 2021, https://www.youtube.com/watch ?v=rkas5 PkJ

Here God takes man (Adam) from the dust of the earth and breathes life into him. Man becomes alive, animated with a divinely given light. We are both matter and spirit, earth and breath. Our bodies are constitutive and integral to who we are and what we are. They are not irrelevant facts that we can alter at will. We are not ghosts in machines, possessing impersonal bodies that we own. Pope John Paul, again, says, "Man, formed in this way, belongs to the visible world; he is a body among bodies."[30] We belong to the visible world, to the world of human action.

We are our bodies. We are physical creatures, not angelic beings. But we are also breath, possessing a spirit that informs us and gives us life—unified whole beings. This is the Catholic anthropology of human existence. This is why work is so important, so human, such a gift of grace. In fact, work is given to us also in the beginning, before the intrusion of sin, as a gift of grace and as a mandate (Gen. 2:15). "This mandate [to subdue the earth]," said the Second Vatican Council, "concerns even the most ordinary everyday activities [so that] men and women ... can justly consider that by their labor they are unfolding the Creator's work and contributing by their personal industry to the realization in history of the divine plan."[31] More recently, Protestant thinkers Chuck Colson and John Eckerd added their voices to the chorus stressing the importance of work:

> First, the church must reclaim its own heritage. That means preaching and teaching the work ethic. Teach diligence, excellence, thrift, respect for property and that through work we participate in Christ's work of redeeming the earth.... Second, the church must teach vocation. Every Christian needs to rediscover and understand that the individual's calling

[30] John Paul II, *Man and Woman He Created Them: A Theology of the Body*, trans. Michael Waldstein (Boston: Pauline Books & Media, 2006), 152.

[31] Second Vatican Council, *Dogmatic Constitution on the Church* (*Lumen Gentium*), in *The Documents of Vatican II, trans.* Walther M. Abbott (London: Geoffrey Chapman 1966), 232 and 243. Although some Protestant theologians have historically criticized the language of man and his work as co-creating (Karl Barth, Stanley Hauerwas, and others), there has been an interesting modern convergence of thought between Catholics and Protestants on the question of the vocation to work. For a historical sketch see Alistair McKenzie, "Faith at Work: Vocation, the Theology of Work, and the Pastoral Implications" (master's thesis, University of Otago, New Zealand, 1997), Theology of Work Project, https://www.theologyofwork.org/thesis-on-vocation-the-theology-of-work-and-the-pastoral-implications-2/historical-developments-in-vocation-and-the-theology-of-work/.

> is at the very heart of faith and that it is imperative that each Christian glorify God with his or her work. [32]

In a most remarkable way, the body reveals the person. In his *Man and Woman, He Created Them: A Theology of the Body*, John Paul II states that "only the body is capable of making visible what is invisible: the spiritual and the divine. It has been created to transfer into the visible reality of the world the mystery hidden from eternity in God, and thus to be a sign of it."[33] In other words, our bodies are sacramental. Each person is relevant. They convey and reveal God himself, after whom we were created.

What happens when the man sees the woman? After naming all other creatures, all having been pronounced good, the man immediately recognizes the woman as one with him. Our bodies speak of communion, of unity, of belonging to each other. Man and woman, just as the cosmos itself was, are gifts to each other. The question of why we have bodies and what is their significance is not frivolous. As Lutheran theologian Joe Keinig states in his book *Wonderfully Made: A Protestant Theology of the Body*, inquiry on the meaning of the body "is not a theoretical question for idle speculation, something for philosophers to consider. It is a practical matter that determines the course of our lives."[34] The question is today more meaningful than ever, because our society is offering a distorted vision of the human person. Any distortion in anthropology affects how we serve those in need.

In Genesis 2:18 something important happens. Earlier, man was presented with all types of beings, and none were suitable to him. God had created all of them by the power of his word. But none are suitable. God then puts man to sleep. From his side he creates woman. Importantly, Adam is for the first time called "*ish*," or male. It is when presented with the woman that man becomes a male! Pope John Paul II in his magnificent *Theology of the Body* identifies the man's sleep as the sleep of nonbeing. Man becomes a being when he encounters woman. God differentiates humanity by making woman from the same substance as man. She is not instantiated at first by his word, as was the case with all other animals, but she is created from the

[32] Chuck Colson and Jack Eckerd, *Why America Doesn't Work* (Dallas: Word Publishing, 1991), 96.

[33] John Paul II, *Man and Woman He Created Them*, 203.

[34] Joe Kleinig, *Wonderfully Made: A Protestant Theology of the Body* (Bellingham, WA: Lexham Press, 2021), 2.

very substance of man. He creates two intrinsically connected modes of being human.

Listen to the joy and delight of the man who recognizes woman: “This one, at last, is bone of my bones and flesh of my flesh; This one shall be called ‘woman,’ for out of man this one has been taken” (Gen. 2:23). This differs from the postmodern and neo-Marxist paradigm that has men and women in a struggle for power. In this view, they are seen as undifferentiated, with their maleness and femaleness being linguistic sorcery devoid of substantive reality and abstracted and decreed from the miasma of undifferentiated matter. Or in other versions they are seen as totally different beings. Instead, the truth is that the maleness and femaleness of humans matter, as they are both sacraments, gifts from God and gifts to each other. From the beginning the man-woman relationship is one of reciprocity, unity, and love, not of power and domination. Power and domination appear in the Genesis account only *after* the fall of man—as sin enters human existence.

In Genesis 1 God uses his word—language—to bring a good world out of nothing. Language is the instrumental cause of creation by God. In Genesis 2 man uses language to name the creatures God created. As Favale tells us, “Divine speech makes reality, human speech identifies reality.” Notice the profound difference between the gender paradigm and the Genesis paradigm. Man uses language to recognize the meaning and purpose God gave to woman, “bone of my bones and flesh of my flesh.” Man recognizes that woman shares his nature but in her own distinctive and “very good” reality. Man recognizes himself in seeing the woman. Naming is always a linguistic response of man who lacks the power to confer substance and purpose, exactly the opposite of what happens in the gender paradigm. Language is good and meaningful only when it aligns with the reality whose substance was created by God. Language is evil when it pretends to the divine power of instantiating reality in opposition to God’s divine creation.

Most gender theorists have constructed a false understanding of reality and of language and are trying to impose it on society. The Christian worldview rejects such falsities. The binary existence of humans is not an illusion, as they pretend. It is at the very heart of human existence. This meaning is intrinsic to human existence and it is intelligible to us. We can recognize it and use language to identify it, but we lack the power to confer substance.

Part 2

The Practical Work of Poverty Relief

7

Poverty

Do you know what poverty is? Most people probably assume that they do. Rarely do we question our knowledge on topics that we have heard about all our lives and that seem to be simple and straightforward. But poverty may be more complicated than you think.

People often define poverty as simply a lack of resources. In part, our view of poverty springs from associations we make based on media images. Social policy problems are commonly represented through the use of powerful symbols; in fact, symbolic representation is the essence of problem-definition in politics and policy discussions. Because they capture the imagination, symbols can be helpful, inducing us to pay close attention to a genuine need. But they also can cause us to suspend our skepticism and our critical thinking about problems. Whoever controls a symbol controls the narrative, and that confers the power of controlling the response. A narrative runs through these images, conveying a vision of how the world works.

A powerful American narrative of our time is that of control and helplessness. This narrative conveys the idea that control has always been in the hands of a few, that most are denied choice and self-determination in any meaningful sense. A narrative component that underpins the story of control and helplessness is *synecdoche*, a figure of speech by which a whole is represented by a single part (e.g., "head" of cattle). Applied to social activism, it is a form of symbolic representation that focuses on a part of a problem that can be visually dramatized—for example, a horror story of destitution or an account of rank injustice. The synecdoche is useful to organize people because it can generate anger. Images of people in extreme poverty can properly place attention on the plight of the poor, but they can also become tools to control the narrative and reduce a problem to one of oppression.[1] The narratives of "oppressed people" or "helpless masses" have the inherent power of confining our responses to a narrow range of options.

The idea that poverty primarily means a lack of things also reflects the fact that we live in an abundant society where wealth seems to surround us. In fact, Americans do live in one of the wealthiest societies in all of human history and, consequently, we take many things for granted and do not associate having them with wealth. We thus tend to identify poverty with people who are not employed and who are living on government assistance, regardless of the actual material quality of their lives. This view of poverty is narrow and ignores what precedes and effects the creation and acquisition of these things.

Here we will offer a different vision of the problem of American poverty, because the very concept of what poverty is ought to be challenged. Shifting the discussion in this way has profound implications for how we respond to the problem. It creates a fresh prescription out of a new description, changing the "normative leap" by which we move from observation to action.[2]

What Causes Poverty?

Many of those who seek to help the poor ask the question, "What causes poverty?" Often, there is an implicit assumption behind this question: that if we get to the "root cause" of poverty, we can create systems to eliminate it. There are several problems with this line of reasoning.

First, the metaphors surrounding poverty may be misleading. "Buried in every policy metaphor," Debra Stone observes, "is an assumption that 'if a is like b, then the way to solve a is to do what you would do with b.' Because policy metaphors imply prescription, they are a form of advocacy."[3] Poverty is often presented as a disease with the power to spread. Certain

[1] Deborah A. Stone, *Policy Paradox and Political Reason* (Glenview, IL: Scott, Foresman, 1988), chap. 6.

[2] "Normative leap" is a term coined by professors Martin Rein and Donald Schön that signifies the subtle jump from description to prescription in policy metaphors. Donald A. Schön and Martin Rein, *Frame Reflection: Toward the Resolution of Intractable Policy Controversies* (New York: Basic Books, 1994).

[3] Stone, *Policy Paradox and Political Reason,* 118.

conditions are called "breeding grounds," and poverty rises at times to the level of an "epidemic." If poverty (a) is a contagion (b), then it can be cured the way a doctor cures b, by intervention to remove the contagion. If poverty is a disease, then we must remove it from those so unfortunate to have contracted it. A moral duty is assigned to "stamp out" the disease, and crusades need to be called to intervene, probably on a long-term basis.

The metaphor contained in the question thus implies an external cause for poverty, which in turn implies a capacity—and possibly an obligation—for others to solve the problem. In a sense, the question objectivizes the poor, who are seen as victims of forces "out there" in American society. Since "the system" necessarily conspires to keep some in poverty, only political action can ameliorate their condition. Many poverty-alleviation programs are built on this "politics first" ideology, designed to empower those who have been left out of the economic mainstream.

Another difficulty is that the question is regularly used to attack the free-market system as the source of the problem. The market cannot provide adequate resources to the poor, in this view, because profit-driven actors impede it through economic and political structures. If the free market is flawed in this way, then we need to "tweak the machine" by intervening in the market. One intervention leads to another, and failure leads to even more intervention as we continually conclude that "we did not do enough." The field of social work, for example, is profoundly influenced by this assumption.[4]

Finally, the question is not very interesting. Not because the poor are unimportant or do not deserve our attention—just the opposite. It is uninteresting because poverty has been the almost universal condition of humanity for thousands of years. It is not difficult to create poverty; it is what comes naturally when the conditions to create wealth are absent. This is why simple solutions such as "giving people stuff" do not work. Wealthy countries have attempted to eliminate poverty by flooding developing countries with aid, to little (or even negative) effect. If only eliminating poverty were as easy as shifting piles of money around!

What is the important question, then? To answer, we need to refocus our attention on human persons and their nature. What is exceptional in the person? What is the basis of human dignity? Inevitably we must talk about

[4] See, for example, D. S. Eitzen, Maxine Baca Zinn, and Kelly E. Smith, *Social Problems*, 12th ed. (Boston: Allyn & Bacon, 2012); and Philip R. Popple and Leslie Leighninger, *The Policy-Based Profession* (Boston: Allyn & Bacon, 1998).

human freedom. As Michael Matheson Miller, director of PovertyCure, succinctly states, "God made us free, and when the political and economic systems reflect our nature, people prosper."[5]

The interesting question does not concern what poverty is. Instead, it concerns what makes people flourish. What is there in the human person that, if awakened, becomes the most efficient instrument for self-realization?

Shifting our focus brings attention to a proper understanding of the person as a moral being made in the image of God, with the capacity for moral and economic self-realization and integral human fulfillment. We begin to see poverty as a problem whose solution is the poor themselves: persons, with all their flaws but also with all their inherent capacities. And we stop seeing it as a political issue or an emotional stimulus to feel sorry for people who are cursed by a universal plague. Then we get to the heart of the matter. We get to the anthropological question that can lead to the political and economic order best suited for people as they really are.

What Causes Human Flourishing?

Simply put, human flourishing is what happens when we freely engage in the wholesome activity, goal, or commitment that enables us to become productive and achieve our full potential. It is whatever motivates us to wake up early in the morning and eagerly go to work. It is what keeps us fresh and alive, interested and busy, excited and motivated to be an active participant in the building of our lives. Flourishing is related to high human functioning that generates creativity, energy, economic initiative, growth, and resilience. Those who fail to flourish experience depression and languish in a life of empty and hollow existence. They see themselves as victims of forces outside of their control. They are not free.

In an important way, human flourishing is connected to self-interest. Self-interest reflects the fact that the best way to know what is good for others is to experience what is good in ourselves. Self-interest is not identical to selfishness. "The 'self' in self-interest is complex," writes theologian Michael Novak, "at once familial and communitarian as well as individual, other-regarding as well as self-regarding, cooperative as well as indepen-

[5] Michael Matheson Miller, PovertyCure Sample Session, video file, Acton Media (2012).

dent, and self-judging as well as self-loving."[6] The knowledge of the good is direct in reference to ourselves, but it is indirect if we know the good only through our perception of its effects in others. That is why Jesus said, "Do to others as you would have them do to you" (Luke 6:31). The matrix that shapes the knowledge of the good is in the self. There must be an end, a purpose, for the actions that we perform; in other words, life must have a point if it is to be worth living. This is what the ancient Greek philosopher Aristotle called *eudaimonia*: flourishing or well-being.

Eudaimonia is a property of our life when considered as a whole and it is good for its own sake. It means literally "the state of having a good indwelling spirit, a good genius." Flourishing is the highest good of human endeavors and is manifested in the pursuit of virtue, that is, in excellent human activity. According to Fr. Robert Sirico, the longtime president of the Acton Institute, "Human flourishing is the holistic unfolding of what God designs people to be. It means having the liberty to creatively and productively exercise our God-given gifts and skills in an integrated way that contributes both to the welfare of other people and to the glory of God." Fr. Sirico goes on to clarify: "While I believe a free economy in a free society is conducive to human flourishing, much more is needed than mere freedom. Human flourishing requires objective standards of right and wrong which are embedded in nature, that is, virtue—the virtues revealed to us through reason and which receive confirmation through Revelation."[7]

When the question of poverty is reframed positively, centering on the human person as the most efficient instrument for his own betterment, we can detach ourselves from the political question and pay attention to the human potential for growth. We can look at the mirror to find the solution there, instead of looking for answers from outside actors or from systems.

Our lives are projects under development, and they can improve if we put some effort into them. Given the reality of human autonomy, the person bears responsibility for the direction of his or her life. Moreover, human beings in poverty should not be seen as a problem to be solved or as victims but instead as persons with creative potential, with capital—that is, a

[6] Michael Novak, *The Spirit of Democratic Capitalism* (1982; repr., Lanham, MD: Madison Books, 1991), 93.

[7] Rev. Robert Sirico, interview by J. Q. Tomank, *Ignitum Today*, September 28, 2012, http://www.ignitumtoday.com/2012/09/28/interview-rev-robert-sirico/#sthash.o3iX2cBf.

resource that may be employed productively.[8] They are beings capable of acts of understanding, creativity, and self-determination. The creative power of a human being is highlighted when we ask the right questions about poverty. "Because all goods and institutions produced or designed by human beings ultimately derive value from the human capital on which they rest, they must foster the development of that capital if they are to be effective in the future."[9]

The eminent economist Gary Becker points to the highly personal nature of this kind of capital: "People cannot be separated from their knowledge, skills, health, or values in the way they can be separated from their financial and physical assets."[10] Since all people possess human capital, we can speak of a universal vocation to be creative and entrepreneurial. The entire discussion of poverty shifts in a positive way toward awakening the human spirit, and we avoid both the atrophy of personal responsibility and the hypertrophy of bureaucracy and centralization.

What Kind of Poverty?

When people think of poverty, the first picture they often have is African children dying of hunger, bloated bellies due to malnutrition, sweatshops where men, women, and children are forced to work for maybe a dollar a day, and beggars roaming the streets of crowded places far away. In other words, they have an image of *absolute* poverty.

Absolute poverty is a measure of poverty that uses a threshold that is the same regardless of context. It refers to what is necessary to afford minimal standards of food, clothing, health care, and shelter. Those who are absolutely poor suffer a severe deprivation of these minimal resources.

---

[8] Capital is not merely physical, tangible products or means of exchange. It resides in the mind, giving value to things beyond their physicality. As the Austrian economist Ludwig von Mises put it, "The mental tool of the market economy is economic calculation. The fundamental notion of economic calculation is the notion of *capital* and its correlative *income*." Mises, *Human Action: A Treatise on Economics*, 260.

[9] Anthony J. Santelli, Jr., et.al., *The Free Person and the Free Economy: A Personalist View of Market Economics* (Lanham, MD: Lexington Books, 2002), 83.

[10] Gary S. Becker, "Human Capital," *EconLib*, https://www.econlib.org/library/Enc/HumanCapital.html.

In the United States, however, absolute poverty is an uncommon sort of poverty. Here, the term *poverty* is generally used to describe a very different condition. Instead of speaking of absolute poverty, we must refer to *relative* poverty. This is a poverty relative to the lifestyle of one of the wealthiest societies in human history. A shift in worldview is needed to understand American poverty. British sociologist Peter Townsend offers the classic definition of relative poverty: "Individuals, families and groups … can be said to be in poverty when they lack the resources to obtain the types of diet, participate in the activities and have the living conditions and amenities which are customary, or are at least widely encouraged or approved, in the societies to which they belong."[11]

Relative poverty refers to the quality of one's life according to a specific societal standard. In the contemporary United States, our standard is unique. For example, the international poverty threshold for some time was one dollar of income per day. The World Bank has over the last couple of decades revised that upward to reflect inflation; in 2022, it raised it to $2.15. Even so, it's obvious that these numbers are meaningless in the context of the United States, where no one would consider an annual income of $800 as adequate to escape poverty. Here, we speak more commonly about a basic living standard called the poverty threshold or poverty line. The poverty thresholds were developed in the early 1960s by Mollie Orshansky, a statistician for the Social Security Administration. They continue to be used and are established annually based on an analysis called the Current Population Survey.

The Orshansky poverty thresholds were adopted by the Lyndon B. Johnson Administration in the 1960s as a working definition of poverty for the purpose of measuring progress in the raft of programs instituted under the auspices of the "War on Poverty." Each year, the US Census Bureau updates the poverty threshold to account for inflation. Additionally, the government utilizes poverty guidelines. These differ slightly from poverty thresholds and are a simplification of the thresholds used for purposes such as determining financial eligibility for certain federal programs.

Total means-tested spending on cash, food, and housing programs is now twice what would be needed to lift all Americans out of poverty. Why then does the government report that over forty million persons live in poverty each year? The answer is that, in counting the number of poor Americans, the Census Bureau ignores almost the entire welfare state: The census counts

[11] Peter Townsend, *Poverty in the United Kingdom* (London: Penguin, 1979), 31.

only a minute fraction of means-tested cash, food, and housing aid as income for purposes of determining whether a family is poor. Furthermore, there seems to be an incentive for the political and bureaucratic class to heighten the number of people in poverty, since government largesse can offer the opportunity for patronage and benevolence, as well as additional power and resources for the "bureaucracies of compassion."

According to the US Department of Health and Human Services, the poverty level for 2023 was set at $30,000 in annual income for a family of four. But this is only one, common standard. There are nearly fifty different federal poverty thresholds varying by family size and type. The total income does not account for government cash and subsidies.

The way these thresholds are calculated is also flawed in continuing to assume (over fifty years after being created) that families spend almost 20 percent of their disposable income on food. Food now accounts for a little over 11 percent of a household's disposable income.[12] The absence of government assistance and the overestimation of basic needs are just two of the many problems with measurements that purport to measure poverty but are based exclusively on income. There are many factors needed for an accurate assessment of a person's material wellbeing, and commonly cited measures of poverty are gravely deficient.[13]

Another common misunderstanding of poverty statistics stems from a failure to appreciate that such numbers usually reflect snapshots in time. People's financial situations are dynamic. It is impossible to ascertain the

---

[12] See graphs at "Food Prices and Spending," USDA Economic Research Service, https://www.ers.usda.gov/data-products/ag-and-food -statistics -charting -the-essentials/food-prices-and-spending/.

[13] For a detailed treatment of the deficiencies of poverty measurement, see John F. Early, "Reassessing the Facts about Inequality, Poverty, and Redistribution," Policy Analysis no. 839, Cato Institute, April 24, 2018, https://www.cato.org/policy-analysis/reassessing-facts-about-inequality-poverty-redistribution. A 2019 study that attempted to account more accurately for all income found that the real poverty rate was 2.3 percent—ten points lower than the official rate of 12.3. See Richard V. Burkhauser et al., "Evaluating the Success of President Johnson's War on Poverty: Revisiting the Historical Record Using a Full-Income Poverty Measure," AEI Economics Working Paper 2019-22, December 2019, American Enterprise Institute, https://www.aei.org/research-products/working-paper/evaluating-the-success-of-president-johnsons-war-on-poverty-revisiting-the-historical-record-using -a-full-income-poverty-measure/.

actual destiny of individuals through time by looking at statistical aggregates at a single instance. In reality, statistics on poverty are merely proxies; that is, approximations of the state of the world we are trying to measure. An additional problem with proxies is that they invite us to believe in the existence of a static group of people in perpetual poverty and another group of people that remain in a permanent state of plenty. We have all heard the phrase, "The rich get richer and the poor get poorer."

Most of the actual people who appear in a poverty measure are moving up or down; they were not poor a year earlier or will not be poor next year. This kind of temporary poverty is obviously less of a concern for society than persistent poverty. Many wealthy people have spent some period of time below the poverty line—perhaps as a graduate student or during a brief period of unemployment. The US Census Bureau reported 46.2 million poor people in the United States in 2010; a sharp increase from the previous year total of 43.6 million. For the past two decades, the number has been at least 35 million people. However, are those counted as poor the same assortment of people? These numbers do not tell us. The inherent pitfall of statistics is that they often miss individual lives because levels of aggregation are often not very useful to properly compare. The actual flesh-and-blood individuals who make up the various income levels shift over time, with some people rising to higher levels and others going down. In other words, America remains a mobile society, where poverty is not destiny.[14]

"One common source of needless alarm about statistics," the economist Thomas Sowell observes, "is a failure to understand that a given series of numbers may represent a changing assortment of people." He captures the problem by relating a joke: "Upon being told that a pedestrian is hit by a car every twenty minutes in New York, the listener responded, 'He must get awfully tired of that!' "[15] Just as it isn't the same pedestrian getting hit every twenty minutes, many of the people in poverty are not the same people year after year.

---

[14] Robert Carroll, "Income Mobility and the Persistence of Millionaires, 1999 to 2007," Tax Foundation Special Report no. 180, June 2010, https://taxfoundation.org/research/all/federal/income-mobility-and-persistence-millionaires-1999-2007/.

[15] Sowell, *The Vision of the Anointed*, 43.

Income Mobility

Is poverty destiny? Is the constituency of various income levels unchanging? Are the rich getting richer because the poor are getting poorer? These are important questions for those who believe in fairness and have an authentic desire to help those in need.

Let us begin with the last assertion. In the United States, as economics professor Steve Horwitz has demonstrated, it is largely a myth that as the rich get richer the poor get poorer.[16] There is no relationship of causality between the increases in the wealth of some and the statistical poverty of others. The allegation is largely based on comparisons of wealth between aggregations of people that miss some fundamental information. It is true that the top 20 percent of income earners in the country have a larger share of income than in the past while the bottom 20 percent of income earners have a lower share. But this statistic glosses over a critical issue: the size of the total income that is being divided.

Consider this question: Would you rather receive a third of a pizza or a fourth of a pizza?

The correct answer (assuming that you are not on a diet and would like as much pizza as possible) is that it depends on the size of the pizza. A fourth of a larger pie might be preferable to a third of a smaller one. A larger economy can benefit all, even if my "slice of the economic pie" is smaller in percentage terms than it was previously. It is crucial to look at the economy as a non-zero-sum game, instead of a zero-sum game. Zero-sum economic reasoning has been inherited from the thought of Karl Marx and sees the economy as a static reality. It says that any addition to the goods enjoyed by one person must mean a subtraction of the goods enjoyed by another. In contrast, in a non-zero-sum situation, goods can increase (or decrease) for both people at once.

A free economy is a dynamic economy, and a dynamic economy is a non-zero-sum game. In a free economy, there is no necessary relationship of causality between the wealth of some and the poverty of others. Why? Because when we pay attention to human flourishing, we discover the engine for economic growth. The solution is to create the conditions for people to bake their own pie. Every person has human capital, everyone

[16] Steve Horwitz, "Are the Poor Getting Poorer?," Lecture, Learn Liberty, Institute for Humane Studies, February 16, 2011, https://youtu.be/vDhcqua3W8?si=cuTh0wTU31GN5FRu

can work toward a better life and grow the economy. In other words, it is possible that as the rich get richer, the poor get richer too.

Data shows that the individual income of the poor has risen over time despite their owning a smaller share of national income. Instead of speaking of "the poor" in abstraction, we must refer to "José Perez and his family" or "John Smith and his family." That is, we must not be caught in a tyranny of numbers, which focuses on statistical inequalities, and instead try our best to look at the individual and the actual condition of the poor. The absolute income of the poor has risen even as their share of income is smaller. If we efface the individuality of persons, the category of "poor" ends up being a plain, meaningless box that hides important information.

Consider the findings of an analysis earlier this century that looked back over preceding spans of time. Regarding the movement of people in and out of income brackets, it found that "there was considerable income mobility in the U.S. economy over the 1987–1996 and 1996–2005 periods." It found, further, that "over half of taxpayers moved to a different income quintile and that roughly half of taxpayers who began in the bottom income quintile moved up to a higher income group by the end of each period. By contrast, those with the very highest incomes ... were more likely to drop to a lower income group and the median real income of these taxpayers declined in each period."[17]

If the poor get richer, then why are there still plenty of people who are poor? As people are displaced from one category, others enter it. In the case of the lower category, it is continually replenished with young people entering the labor force, immigrants, and some who fall from a higher income level.

Many people start at the bottom only to eventually move up, and some reach a higher income level but later fall into poverty for a number of reasons. Among the reasons for descending into poverty are the sudden death of a provider, divorce, sickness, mental illness, economic downturns, and failed business ventures.

A number of studies have considered the movement of individual households over time. A study by Sawhill and Condon in 1992 examined income mobility, focusing on individuals between the ages of 25 and 54 in 1967 and 1977 to find what happened to their incomes over the subsequent decade (1967–1976 and 1977–1986). They found that 44 percent of families in the bottom quintile in 1967 had moved to a higher quintile by 1976. In addition,

[17] Gerald Auten and Geoffrey Gee, "Income Mobility in the United States: New Evidence from Income Tax Data," *National Tax Journal* 62 (no. 2, June 2009), 301.

47 percent of those poor starting in 1977 had moved out of poverty by the end of the decade. A 1996 study by McMurrer and Sawhill found that mobility rates have remained about the same in the twenty-year period since the 1976 Sawhill and Condon study. Gottschalk (1997) analyzed the 1974–1991 period and found that 42 percent of households remained in the bottom quintile while 53.9 percent remained in the top quintile of income. Bradbury and Katz examined mobility for three periods: 1969–1979, 1979–1989, and 1988–1998. For each period they found that roughly 50 percent of those in the bottom and top quintiles maintained the quintile positions they held at the beginning of each ten-year period. A Treasury Department study by Auten and Gee (2009) confirmed that about 50 percent of households move out of the bottom quintile and the top quintile within ten years. The study also found that the income mobility trend had been largely unchanged over the preceding twenty years.[18]

The bottom line is that income mobility continues to be real in America, regardless of who controls the political machinery in Washington. The underlying free-market processes still allow the poor to move up the income ladder within a decade or so. The conventional understanding of what causes poverty is outdated and based on erroneous assumptions about the human person. Its static view of "the poor" obscures the fact that a free economy remains viable in America for those who, using their skills and effort, choose to better themselves.

Poverty by the Numbers

Even if there is income mobility, some might say, that does not mean that poverty is not a problem. Isn't radical inequality of wealth an injustice? What about the suffering of those who live in poverty?

> Even though the American economy is booming, prosperity has not filtered down to the 36.5 million poor people in the United States, including 4.5 million children. A report by the Children's Defense Fund indicates that the gap between rich and poor is increasing. American corporate CEOs earned 41 times more than their workers in 1960, but by 1995 CEOs were paid 185 times as much. The average CEO

[18] These studies are summarized in Carroll, "Income Mobility and the Persistence of Millionaires," 4. See also Michael Cox and Richard Alm, *Myths of Rich and Poor: Why We're Better Off Than We Think* (New York: Basic Books, 1999).

in 1995 earned more every two days than the average worker earned in a whole year.[19]

This passage comes from a social work textbook, which is used to train social workers to go into communities and work as community organizers. The solution proposed by the textbook is commonplace among those engaged in community organizing: change the social and political structures of society to make them more just according to political premises that place the state at the center.

In this view, we must become social engineers—attempting to influence or create changes in society from a position of authority and power—because the foundational structures of society are making the poor eternal victims of a system that is getting more and more oppressive. Even during economic boom times, prosperity eludes the poor and the immense wealth of some is the direct cause of the poverty of others. We already showed that a great number of poor people actually leave the ranks of the poor in a relatively short period of time, prosperity being within their reach. But what are the actual living conditions of the poor?

Destitution is not the word we should use for the vast majority of American "poverty." Most poverty does not imply the inability to meet basic needs. In fact, most people's understanding of poverty does not match the way the government defines it, as falling below a certain income level, irrespective of whether those defined as poor have access to resources adequate to meet their basic needs.

If poverty is understood as destitution, very few of the more than forty million people deemed poor by the federal government meet that standard. As scholar James Q. Wilson has stated, "The poorest Americans today live a better life than all but the richest persons a hundred years ago."[20] While economic hardship exists in America, it is limited in scope and often provoked by a number of non-economic factors. The perception of destitution and relative squalor is one bolstered by political rhetoric and media reports that focus on non-representative cases such as homelessness and hunger.

---

[19] Brueggemann, *Macro Social Work*, 25.

[20] James Q. Wilson, *The Marriage Problem: How Our Culture Has Weakened Families* (New York: HarperCollins, 2002), 1, cited in Robert Rector and Rachel Sheffield, "Air Conditioning, Cable TV, and an Xbox: What is Poverty in the United States Today?" Heritage Foundation Backgrounder no. 2575, July 19, 2011, http://www.heritage.org/research/reports/2011/07/what-is-poverty#_ftn3.

Often, the narrative is supported by community activists and social workers whose experience is centered on such non-representative cases.

American standards of living have only risen since the time Robert Rector summarized the state of the American poor using data from the US Census:

> In 2005, the typical household defined as poor by the government had a car and air conditioning. For entertainment, the household had two color televisions, cable or satellite TV, a DVD player, and a VCR. If there were children, especially boys, in the home, the family had a game system, such as an Xbox or a PlayStation. In the kitchen, the household had a refrigerator, an oven and stove, and a microwave. Other household conveniences included a clothes washer, clothes dryer, ceiling fans, a cordless phone, and a coffee maker.
>
> The home of the typical poor family was not overcrowded and was in good repair. In fact, the typical poor American had more living space than the average European. The typical poor American family was also able to obtain medical care when needed. By its own report, the typical family was not hungry and had sufficient funds during the past year to meet all essential needs.[21]

It is important to recognize that the term "typical family" is a proxy, a measurable variable used in place of a variable that cannot be measured. There are families that are not typical. Although a sizable number of poor households in America do not experience abject conditions, some families do experience hardship. For a family that does not fit the norm, knowing of the norm is not going to help them. It is irrelevant to them that the frequency of deprivation among poor people is not as high as some say, because their family is suffering. We should never dismiss the actual fear and insecurity of those who find themselves in distress. When we fail to recognize the reality of suffering, we become ineffective in our quest to offer a new path. The path of human flourishing, connected as it is to freedom and responsibility, closes when we fail to empathize.

Yet, accurate information about poverty is essential precisely because the absence of it may impede the proper care of those who are really in need. Robert Rector identifies the problem: "Exaggeration obscures the nature, extent, and causes of real material deprivation, thereby hampering the development of well-targeted, effective programs to reduce the problem."[22]

---

[21] Rector and Sheffield, "Air Conditioning, Cable TV, and an Xbox."

[22] Rector and Sheffield, "Air Conditioning, Cable TV, and an Xbox."

When exaggeration and waste are commonplace, we find ourselves at a disadvantage when we try to help others. Moreover, the data that is most widely publicized is from the United States Census annual report on income and poverty and it contains no description of the living conditions of the poor. The absence of context and specificity produces a caricature of the problem, impeding our efforts to effectively address those who are truly in need.

Even as we continue to strive strenuously to ensure that all people are able to live in dignity, we do well to keep the big picture of poverty in proper perspective. Arthur Brooks has highlighted the world's achievements in combating poverty: "According to Columbia University economist Xavier Sala-i-Martin, the percentage of people in the world living on a dollar a day or less—a traditional poverty measure—has fallen by 80% since 1970. This is the greatest antipoverty achievement in world history." Depicting poverty as an ever-worsening situation is simply inaccurate. It was not direct government aid or even private charity that brought about this spectacular decline in poverty. "That achievement is not the result of philanthropy or foreign aid," Brooks notes. "It occurred … thanks to global free trade, property rights, the rule of law and entrepreneurship."[23] Remembering that the normal working of the market in the context of well-functioning basic government institutions is the primary means of wealth creation is critical as we consider how best to assist those who remain in need.

Preoccupation with income inequality misses the important question of the quality of life of the poor. The discussion seems to be based on a view that places the state as the primary institution to assure the common good through the redistribution of what, by and large, was earned in the first place. If income inequality were a reflection of the worsening of the living conditions of most people, it would be a most important topic, but that is simply not the case. Moreover, a focus on redistribution sees some as passive recipients instead of active participants. Nothing could be more demoralizing to the truly struggling poor.

When we discover that it is human flourishing that is the answer, we can better find the means for families to improve their prospects. Better neighborhoods are built by people and sustained by them through their efforts, their values, their commitments, and their engagement in sound

[23] Arthur Brooks, "Republicans and Their Faulty Moral Arithmetic," *Wall Street Journal*, March 3, 2013, https://www.wsj.com/articles/SB10001424127887324338604578326350052940798.

economic activity. In fact, collective entities are better discernible through the action of individuals, an approach that has been termed *methodological individualism*. This understanding is different from *atomistic individualism*, where individuals are seen as islands unto themselves. We must always stand against both the idea of community that renders the individual as scenery in the drama of collective action and the idea that human beings are wholly disconnected from other persons and therefore have no social obligations.[24]

Trade-Offs or "Solutions"?

Exaggeration of the nature of a problem often leads to centralized and collectivized solutions that ignore the possibility of systemic and localized answers. If one sees a vast number of people in a condition of poverty—and does not have good, specific information about that condition—it is easier to prefer bureaucratized solutions, as the problem may seem overwhelming.

A sense of dismay may lead to calling for immediate solutions coming from government and a desire to fix the problem through political means that nationalize answers to the problem. But can we always fix every problem? Can we "unbake" the cake of reality? What should be our attitude in the face of poverty? In the quest for solutions there are two archetypes that need to be considered.

The Utopian Solution

In the utopian system, solutions are out there waiting to be found, like when you go on an Easter egg hunt.[25] If we cannot find them, it is because external forces impede progress, some people are indifferent, or we have not relied on the wisdom of experts knowledgeable and bold enough to take charge of solving the problem. Implicit in the utopian solution is affirmation of an expanded differential knowledge and mental capacity in the human mind accompanied with a powerful sense of moral indignation. Such knowledge is often deposited in the minds of experts who can guide a series of processes in our quest for a solution.

"If a terrible simplificateur is someone who sees no problem where there is one, his philosophical antipode is the utopian who sees a solution where there is none.… Extremism seems to occur most frequently as a result of

[24] See Mises, *Human Action*, 41–44.

[25] See Sowell, *Vision of the Anointed*, chap. 5.

the belief that one has found (or even can find) the ultimate, all-embracing solution."[26] In the utopian mindset, there are intellectual and political solutions to the problem, but "they" (often referring to whoever opposes funding the quest) refuse to allow them. The inherent constraints of a situation are often brushed aside because "something needs to be done and we know what it is." It is important to notice that utopianism begins in the mind. Its starting point is in the human imagination, and it must then be transferred to reality. In this view, two of the most important factors needed to solve the problem are political mobilization and social imagination.

The Realist Solution

For the realist, we cannot change the nature of most things—and definitely not human nature. As the human person does not have the expanded capacity some assume, there are not many "solutions" to the problems of human existence. We can share a desire for a better situation without sharing faulty assumptions as to the extent of our knowledge and control.

In this view, our options are constrained by the reality of human fallibility and the limitations of material existence; we must be humble about ourselves. The reality of suffering is inherent in the deficiencies of human existence, and we often have inadequate knowledge and resources to change things. The great virtue that springs from the realization of our fallibility is prudence. This cardinal virtue was defined by Aristotle as *recta ratio agibilium*, "right reason applied to practice."

In acting prudently, we acknowledge our limitations and seek advice. We also understand that seeking the advice of history and tradition is important; that is, the realist viewpoint starts from the base of the unarticulated and incremental experience of many people to find needed knowledge and guidance from what has worked. In narrowing the scope of concentrated, intentional, and expanded knowledge, we prefer the diffused and shared knowledge of those who now and in the past have dealt with the problem.

The realist vision still accepts human limitation in the choices we make, thus accepting that "if I tighten that screw here, I might be breaking something else there." That is, we face the reality of *trade-offs*. Humbly, we accept that there may not be categorical solutions to poverty, and that might be why Jesus said, "The poor you will always have with you" (Matthew 26:11). From the limited options available for poverty alleviation we

[26] Watzlawick, Weakland, and Fisch, *Change*, 48–49.

choose incrementally what can best help us find answers, treading patiently on a path we know can never bring about heaven on earth. Some "unmet needs" will remain unmet, and poor people will still exist in our society. The important thing is not to try to plug every hole of need but to remain faithful to the best processes for making trade-offs and correcting inevitable mistakes. The problem of poverty does not reside first in a lack of desire to fix things but instead in the inherent reality of the human person and the innate imperfection of social processes.

There is a systemic causation to social problems that no wise and knowledgeable group of planners and schemers can fix from above. Systemic causation arises from the interaction of many individuals and the inherently conflicting ends at play in that interaction. From the trial and error of human experience, a set of legal traditions, family ties, and social customs has risen through time, and we can use it to move forward. Experience helps us find what works and improve it and what does not and discard it. The realist position recognizes that to improve human existence means to find better ways, not ultimate answers. Sin is ineradicable, so we might as well create systems that recognize that fact. Democratic capitalism's "political economy, while depending upon a high degree of civic virtue in its citizens," Michael Novak notes, "is designed for sinners. That is, for humans as they are."[27]

In a system where humans interact, incentives are crucial. Whether these incentives are legal or economic, they create the conditions to maximize desired outcomes. A great incentive for a man to go and work hard might be his family ties and commitments. Another person might have the incentive of earning more or creating something no one else has created before. If you incentivize work, you will probably get more working people; if you incentivize need, you'll get more needy people. Given that solutions for the most part escape us but trade-offs are unavoidable, the best way to maximize success is by creating incentives toward positive outcomes.

What is needed is not a group of "anointed" ones with greater knowledge, because such a view favors a non-moral exercise where third parties become the decision-makers and choice is transferred to bureaucracies. The money goes from your pocket to the state and from there to the "bureaucracies of government compassion." Instead, what is needed is a system that limits the state and fosters a broad diffusion of power, taming the totalistic impulse.

[27] Novak, *Spirit of Democratic Capitalism*, 85.

8

A Brief History of Government and Relief

Government, by its nature, produces no good from adjacent opportunities, which are decentralized and require local knowledge. Thus, the welfare state uses resources like a blunt instrument.... The state with all its functionaries cannot hope to reproduce the profound connections created by local circumstances among real neighbors.

— Max Borders[1]

The beginning of the welfare state might be traced to England's Elizabethan Poor Law of 1601, by which the Crown took charge of what had been the responsibility of the church for the relief of pauperism. Government involvement in welfare functions gradually spread and increased across Europe, giving rise in the late nineteenth century to the modern *welfare state*. The modern welfare state conveys the idea that the government is the major actor in securing the common good and providing social protection. It was initially conceived in Germany under the government of the first chancellor of the German Empire, Otto von Bismarck. Ironically, Bismarck created his welfare system to prevent a radical socialist takeover. His paternalistic system also aimed to unify the nation and bring industrial workers under the control of the state. Bismarck affirmed that the state should offer the poor

[1] Max Borders, *Super Wealth: Why We Should Stop Worrying about the "Gap" between the Rich and Poor* (Sioux Falls, SD: Throne Publishing, 2012), 320.

"a helping hand in distress.... Not as alms, but as a right to maintenance."[2] The individual has a claim against the state and the state has an obligation toward the individual. He called his system "state socialism."

Early American welfare efforts were indebted to British Poor Law. For example, Rhode Island adopted it with almost no revision. The new country relied primarily on the kindness and generosity of individuals through basic and simple communities or private charities to fulfill the task of poverty alleviation. Most governmental involvement was at the local level, through "outdoor relief" (aid granted outside residential institutions) and poorhouses, and it focused on the most vulnerable. Nineteenth-century New Yorkers, for example, built scores of private charitable homes, each serving a different group in need—and with a different colorful name. One of those was the "Home for the Friendless." Built by the American Female Guardian Society in 1847, the home's mission was "to protect, befriend, and train to virtue and usefulness those to whom no one seemed to have thought or pity."[3] Government appropriations remained small. Relief was offered primarily to the elderly, the sick, the disabled, and destitute women and children. Private help often surpassed that of local government efforts, and there was strong societal resistance to the idea of federal intervention.

An example of that resistance was the consensus among the Founding Fathers that federal intervention was not proper in this sphere of life. James Madison, acknowledged father of the Constitution, is a good example. When Congress appropriated $15,000 for relief for French refugees fleeing from San Domingo to Baltimore and Philadelphia, Madison stated, "I cannot undertake to lay my finger on that article of the Constitution which granted a right to Congress of expending, on objects of benevolence, the money of their constituents."[4]

Most of the private efforts were religious in nature. These have been accounted for in great detail in Marvin Olasky's *The Tragedy of American*

---

[2] As quoted in Moritz Busch, *Bismarck: Some Secret Pages of His History*, condensed ed. (New York: Macmillan, 1899), 404.

[3] *King's Handbook of New York City* (1892), quoted in "The 19th Century 'Home for the Friendless,'" *Ephemeral New York*, September 13, 2010, https://ephemeralnewyork.wordpress.com/2010/09/13/the-19th-century-home-for-the-friendless/.

[4] Quoted in Gary Porter, "The United States Constitution as a Bill of Rights," Constituting America, https://constitutingamerica.org/90day-aer-the-united-states-constitution-as-a-bill-of-rights-guest-essayist-gary-porter/.

Compassion.[5] By the turn of the twentieth century, however, both public and private charity were in the midst of a transformation. The rise of "progressivism" in America began to alter the nation's attitude toward government and with this, the attitude toward federal intervention in relief efforts. One important attitudinal change was the belief that "experts" could better attend social problems than ordinary individuals. Government began to be conceived as a problem solver.

The idea of government and experts solving social issues can be termed social engineering. The key to understand social engineering resides both in the intentionality and the locus of efforts. Systemic processes are seen as unable to solve problems too big and too complex; thus the need for expertise and programs. Government is seen as the best place to find the experts and the resources to fix things.

By the late 1800s the federal government began to intervene in relief efforts to help disabled veterans and widows and to assist victims of floods in 1867, 1874, 1882, and 1884.[6] Traditional charitable activities gradually gave way to increased government intervention, and with the advent and development of the Child-Saving Movement, government's presence in charity work was here to stay. The creation of the Children's Bureau and the establishment by many states of welfare programs called "mother's pension" were important steps toward eventual government control and the subsequent expansion of the welfare state.

The wisdom of the Founders concerning the role of government, as expressed by Thomas Jefferson, had by then been long dismissed: "Still one thing more, fellow citizens—a wise and frugal Government … shall leave them otherwise free to regulate their own pursuits of industry and improvement, and shall not take from the mouth of labor the bread it has earned. This is the sum of good government, and this is necessary to close the circle of our felicities."[7]

The 1920s saw a number of efforts to increase state and federal government intervention and a push for increased expert intervention. The language also changed. For example, "relief" became known as "public welfare." Not

---

[5] See Olasky, *Tragedy of American Compassion*, 6–24.

[6] See Michael D. Tanner, *The Poverty of Welfare: Helping Others in Civil Society* (Washington: Cato Institute, 2003), chap. 2.

[7] Thomas Jefferson, "First Inaugural Address," March 4, 1801, https: //avalon .law.yale.edu/19th_century/jefinau1.asp.

only public charity changed; private charities also began to depend increasingly on a professional class, exemplified in the social worker. Paid staff replaced volunteers, and schools of social work were rapidly established.[8] During this early development of the welfare system, African Americans were for the most part excluded from receiving relief, especially in the South. As many private charities refused to help them, Blacks often created their own charitable associations.

Fraternal organizations and mutual aid societies became an important source of support within the African American community. Hundreds of Black lodges and fraternal groups formed an important web of support—these were often segregated chapters of larger organizations such as the Elks, the Masons, and the Loyal Order of the Moose. Others were created by Blacks and were all-Black, such as the Grand United Order of Odd Fellows, the Independent Order of Saint Luke, and the United Order of True Reformers. The latter two were founded by ex-slaves after the Civil War and initially specialized in sickness and burial insurance.[9] African American membership in fraternal societies was enormous. In 1916, there were over 300,000 Blacks in the Odd Fellows and 250,000 in the Knights of Pythias.

The importance of fraternal societies went beyond material assistance, as they became basic communities and centers where Blacks found support, friendship, and the communication of a set of values that built good character. They built orphanages and homes for the sick and offered a form of life and health insurance. They fed the hungry, clothed the naked, and offered a home for the homeless.

This was accomplished without government assistance. A number of factors could be mentioned for the decline of fraternal communities among Blacks, but there is no doubt that the expansion of the welfare state was a major one. These organizations remained a thriving force well into the

---

[8] Michael Katz, *Improving Poor People: The Welfare State, the "Underclass," and Urban Schools as History* (Princeton, NJ: Princeton University Press, 1995), 4; See also Tanner, *The Poverty of Welfare*, 18–19.

[9] David Beito, "Mutual Aid, State Welfare, and Organized Charity: Fraternal Societies and the Deserving and Undeserving Poor, 1900–1930," *Journal of Policy History* 5, no. 4 (Fall 1993): 419–34, cited in Tanner, *Poverty of Welfare*, 20. See also David Beito, "From Mutual Aid to Welfare State: How Fraternal Societies Fought Poverty and Taught Character," Heritage Foundation, July 27, 2000, http://www.heritage.org/research//lecture/from-mutual-aid-to-welfare-state.

1930s, but with more welfare benefits being available to Blacks an important reason for their existence was lost.

The New Deal and the Great Society

The Great Depression was a difficult period in our nation's history. At its worst point there were some thirteen million people unemployed, about 24.8 percent of the labor force in 1933. Over the 1929 to 1933 period, economic production fell by half and disposable income dropped 28 percent. By 1933, there were 12.8 million unemployed. This was the context for central planning and federal expansion.

With the economic collapse came a great push to increase federal intervention in the economy and to provide relief; as usual, a crisis created a need for immediate solutions and government intervention. Local governments looked to the states for help, and the states increasingly looked toward Washington. The professional class of social workers demanded federal action, and various groups of reformers and radicals marched into Washington to second this demand. In Congress, representatives who perceived the sentiment of their constituents turning toward government joined the cause. Although President Herbert Hoover initially opposed federal provision of relief, he eventually caved to popular pressure.[10]

A common explanation for this development—at the time and ever since—is that capitalism and the free-market economy produced the collapse, so the only way to prevent the inherently destructive forces of the system was through government intervention. It was the "laissez-faire" attitude of Hoover, this interpretation continues, that precipitated the economic catastrophe, when it could have been headed off with some timely intervention. In reality, Hoover dramatically increased spending on relief programs and subsidies and government intervention in the economy was on the rise. So much so, that candidate Roosevelt accused Hoover of presiding over the greatest spending administration in all of history.[11]

However one reads this chapter of history, it is certainly true that the welfare state grew exponentially following the landslide election of President Franklin Roosevelt in 1932. He gained power with a promise of austerity,

---

[10] Tanner, *Poverty of Welfare*, 23–24.

[11] See Lawrence W. Reed, *Great Myths of the Great Depression* (1981; repr., Midland, MI: Mackinac Center, 2010), 5.

balancing the budget, and sound monetary policy, but wasted no time in expanding the welfare state beyond anything our country had ever seen. His Federal Emergency Relief Act was the first federal law that did not limit welfare to widows or people with disabilities, including as it did "all needy unemployed persons and/or their dependents." The federal government intervened not only through grants to the states but increasingly in a direct manner, tying the individual citizen to the national state in an unprecedented way. "President Roosevelt and the New Deal forever changed the face of welfare in America," Michael Tanner claims. "Between 1932 and 1939 welfare spending at all levels of government ... increased from $208 million to $4.9 billion. At the same time, the New Deal dramatically increased the federal role in welfare. In 1932, 97.9 percent of all government welfare spending was at the state and local levels. By 1939 such spending had declined to just 37.5 percent."[12]

This created a straight line to the federal government through public works jobs, direct relief, and social insurance. Roosevelt's rhetoric decrying dependency on relief did not match his actions, as he exponentially increased relief programs. By 1934, there were twenty million people on the dole, and with the Social Security Act of 1935 came the Aid to Dependent Children program (later Aid to Families with Dependent Children, AFDC), which is today Temporary Assistance for Needy Families (TANF).[13] Initially a very small program intended only for widows and families with an absent or disabled father, the program is now a behemoth.

During the 1950s AFDC and other relief programs grew in spite of rapid economic growth. By 1956, about 2.2 million people were receiving aid, and things were soon to expand even more. After the assassination of President John F. Kennedy, Lyndon Johnson embarked on a massive transformation of the notion of the place of government in society with his Great Society plan that would include a War on Poverty, the unofficial name given to legislation first introduced by President Johnson during his State of the Union address on January 8, 1964. Medicare, Medicaid, Head Start, a number of job training, health care, and direct aid programs, and an expansion of AFDC soon ballooned the size of government and added

[12] Tanner, *Poverty of Welfare*, 26.

[13] See Susan W. Blank and Barbara B. Blum, "A Brief History of Work Expectations for Welfare Mothers," *Welfare to Work* 7 (no. 1, 1997): 29–30.

millions of people to the rolls of federal aid. By 1972, close to ten million people were on AFDC and other welfare programs.[14]

With such growth came a political incentive to maintain and expand these new initiatives, and the following administrations of Presidents Nixon, Ford, and Carter all added new anti-poverty programs. Spending more than tripled between 1965 and 1975, and a number of court decisions struck down state laws that contained limiting criteria for aid, strengthening the understanding of welfare benefits as a "right."[15] Since then—albeit with some retrenchments focused on reducing its size and scope—the welfare state has become a prominent feature on the face of our nation.

The legacy of the Great Society was not the elimination of poverty but the institutionalization of welfare and the definitive federalization of poverty alleviation efforts. Long gone was the initial residualist conception of welfare, whereby helping those in need was a function primarily of families, churches, and private charities.[16] The institutional conception, where the nation-state provides a broad range of social services and economic protections, was here to stay.[17] With welfare seen as a basic institution of society and more people hooked on the dole, the stigma formerly attached to a life of dependency was removed. Efforts have been made to offer universal schemes of federal benefits instead of selective systems, because "if we

---

[14] Olasky, *Tragedy of American Compassion*, 182.

[15] Robert Rector and William Lauber, *America's Failed $5.4 Trillion War on Poverty* (Washington, DC: Heritage Foundation, 1995), 11. See more at http://www.downsizinggovernment.org/hhs/welfare- spending#_edn9.

[16] In the *residualist conception*, social welfare is not a major institution but a set of activities of individuals and groups within society. Residualists believe that it is inappropriate to view social welfare as a basic community alongside other communities such as the family, the business community, the neighborhood, or churches. Social welfare is truly a safety net to catch those who find themselves in hard times and restore them or take care of those who are permanently unable to take care of themselves.

[17] See Neil Gilbert and Paul Terrell, *Dimensions of Social Welfare Policy*, 5th ed. (Boston: Allyn and Bacon, 2002), 29–32. In the *institutional conception*, social welfare is a distinct institution in society, not merely a safety net. It is not supposed to carry the stigma of the "dole" and conceives welfare benefits as a right. Government has a primary role in securing social welfare, because the main causes of poverty are institutional.

are all on the dole, there is no stigma."[18] The organization of the welfare state in America began with a focus on local governments and aid to those in desperate need—those victimized by a calamity and unable to work. Later, federal intervention increased, but the system was still conceived as the provision of social insurance and a "safety net," primarily offered to the neediest people. Eventually, however, eligibility became less categorized and less tied to work and moved to include a greater number of people. With every crisis, there has been an expansion both in scope and spending. The next phase has seen a call to enact egalitarian and redistributive principles with universalist intentions, tying the entire population to benefit and moving even beyond citizenship.

One terrible consequence of statist universal schemes is the death of philanthropy. "If the state assumes the prime responsibility for helping those in need," Samuel Gregg points out, "it is little wonder that the philanthropic impulse with commercial society begins to diminish."[19] This is the reality in many countries, where government dominates the charitable realm to the point where private initiative barely exists. In the United States, the private charitable sphere remains robust, thanks to the strong and resilient tradition of mediating institutions. But these private efforts often find themselves at odds with or crowded out by government programs; instead, government should be encouraging such efforts as more efficient and humane.

THE IDEOLOGY OF POVERTY AND WELFARE

As the foregoing history shows, although the welfare system began its development early in the twentieth century, it was not until the 1960s that we saw a massive financial and ideological commitment to institutionalized

---

[18] Under a *selective* system, benefits are available based on individual need. Selectivity can apply both to welfare systems offered by the state as well as those provided by other institutions in society. Families and individuals demonstrating need should have priority in getting help. Means-testing is a way of being selective. In contrast, *universalism* posits that welfare benefits must be available to the entire population as a basic right. Universalists see social policy as the proper response of society because all citizens are "at risk" in the sense that all suffer life problems at one time or the other. The government's role is expansive, so as to be able to respond to these needs.

[19] Samuel Gregg, *The Commercial Society: Foundations and Challenges in a Global Age* (Lanham, MD: Lexington Books, 2007), 105.

aid. This evolution went hand-in-hand with a transformation of the ideas behind welfare provision.

The dimensions of welfare policy have changed based on what seems to have been a new ethos and a new social understanding of poverty and social action. The first dimension was the federalization of welfare. A unitary vision of society was adopted, whereby the federal government took control of dispensing aid. The second was the comprehensive nature of the system. The number of programs addressing an array of areas of life increased and continues to expand. The third was the meaning of the system. From a system conceived as a safety net we moved toward a system that sees welfare as a basic institution of society.

The turmoil of the 1960s and the growing call for federal action took over the national conscience and the understanding of poverty and how to alleviate it. The institutionalization of welfare was underway then in full force, expedited by President Johnson's War on Poverty. Poverty began to be seen as the result of structural realities in society. People were victims of a system that kept them in poverty. If poverty was entrenched, then the poor were trapped in the pressing needs of the moment, working so hard to meet basic immediate needs that they could not be expected to advance beyond this state. Frustrated and exhausted by exigency, they lacked the time, resources, and inclination to engage in second-order activities that could help them get out of poverty. In other words, external forces prevented them from moving forward.

What was a good and caring society to do? Intervene to meet these needs and alleviate the pressures of a life in the bondage of immediacy. And intervene we did, massively.

With most of the basic needs taken care of, this way of thinking goes, the poor will then have the resources, time, and inclination to change. The theory was that welfare would lessen dependency. For example, President Kennedy stated that a war on poverty must be undertaken "to help our less fortunate citizens help themselves." He added, "We must find ways of re-urning far more of our dependent people to independence."[20]

We would spend money to create programs and bring people up from dependence into independence. President Johnson spoke likewise: the creation

[20] "Public Welfare Program—Message from the President of the United States" (H. Doc. No. 325), *Congressional Record*—House, February 1, 1962, 1405, cited in Sowell, *Vision of the Anointed*, 9.

of federal welfare programs was intended to make "taxpayers out of tax-eaters" and "give a hand, not a handout." When his poverty-alleviation legislation passed, he proclaimed, "The days of the dole in our country are numbered."[21]

We can see that the rhetoric of the War on Poverty was aligned with the ethos behind the initial, residualist understanding of poverty alleviation: we intervene to restore people to a condition of self-sufficiency, and the aid is not a right but an instrument to uplift, empower, and motivate. Yet the problem was that the system created a set of incentives pressing against the reality of human nature. What occurred was contrary to the intended purpose of lessening dependency, because the anthropology behind the system was incorrect. Simply put, the system misunderstood the human person. In so doing, it created an incubator of dependency that instead of eliminating poverty made it a permanent fixture. The avalanche of aid did move people out of official poverty but not out of dependency. With the passing of time, dependency rose and so did official poverty, as the line of demarcation continued to move upward.

Such was the failure that there were more officially poor people in 1992 than in 1964, when the War on Poverty began. The reality is that the human person responds to incentives, and massive aid offers an incentive for permanence in the condition of poverty. The longer the aid is given and the more comprehensive the set of benefits is, the stronger is the tendency to acquire and not lose them. Eventually, people see these benefits as a right, as an absolute necessity, and see as "mean-spirited" those who even suggest that the benefits should someday be halted. Thus is put in place the incentive for the creation of a permanent underclass, more or less well-fed but still in official poverty.

The very forces of incentive behind a program created for the purpose of lessening poverty conspired to create a system with the opposite, unintended consequence of strengthening dependency, which triggered a further expansion of the welfare system. "The so-called 'social safety net' has become a sticky web that ensnares people—rich and poor—keeping them in a kind of economic torpor," Max Borders observes. "Those who might be Makers increasingly become Takers."[22]

---

[21] See Marjorie Hunter, "Johnson Signs Bill to Fight Poverty: Pledges Era," *New York Times*, August 21, 1964, 1, cited in Sowell, *Vision of the Anointed*, 10.

[22] Borders, *Super Wealth*, 181.

Moreover, these innate forces of incentive built into the system helped move welfare to its next level: institutionalization. The next phase of institutionalization required a justification for the failures of reducing dependency. There have been two main explanations: (1) We did not invest enough; and (2) We would have been even worse off if we had not intervened.

The initial goal was soon ignored in favor of a new one: reducing official poverty by the redistribution of resources. The transfer of resources from some to others became the overarching goal. The test for whether a program was successful was no longer whether dependency was reduced but whether a given program personally benefited a recipient. It would be hard to find an instance of failure under such a premise. More importantly, a system where reducing dependency is no longer the main goal creates the incentive for a broken, divided society, with those who produce on one side and those who do not on the other. People might desire to work, but the system creates a powerful contrary incentive not to.

Even though poverty rates had been going down for generations, the programs were deemed successful by offering a non-falsifiable explanation. As one commentator put it, "The question is not what the bottom line is today—with poverty up—but where would we be if we didn't have these programs in place?" Using this criterion, one is free to speculate: "I think we'd have poverty rates over 25 percent."[23]

With this justification in place, it is logical to conclude that more spending will serve more people, thus creating a successful program. The truth is that the poor were not helpless victims moved by structural forces outside of their control but creative subjects with the moral capacity for self-realization. The poor were struggling, but the struggle itself was the very instrument by which they could escape poverty. Once that instrument was removed, harm was done regardless of the amount of money invested in propping them up. The welfare state became an awful waste of social capital.[24] Poverty was going down in America way before we "changed our mind" about how to

[23] See Lucia Mount, "U.S. War on Poverty: No Sweeping Victory, But Some Battles May Have Been Won," *Christian Science Monitor*, September 19, 1984, 3–4, cited in Sowell, *Vision of the Anointed*, 15.

[24] See Malloch, *Doing Virtuous Business*, 11–17. Social capital is a set of desirable conditions manifested in persistent relationships within interactive communities. Positive conditions for human flourishing emerge from social networks built on trust and reciprocity. Under conditions of genuine economic liberty and a cultural ethos that nurtures virtue, people learn that being trust-

tackle it. Fathers were working two jobs and mothers would sew garments and ration meals at home. Life was tough, but these people sacrificed to raise their children into a better life. They were willing to sacrifice and delay gratification, and their sacrifice paid off.

The Results of the Welfare System

Federal intervention in the form of relief programs and services since the mid-sixties has been massive. From a few minor programs in the early twentieth century the federal government grew by the 2010s to include dozens of programs spread across a variety of federal departments and agencies. Spending by federal and state governments combined on means-tested programs designed for the poor now exceed a trillion dollars per year.[25]

The third phase of welfare reform, with its drive toward full institutionalization, has been defended by many in view of some attempts at reform. During the 1980s many states experimented with different models but were often attacked by those who saw welfare as a right. A writer for *The Nation*, for example, denounced work requirements ("workfare") as "indentured servitude."[26] When welfare reform passed in 1996, many predicted a doomsday scenario. The best example might be an often-cited Urban Institute study that predicted over one million children thrown into poverty by the reform.[27] In an editorial with the vivid title "Look Ma! No Net!" *The Nation* claimed that "conservative estimates suggest an additional 1.2 million children will be denied help."[28] At the time, referring to President Bill Clinton and

---

worthy and playing fair tend to create more and better opportunities in the long run than cheating and being opportunistic.

[25] Robert Rector and Vijay Menon, "Understanding the Hidden $1.1 Trillion Welfare System and How to Reform It," Heritage Foundation Backgrounder no. 3294, April 5, 2018, https://www.heritage.org/welfare/report /under standing-the -hidden-11-trillion-welfare-system-and-how-reform-it.

[26] Valerie Polakow, "On a Tightrope Without a Net," *The Nation*, May 1, 1995.

[27] See Sheila Zedlewski, "Potential Effects of Congressional Welfare Reform Legislation on Family Incomes," Urban Institute, 1996. A *New York Times* columnist, Bob Herbert, used the study to attack reform as "creepy": Bob Herbert, "In America; The Mouths of Babes," *New York Times*, July 22, 1996.

[28] "Look Ma! No Net," editorial, *The Nation*, December 11, 1995.

moved by the dire predictions of the "experts," a representative of his own party exclaimed, "My president will boldly throw 1 million into poverty."[29]

The results of reform were very different from the wild predictions. Official poverty did not increase; in effect, it decreased. Millions of children did not wake up under bridges, and welfare rolls were reduced at one point by 60 percent. The year before welfare reform was made law, the poverty rate was at 13.8 percent, and it declined to 11.7 percent by 2003. Among African American children poverty went to its lowest percent in history. Instead of 2.6 million additional children in poverty, there were 3.5 million fewer children in poverty.

Anecdotal cases of families who suffered hardship after welfare reform can be located, of course. One study, for example, found that 38.7 percent of former welfare recipients were unable to pay a utility or housing bill at least once during the year after leaving welfare.[30] The reality is, however, that some families at times had these problems before welfare reform and there is no good reason to believe that private charities cannot suffice for assisting these families.

Yet, reform was limited to only one welfare program and welfare spending continued to rise considerably. As mentioned, more than a hundred federal anti-poverty programs exist, administered by a number of agencies and departments. The exact number of programs fluctuates periodically depending on congressional appropriations, but the clear trend is for growth. As of 2012, at least 106 million Americans receive benefit from at least one of these programs.[31]

Poverty has not receded due to greater federal involvement, more anti-poverty programs, and billions of dollars spent. The policies of welfare have been an abject failure. Not only have these policies been a failure but their cost has a potential nefarious effect on the most vulnerable as insolvency is a real possibility for the future. Poor children deserve better schools, and needy people deserve systems that bring help closer and attend to local needs assessed by local people. The welfare state impedes these

[29] Representative Charles Rangel, cited in Jeff Jacoby, "Welfare Catastrophe? No, It's a Modest Reform," *Boston Globe*, August 6, 1996.

[30] See U.S. Conference of Mayors, "Status Report on Hunger and Homelessness in American Cities," Washington, 2000, cited in Tanner, *Poverty of Welfare*, 51–52.

[31] Michael Tanner, "The American Welfare State: How We Spend Nearly $1 Trillion a Year Fighting Poverty—And Fail," Cato Institute Policy Analysis no. 694, April 11, 2012, 3.

goals by centralizing and bureaucratizing poverty alleviation efforts. The money goes to Washington, where it is eaten up by federal "bureaucracies of compassion," with only a fraction ending up where it should, in the hands of the deserving poor.

A conservative estimate shows that government redistributive agencies absorb two-thirds of every dollar budgeted to them. That leaves only one-third of the dollar for the subsidy recipient. If we add to that the cost of taxation imposed on the taxpayer (in the form of time and expenses to comply with tax law), the actual cost of delivering each dollar of subsidy to recipients is nearly five dollars. To spend five dollars in the process of delivering only one is not an efficient system.[32]

Finally, when one follows the money thrown at anti-poverty programs—many trillions of dollars in state and federal spending since the 1960s—and examines the declared goals for the effort, it is difficult to avoid agreeing with President Ronald Reagan when he said, "In the sixties we waged a war on poverty, and poverty won."[33] Not only did welfare grow exponentially since the New Deal but it became increasingly federalized. Historical data showing the relationship between the resources spent on poverty and poverty rates shows no relationship of causation (in effect, no correlation) between greater government expenditures and the lowering of poverty rates.[34]

In fact, poverty had been going down exponentially before the federal government spent more than $50 billion in federal anti-poverty efforts during the late 1960s. Since then, poverty stabilized but welfare spending skyrocketed.[35] One reason for this failure is the perverse incentive structure created by a welfare system that is inadequately concerned with the danger of cultivating dependency.

One crucial, long-term factor in avoiding or escaping poverty is simple and straightforward: having a job. Yet, the incentives built into the welfare

[32] See James Rolph Edwards, "The Cost of Public Income Redistribution and Private Charity," *Journal of Libertarian Studies* 21 (no. 2, Summer 2007): 8–9.

[33] Nicholas Lemann, "The Unfinished War," *Atlantic Monthly* (December 1988): 37.

[34] Tanner, *Poverty of Welfare*, 32.

[35] See Dylan Matthews, "Poverty in the Fifty Years Since 'The Other America,' in Five Charts," *Washington Post*, July 11, 2012, http://www.washington post.com/blogs/wonkblog/wp/2012/07/11/poverty-in-the-50-years-since-the-other -america-in-five-charts/.

system conspire against making that decision. In terms of economic calculation, the welfare system makes work irrational. Too often welfare benefits (which are tax-free) exceed work income. A 2013 study summarized the situation at that time. In thirty-five states, welfare paid more than a minimum wage, even after accounting for the Earned Income Tax Credit. In twelve states, an individual getting a job equal to welfare benefits would see a decline in income. In thirty-three states, the equivalent wage value of welfare had increased since 1995. The largest increase was in the states of Vermont, Hawaii, the District of Columbia, and New Hampshire. In thirteen states, welfare paid over $15 per hour. In eleven states, welfare paid more than the average pre-tax first-year wage for a teacher. In thirty-nine states, it was more than the starting wage of a secretary.[36]

Federal and state welfare-program work requirements have been varied and fluid over the last couple of decades, but leniency during the Covid pandemic certainly contributed to a rise in the problem of government assistance fueling the avoidance of productive work. According to one early 2023 estimate, food stamps and Medicaid combined provide more than $400 billion annually to able-bodied American adults.[37] A persistent trend of declining labor force participation by able-bodied men of prime working age points to the need to ensure that work is not disincentivized.[38]

In spite of attempts to reform and calls for ending welfare as we have known it, the welfare state has become institutionalized and its justification appears to have shifted. It seems no longer like a "safety net" focused on restoring the individual to independence but instead a permanent fixture of modern America. "If only government assistance *were* a last resort!" Fr. Robert Sirico laments. "The displacement of charity by welfare has left

[36] Michael Tanner and Charles Hughes, *The Work Versus Welfare Trade-Off: 2013*, Cato Institute, August 19, 2013, 3–4, https://www.cato.org/white-paper/work-versus-welfare-trade-2013.

[37] Michael Greibrok, "Universal Work Requirements for Welare Programs Are a Win for All Involved," Foundation for Government Accountability, May 17, 2023, https://thefga.org/research/universal-work-requirements/.

[38] See, for example, Nicholas Eberstadt, "Education and Men without Work," *National Affairs* (Winter 2020), https://www.nationalaffairs.com/publications/detail/education-and-men-without-work.

people's most fundamental moral and spiritual needs unmet—and in the process actually perpetuated material poverty."[39]

During a good portion of the early history of our country, poverty was understood as a function of individuals and basic simple communities such as the family and the church. Government acted as a supplement to the activity of other civil society communities, and the federal government was mostly absent from that effort. That traditional understanding was incrementally challenged by a more collectivist and unitary understanding that saw poverty as structural in nature and its alleviation as a function primarily of the federal government. The New Deal and then the Great Society offered impetus to that new understanding and supplied wind to the sails of the welfare state. Modern welfare programs foster dependency rather than self-reliance. Moreover, the type of poverty we refer to here is of a very different nature than what most people associate with poverty. The quality of life experienced by America's poor would be the envy of most people, in most other parts of the world, through most of history.

In the end, we can see how poverty has become something very different from lacking resources. It is something that penetrates the soul instead of something one lacks externally. True poverty, as opposed to material deprivation, can be seen as the unrestrained appetite for comfort acquired without effort, leading to apathy and vices such as laziness and envy. Too often, human dignity is degraded rather than enhanced by the contemporary welfare state.

---

[39] Sirico, *Defending the Free Market*, 115.

9

Human Dignity

A specter is haunting the Western world: the underclass. This underclass is not poor, at least by the standards that have prevailed throughout the great majority of human history.... In certain respects, indeed, it enjoys amenities and comforts that would have made a Roman emperor or an absolute monarch gasp. Nor is it politically oppressed: it fears neither to speak its mind nor the midnight knock on the door. Yet, its existence is wretched nonetheless, with a special wretchedness that is peculiarly its own.

—Theodore Dalrymple[1]

Everything we do in poverty-alleviation efforts must center on the human person, be for the sake of the human person, and consider first and foremost the human person. Why? What is so important about the human person?

It might be best to begin by answering this question: What, fundamentally, *is* a human person?

The Human Person

Christian anthropology approaches this question by looking at the person in relation to God. That relationship is possible due to the original condition of the human person made in the image of God—the *imago Dei*. The image

[1] Theodore Dalrymple, *Life at the Bottom: The Worldview That Makes the Underclass* (Chicago: Ivan R. Dee, 2001), viii.

of God (Genesis 1:26) is the starting point of theological anthropology and the necessary foundation for the creation of systems of care that understand well the subject at hand. Steve Corbett and Brian Fikkert summarize the connection: "The crucial thing is to help people understand their identity as image bearers, to love their neighbors as themselves, to be stewards of God's creation, and to bring glory to God in all things."[2] However, one need not adhere to Christian theology to notice certain things about humans that assist us in understanding human dignity.

We believe that humans are exceptional because they possess a double capacity: reason and will. This dual capacity makes humans *moral* beings, subjects of meaning who can make or break their lives by the things they believe and the things they choose to do. That is, we can direct ourselves to integral human fulfillment. In a way, we *become* what we believe and do. The grandeur of the human person resides in that incredible capacity for knowing and doing. That capacity is innate and is addressed to certain human and social goods: truth and virtuous acting. We have reason and volition (a will) so that we can know the truth and do good. In short, we are free.

A correct understanding of the human person goes from an original condition or state to a historical reality, in which we see people at times choosing error instead of truth and doing evil things (what Christians call sin) instead of acting rightly. In other words, there is in us a potential that is actualized one way or the other precisely because we are free to believe and choose. If we deny human freedom, we deny human dignity. When a person does so, the Reformed theologian Reinhold Niebuhr wrote, he "contradicts himself within the terms of his own essence. His essence is for free self-determination. His sin is the wrong use of his freedom."[3] Freedom places the person on a journey to completion, an eschatological thrust toward fulfillment. That is, our lives are dynamic, complex, and incomplete. Dignity is existential.

When the immediate biological possibilities of animals are fulfilled, they tend to return to rest. Yet, with persons there is a dimension that moves us forward with an eye on inquiry and further realization. This dimension can lay dormant if we build our systems of care with an erroneous anthropology.

The centrality of the human person is an ancient belief. From Thomas Aquinas and the scholastic thinkers of the medieval period to the eighteenth-

[2] Corbett and Fikkert, *When Helping Hurts*, 145.

[3] Reinhold Niebuhr, *The Nature and Destiny of Man*, vol. 1 (New York: Charles Scribner's Sons, 1949), 16.

century French physiocrats, from Adam Smith and his classic *The Wealth of Nations* to modern Austrian economic thinking, the human person is seen as exceptional.[4] Every project attempting to address human needs is built upon a given understanding of the human person. This understanding is very often undeveloped or hidden within the systems in place and the activities performed, but it is never absent.

Unfortunately, there is ingrained within the processes of many systems of care an incomplete understanding of human dignity that avoids the existential burden. Most service-oriented organizations emphasize these two questions: What we are going to do for people (benefits)? And what are people entitled to (rights)?

"Rights talk" is everywhere in our society, and human dignity is often filtered through the prism of that chatter. The difficulty is not with the notion of rights itself but with its disconnect from social responsibilities and institutions. There exists, as Jordan Ballor tells us, a "hyper-individualism" that centers on claiming rights.[5] Therein lies the problem that confronts those attempting to serve others: a need to account for the legitimate social and moral claims upon each person by our friends, family, and neighbors. Duty and obligation are essential features that spring from a correct understanding of human dignity.

Service-oriented people very often ask themselves, "Who is my neighbor?" (Luke 10:29). This is as it should be. But we also need to let those we serve ask the same question of themselves. "The reality of human sinfulness means that there will always be people who are in need," Ballor points out. "But the fact that they are people, created in God's image with authority, responsibility, and dignity, means that we must help and be helped in particular ways."[6]

As noted earlier, there is something in every person that makes him or her unique and unrepeatable—exceptional. We call this reality *intrinsic* because it is in every person by virtue of being a person. Mother Teresa and Adolf Hitler, Pol Pot and Billy Graham, all had an intrinsic capacity of reason and volition. They all mirrored the Creator in the possession of such power. What they chose to do with those capacities—what they became as a result of those choices—differed dramatically.

---

[4] Donohue-White et.al, *Human Nature*, 1–9.

[5] Ballor, *Get Your Hands Dirty*, 3.

[6] Ballor, *Get Your Hands Dirty*, 9–10.

Many systems of care rely exclusively on this side of the coin of human dignity and end up embracing biological reductionism. Instead of accepting an integrated understanding of the human person, they embrace a dualism where the body is attended to, to the detriment of the spiritual and existential. The vital dimensions of existence become the center of activity and all they do is address material needs.

The passivity and slumber that ensues after animal activity in light of their nature is incentivized when our systems of care fail to address in its fullness the reality of human beings. The other side of human dignity, the existential, is the one that actualizes the potentialities intrinsic to our nature. That is, we take what we were given and we build something with it, one way or the other. It is with reference to the quality of what we build that we can begin to see a difference between Adolf Hitler and Pol Pot on one side and Mother Teresa and Billy Graham on the other.

The systems of care we create and the understanding of human dignity they are built upon will allow us to see human beings as either passive recipients of magnanimity in perennial search for security on one hand, or on the other as active participants in a life that is uncertain, dynamic, and risky but also essential in finding meaning and purpose and striving for completion.

The shadow of materialism hovers over many systems of care that depersonalize and instrumentalize the poor. As material things are central in meeting biological needs, the poor themselves are at times seen as an undifferentiated mass of humanity whose needs are the door to acquire the material goods to be distributed.

Immense energies are invested in the process of gaining resources to acquire these goods, and the poor—and their stories of need—are used for that purpose. The poor become the instrumental narrative in a sad story of deprivation that in turn fills coffers of transactional systems of care and support. In these systems, the key component is the transfer of goods and services, not the person and all the components of his or her dignity.

Transactional systems are utilitarian. Following the thought of the English philosopher John Stuart Mill, they emphasize the general welfare by maximizing the sum of human happiness. This view reduces values to preferences and desires, admitting no qualitative distinction of worth in terms of the choices people make. Just give them the things they need and leave questions of values to them. These systems reject the possibility of meaningful categorization among the poor.[7] Yet, as we will explore further, such categorization is necessary if we seek to genuinely understand and therefore genuinely assist those in need. Recognition of the nature and dignity of the person is the foundation for discerning what is truly needed to improve a person's situation and actualize his or her potential.

The Response Needed

Human dignity requires a recognition of the human person as a body-soul unified whole. The fact of human consciousness and their spiritual character makes persons subjects capable of transcending their biological reality and participating in authentic human action that connects them with the world through discovery, creativity, and self-determination.

The Freedom and Virtue Institute's self-reliance clubs are an example of projects that focus not on passivity but on active participation and character development. In dozens of schools across the United States and beyond, students participate in extracurricular organizations such as gardening or service clubs. Students work, learn economics, and earn funds with which they can meet all their educational needs. The clubs' effectiveness is due to connecting rewards with accomplishment.

Systems of care that affirm the subjectivity of the poor have a better chance of avoiding the staleness of transactional engagements where the poor are provided with material goods and services and helped to connect to the manacles of bureaucracies offering additional help. The spectacle of long lines of people waiting to get "stuff" is the image of idleness and docility.

Promoting the creation of simple systems of encounter and productivity alters the exercise and stimulates engagement and activity. As subjectivity is open-ended and existential, each person is seen in his or her unique reality, demanding from us closer attention to each individual person. In biologistic systems based on the transaction of goods and service, we might think that we already know what a mass of undifferentiated people need. There is not much discovery to be made there. In personalist systems, however, the discovery of the deeper human need is an everyday adventure. Every individual is seen as unique and unrepeatable, made in God's image, with

---

[7] See Michael J. Sandel, "The Political Theory of the Procedural Republic," in Richard John Neuhaus, ed., *Reinhold Niebuhr Today* (Grand Rapids: Eerdmans, 1989), 19–23.

an intrinsic capacity to transcend biological reality; a being called to greatness. The poor are not seen condescendingly as "little" or unimportant but instead as "giants in the making." As that reality may be difficult to descry at first, it is often the case that organizations need to invest in "baby steps" in the right direction.

A correct understanding of the human person also demands a respect for the communal aspect of the person. The *imago Dei* refers not only to the uniqueness of individuality but also to the communal dimension of self. We are beings created in relation to others; we do not pop up from the ground but are born from others, brought into relationship from the very moment of conception. We need each other! The rationale for our communal life goes beyond mere utilitarian necessity. We are in relation to others because relationships are rooted in the deepest orientation of the human soul. There is a social reality inherent in our beings, and human fulfillment is contrary to isolation and the radical individualism of atomistic conceptions. We respect the individual person because he or she is one of us and one with us and because in each we see a glimpse of what it is to have dignity.

Finally, a correct understanding of the human person demands that we are honest about the reality of sin. The actual situation of the human person, the historical context of man, is marred by rupture of relationships: rupture with God and rupture with others. We only need to look around to see the reality of our inhumanity to each other and the sorry state of our condition. We are often inclined to corruption, to immanence, to vice and death. Our response to human dignity must take into consideration the various ways that human dignity is injured by some people against others and by our own actions. No matter the diversity of our religious or philosophical commitments, we are capable of recognizing a common set of moral norms. As human beings, we have a common sense of what it means to treat others with dignity. "There is something in the way we humans are wired," Lawrence Reed insists. "Down deep within us we have a sense of what is right and what is wrong, what is good and what is bad. And when we ignore our wiring, something within us— that voice we call our conscience—cries out to us. In complex situations, the voice can be difficult to discern, but we cannot really deny that it is there."[8]

The poor are human beings also, with the same inclinations to evil and the same potential for good. They are not immune to the temptations of

[8] Lawrence W. Reed, *Are We Good Enough for Liberty?* (Ottawa, IL: Jameson Books, 2018), 12.

vice, just because their material resources are fewer than others'. In short, we need to resist the temptation to romanticize the poor!

We must learn how to address the poor with a realism that avoids doubtful models based on how we think things ought to be. Instead, we must consult them directly, letting the poor speak for themselves regarding the totality of their reality.

Back to the Things Themselves

The philosophical school of phenomenology might prove useful to us as we engage in an honest assessment of who the poor are. Originating with German philosopher Edmund Husserl (1859–1938), this approach can be summarized by Husserl's motto, "Back to the things themselves."[9] Phenomenology focused on the world of experience and what is manifested through human experience. This "intuition" assists reason and enables one to provide a more complete foundation for reasoning by giving a more complete account of what is immediately given in experience.

Using the phenomenological approach, we can ask the question, "What is it to exist as a poor person?" In being honest about the poor, we must avoid any sort of reductionism, where a single characteristic exemplifies the person. It is very often the case that adopting single notions such as "the oppressed" or "the deprived" or "the humble" closes our work to the complete picture and prevents us from appreciating the uniqueness of the reality being addressed. That is, we must resist the temptation to see reality as mediated through conventional ways of thinking, stereotypes, lofty ideals, plausible paradigms, or antecedent ideological commitments. No, let us get "back to the things themselves." Do not assume things about the poor. Get to know them as individuals.

Phenomenology bears affinity with Christianity in its rejection of the priority of the mind above the essence of things in themselves. The human person is subjective and irreducible, and we must have the courage to encounter the poor in their reality to have a good understanding of their uniqueness.[10] Our response to the reality of human dignity

[9] Edmund Husserl, *Logical Investigations*, ed. Dermont Moran, 2nd ed., vol. 1 (1900; repr. London: Routledge, 2001), 168.

[10] Russell Shaw, ed., *Our Sunday Visitor's Encyclopedia of Catholic Doctrine* (Huntington, IN: Our Sunday Visitor Publishing Division, 1997), 499–502.

requires a commitment on our part that can be summarized in the following guidelines:

> ***Be cognizant of the uniqueness of each person.*** In doing so, we must avoid a paternalism that offers condescension and pity and a biologism that focuses exclusively on material needs.
>
> ***Be cognizant of the greatness of the human person.*** For every person our expectations must be high. Condescension and paternalism are detrimental to any meaningful relationship.
>
> ***Be realistic about each person and the human condition.*** Balance general expectations with individual reality: the reality that humanity—and each of its individual members—is fallen and broken.
>
> ***Be willing to create systems that emphasize the creative and existential dignity of the person.*** At times, these systems require that you not respond emotionally and that you keep your good intentions in check.

Finally, human dignity speaks of a condition in humanity that we must recognize before we move into action. Reflection must precede activity. Right order precedes and informs right action.

HELPING THE POOR AS PERSONS

The foregoing discussion should make clear that every ministry or charitable endeavor must dedicate time and study to understanding what it means to be a person. Changing the point of departure—from what people *need* to who individuals *are*—is essential to finding solutions to poverty.

The subject matter of sociology is society; thus it searches for social determinants of behavior. Many organizations operate under a truism that remains in the background of action: systems are to be blamed for conditions, and the institutional framework of society is the source of social problems.

Yet, if we begin with the person and then move to the structures of social interaction, we see a picture that will allow us to create structures that better serve the person. The importance of right order ought to be remembered in our work with the poor: first things first. First it is the dignity of persons made in the image of God, followed by a rational assessment of real needs, then our good intentions, and, finally, our activity. It should not be our will or our feelings that come first, it should be reason—which provides us with good reasons. Our good intentions cannot serve as a substitute for the truth about human persons. Our will to move forward must retreat and patiently await the commands of reason. How hard it is for us to prudently place ourselves among the scenery in the drama of the poor's quest for a better life instead of seeking the limelight of protagonism!

The dignity of the poor is to be discovered not only in the truth of their natural endowments (that is, in the twofold capacity of reason and volition) but more importantly in the actualization of that dignity: in the things they believe and the choices they make. Freedom is a burden! Booker T. Washington recalled upon hearing news about emancipation:

> For some minutes there was great rejoicing, and thanksgiving, and wild scenes of ecstasy.... The wild rejoicing ... lasted but for a brief period, for I noticed that by the time they returned to their cabins there was a change in their feelings. The great responsibility of being free, of having charge of themselves, of having to think and plan for themselves and their children, seemed to take possession of them. It was very much like suddenly turning a youth of ten or twelve years out into the world to provide for himself.... Was it any wonder that within a few hours the wild rejoicing ceased and a feeling of deep gloom seemed to pervade the slave quarters?[11]

The creation of systems that make the poor protagonists of their self-realization is vital for effective and dignity-honoring poverty-alleviation work. As the conscience of our poverty-alleviation efforts, the truth about the human person places limits on how we go about our work, in a way similar to how the Constitution, informed by the Declaration, tames the totalistic impulse of majority rule.

Any attempt to help the poor must reject the idea of the poor as passive recipients of magnanimity, as victims of forces outside their control. The implicit message of some poverty-alleviation efforts is that they intend to stay put to organize for more government benefits or handouts from ministries or nonprofits.

An efficient system of distribution of goods that serves the purpose of making volunteers happy is not necessarily a good program for the poor. Programs that fail to respect right order promise not to solve our social

[11] Booker T. Washington, *Up from Slavery: An Autobiography* (New York: A. L. Burt, 1900), 21–22.

problems but to make them permanent. A respect for right order envisions personal, moral, and cultural change, not just the redistribution of resources.

Right order calls us to see the poor as active participants in their moral journeys in life. They are capable of virtue. And, as Heinrich Rommen tells us, "Virtue is right reason. Nature and reason are one."[12] Our good intentions ought not to be at the helm of our service. Confusing the right order of service makes us activists and "do-gooders," not faithful servants.

Right order invites us to a faithful presence among the poor, to be partners in their struggles: to suffer with them, cry with them, laugh and rejoice with them—but always refraining from acting for them, as surrogate parents of infantilized paupers. When we see action as imperative and demand any means necessary, boundless power is given to "do-gooders" and government bureaucrats. We should resist this temptation. We are not to measure our success by the level of services we offer, often financed with the loot of confiscated money that Pharaoh took from the people; a loot that feeds the coffers of the bureaucracies of false governmental compassion. Christians must understand that what comes first is a dignity that demands restraint. Human dignity demands that we pay close attention to and emphasize human agency in understanding what causes people to flourish.

In short, human dignity is the actualized potentiality of human flourishing toward integral human fulfillment.

---

[12] Heinrich A. Rommen, *The Natural Law: A Study in Legal and Social History and Philosophy*, trans. Thomas R. Hanley, OSB (orig. German, 1936; Indianapolis: Liberty Fund, 1998), 33.

10

How to Help: Guidelines for Thought and Action

Practically speaking, how do we achieve these goals? How do we ensure that we are focused on the person rather than on systems; that we are ordering our efforts rightly by placing thought before action; that we are empowering rather than infantilizing the poor?

There is a tradition of effective compassion that runs through history, inspiring the best charitable activity, manifested in a variety of religious and secular contexts. This tradition provides several principles that can guide our work.

Subsidiarity

Subsidiarity is one of the key principles in Catholic social thought, though it has been appreciated and applied far beyond Catholic circles. This tenet holds that the activity of simpler and smaller communities ought not be impeded by the intervention of larger and more complex organizations. It attempts to tame the temptation to centralize, and it buttresses individual responsibility within basic communities and limited government. The term comes originally from the Latin *subsidium*, which referred to Roman military reserve units that were always ready to assist in battle. During the Middle Ages, *subsidium* referred to a second line of defense, a back-up or reserve that would come to aid first lines of attack. Eventually, the term came to mean "aid" or "assistance."

In modern times, the principle was intimated by Pope Leo XIII in his 1891 encyclical letter *Rerum Novarum*. His concern was to offer a response to the collectivistic views of society being advanced in Europe by socialists and communists. Pope Leo stressed that God reigns over the social realm but in a mediated fashion. He has entrusted to his creatures a measure of his authority over any function they are capable of performing. This mode of governance shows great respect for human freedom and sees any person entrusted with authority as a minister of divine providence. Leo wrote, "The contention, then, that the civil government should at its option intrude into and exercise intimate control over the family and the household is a great and pernicious error."[1] Forty years after *Rerum Novarum*, Pope Pius XI articulated the principle more explicitly in *Quadragesimo Anno*:

> Just as it is gravely wrong to take from individuals what they can accomplish by their own initiative and industry and give it to the community, so also it is an injustice and at the same time a grave evil and disturbance of right order to assign to a greater and higher association what lesser and subordinate organizations can do. For every social activity ought of its very nature to furnish help to the members of the body social, and never destroy and absorb them.[2]

Finally, Pope John Paul II reiterated the principle in the 1990s: "A community of a higher order should not interfere in the internal life of a community of a lower order, depriving the latter of its functions but, rather, support it in case of need and help to coordinate its activities with the activities of the rest of society, always with a view to the common good."[3] We can see here how subsidiarity opposes any form of collectivism and looks skeptically at government interventionism.

Society is not reduced to or collapsed within the affairs and institutions of the state. The life of the individual person and the activity of basic communities are not grants of magnanimity flowing from the state. Every encroachment of the political system on the basic communities of society reduces human freedom and produces harmful and even destructive unintended consequences. The social nature of the human person is best expressed in the context of his or her everyday affairs within simple and

---

[1] Leo XIII, encyclical letter *Rerum Novarum* (May 15, 1891), §14.

[2] Pius XI, encyclical letter *Quadragesimo Anno* (May 15, 1931), §79.

[3] John Paul II, encyclical letter *Centesimus Annus* (May 1, 1991), §48.

natural free associations such as the family, the neighborhood, the church, civic groups, mutual aid societies, the business community, and the local government. In these relationships, the human person remains at the center of social action and as the matrix to understand his or her life.

Subsidiarity is the "how" that responds to the natural, moral obligation to help one's neighbor. As individuals are social beings, it follows that there is also an institutional duty to assist others. Subsidiarity then also speaks of the relative place of communities within the social order and how each relates to the others. It is necessary to understand how human persons interact with others within the various communities to which they belong and how these communities operate in relation to each of their members.

The principle of subsidiarity can assist us in this understanding. An early, partial definition of subsidiarity can be found in the thought of Thomas Aquinas: "It is contrary to the proper character of the State's government to impede people from acting according to their responsibilities—except in emergencies."[4] Here we can see that government (that is, the political community's apparatus for making and implementing decisions) should generally abstain from intervening in the autonomous life of individual members of a community. Not even under the guise of promoting the good of a complete community can government intervention in the affairs of individuals be conceived as limitless. Because government's assistance should not be anything less than geared toward the fulfillment of its citizens, a respect for their autonomy must prevail, as authentic fulfillment demands that people have the opportunity to choose for themselves. Subsidiarity and its hierarchy of mediating institutions keeps the human person at the center of social action.

Here, we are not limiting the principle to governmental activity; it applies to any other higher authority. There exists interplay between assistance and noninterference of higher bodies (such as government, corporations, and nongovernmental organizations) in the affairs of individuals as they live their lives within more basic communities, that is, those communities to which they belong directly.

We must first consider efficiency. The principle of subsidiarity recognizes the limits posed to authorities in gathering relevant information and responding properly to needs. Invariably, the complexity of the task leads to bureaucracy and to the generalization of rules; that is, the depersonalization of care. Bureaucracy is the necessary response to complexity.

---

[4] Thomas Aquinas, *Summa Contra Gentiles*, bk. III, chap. 71, no. 4.

Bureaucrats devise plans and create rules that cannot look at the deeper human need. The "experts," often knowing less than they think, tend to attribute social order to rational design and conscious intention. This is what Friedrich Hayek called the "pretense of knowledge" that leads to the "synoptic delusion." The delusion refers to the notion that a single agent or entity can comprehend and attend the massive range of information present in a given system or situation. Hayek criticized the tendency to ascribe all evident order to the design of higher authorities, leading to personifying the concept of "society" or "the state" and thus attributing responsibility and purposefulness to an abstract mental construct.[5] Such naive or animistic thinking is characteristic of all schools of totalitarian, socialist, and interventionist thought. Unintended consequences are always present, but they are heightened with responses that are distant. Common sense says that if I am going to help the poor man at the door, I will do it better by engaging the unique person in front of me directly. Data and statistics might be helpful, but they are not what the person needs.

The proper knowledge of the real problem assists us in the art (not science) of prudential decisions about how to help. Prudence is necessary to know the limits of our interventionism. But more than prudence is necessary.

First, we must respect individual autonomy as an essential requirement if people are to act in pursuit of basic human goods. The question of an efficient way of assisting people is secondary to a respect of their integral liberty. "Subsidiarity has … less to do with efficiency than with people attaining integral liberty," writes Samuel Gregg. "A basic requirement for realizing this liberty is to act and to do things for ourselves—as the fruit of our own reflection, choices, and acts—rather than to have others do them for us."[6] This liberty is the one that allows people to act for themselves, instead of becoming wards of others.

This liberty is also a universal and essential component of human nature. "To be aware of what human beings have sacrificed for freedom is to understand that freedom is not a garnish on life but one of the central quests of the human experience," says Fr. Robert Sirico. "The human heart has a natural orientation toward liberty. We are built this way, regardless of our religion

---

[5] For a summary of Hayek's views, see Chris Matthew Sciabarra, "Dialectics and Liberty: A Defense of Dialectical Method in the Service of a Libertarian Social Theory," *Foundation for Economic Education*, September 1, 2005, https://fee.org/articles/dialectics-and-liberty/.

[6] Gregg, *On Ordered Liberty*, 60–62.

or ethnicity; indeed, all men are endowed with liberty and a deep desire for it."[7] To honor this liberty, we must recapture the distinctions that older approaches to charity recognized. As Marvin Olasky points out, "Today's believers in 'liberation theology' often argue that God is on the side of the poor, but the older distinction showed God backing the mistreated poor and chastising those who had indulged in indolence."[8]

Second, we must recognize a limit to our good intentions and desire to help. We must bow before the reality of individual choice, even as we propose and incentivize. It can be extremely tempting to assume that we know better, and given the power that communities of a higher order often have, it can be difficult to resist a desire to move into action and bypass individual choice and the life of basic communities. Yet, even if people act unreasonably, we must accept that it is not our place to prevent every evil.

I have encountered this difficult reality in my own work with the poor. Some years ago I was opening the doors of a ministry I directed in Fort Myers, Florida, when a young Haitian man approached me. He was crying. I immediately let him in and soon heard of his desperate situation. "I am homeless and desperate. Could you give me enough money to pay for a motel for a week?" he asked. I was ready to give him a check when something told me to wait. It was just a sense that I needed to hear more. After a long conversation—and a few phone calls—I found out that he had been dismissed from two shelters for misbehavior.

Reluctantly, he allowed me to drive him to his family's home. There I was greeted by a nice lady living in a middle-class neighborhood. Lo and behold, his mother had no other choice but to let him go, as he was using drugs, disrespecting her, and causing havoc. I realized then that I had no responsibility toward him but to encourage him to repent and mend relationships he had broken. Only then I could come alongside the family to assist if need be.

Subsidiarity holds that needs are better served locally and that liberty is the best instrument in pursuing the goods of human nature that help people flourish. A rationalism that seeks to subject all social phenomena to deliberate rational control from detached experts with power is not the best way to help people; it leads to bureaucracy and utopian solutions that miss the reality of the individual person.

---

[7] Sirico, *Defending the Free Market*, 29.

[8] Olasky, *Tragedy of American Compassion*, 4.

SPHERE SOVEREIGNTY

The faces of poverty are diverse, but every single poor person is a subject of meaning with the moral capacity for self-realization. His or her integral liberty must be recognized and respected as each treads a path that only he or she can trace. *Sphere sovereignty* conceives the social order in an organic fashion, with varied social communities ordered toward the good of the whole and no individual organ lording over others.

Sphere sovereignty was first formulated at the turn of the twentieth century by the Dutch theologian and statesman Abraham Kuyper (1837–1920). "We understand hereby, that the family, the business, science, art and so forth are all social spheres," Kuyper wrote, "which do not owe their existence to the State, and which do not derive the law of their life from the superiority of the State, but obey a high authority within their own bosom; an authority which rules, by the grace of God, just as the sovereignty of the State does."[9]

Sphere sovereignty is a neo-Calvinist concept that looks at the social order in an organic fashion. It is based on the idea that every part of human life exists equally and directly "before the face of God." An organic constitution of society demands respect for all societal spheres and challenges statist conceptions of society. Each sphere of life has its own distinct responsibilities and competence and stands equal to other spheres of life. Sphere sovereignty implies decentralization and places limits on state authority.

Sphere sovereignty attempts to explain the limits of state action with reference to the sovereignty of Christ over society and history. There is a broad continuity and kinship between subsidiarity and sphere sovereignty. There are, however, differences in the approach to the question of the roles and places of various social organs within society. Sphere sovereignty insists on an organic constitution of society, with the state being but one organ alongside others; the state is not to be seen as the parent that magnanimously allows space for other civil society communities.

This organic constitution can be simply explained by the analogy of the human body as a complete organism. Each part of the human body is ordered toward the good of the whole according to the proper end of each part. Each part separately constituted is imperfect on its own. Instead, its reality and purpose are understood in relation to the rationale of the entire organism of which it is a part. Each part has its intended purpose, features,

[9] Abraham Kuyper, *Lectures on Calvinism* (Edinburgh: T&T Clark, 1899), 116, as quoted in Ballor, *Get Your Hands Dirty*, 146.

functions, and significance, but is to work in coordinated fashion with the rest for the good of the whole. Mutually reinforcing each other and acting in complementary fashion, each organ contributes to the common good.

Society is similarly constituted. Each social institution within the body politic relies immediately and directly on God for its existence and authority, not depending on the mediation of any other social organism. God has established authorities of various kinds, and they constitute his mediated sovereignty among humanity.[10] No individual organ can be reduced to another, and each requires, and fosters, particular virtues for the attainment of human flourishing. Each sphere has its own centrality and beauty and is essential for the proper ordering of society.

More importantly, each individual person also has a measure of responsibility and authority that cannot be taken away or transferred. Responsibility for the social order does not accrue only to institutions but also to individual human beings in their concrete circumstances of life.[11] Why is that? Why not let institutions with their resources and power have the task of being responsible for the good of others?

One way of answering that question is that God wanted to bestow on human beings, using the phrase from Blaise Pascal, "the dignity of causality."[12] Made in God's image, each person has a responsibility to become an instrument of God in the temporal sphere. The state cannot be seen as a substitute for Christian voluntary action, as it seems to become when religious leaders exhibit a consistent tendency to justify the welfare state. The welfare state has become a proxy for Christian action, and a defense of endless governmental interventions is seen as compassion. The organizational principle for Christian compassion cannot be state activity, and a commitment to biblical compassion ought not be reduced to support for more zeroes at the end of government program allocations. This is damaging to our society and to those we intend to help. "No self-government can stand where individuals choose to live as slaves and wards," Michael Novak warns. "Just as tyrannies may on occasion be benevolent, the

---

[10] See Jordan Ballor, "A Society of Mutual Aid" in Wim Decock et al., eds., *Law and Religion: The Legal Teachings of the Protestant and Catholic Reformations* (Bristol, CT: Vandenhoeck & Ruprecht, 2014), 9–21.

[11] Ballor, "A Society of Mutual Aid," 16.

[12] Blaise Pascal, *The Thoughts, Letters, and Opuscules of Blaise Pascal*, ed. O. W. Wight (New York: Hurd and Houghton, 1864), 399.

powerful modern state may also be paternalistic, providing for the material welfare of its citizens in exchange for the surrender of self-government."[13]

A simple way to differentiate between subsidiarity and sphere sovereignty is to see each as different intellectual angles to the question of the right ordering of society. Subsidiarity can be seen as a hierarchical model looking at the vertical relationship between "higher" and "basic" communities or institutions. Sphere sovereignty envisions an organic relationship, focusing on the ultimate end or purpose (telos) of each organ within society.

As members of various organs with their own constitution and relevance, human persons are called to participate fully in the life of each community. That is, we are all called to *oikonomia* (stewardship). In collectivist conceptions of society offering a unitary vision of the good and often led by the state as the primary and leading community, stewardship is transferable and mediated through state organs to which we are tied only secondarily. Unitary and centralized systems can induce citizens to find excuses for inaction. We can simply say, "I pay my taxes, the poor are being fed, nothing is broken," or, "I tithe, go to church, pray a little, what else do you want?" These are not examples of stewardship; these are alibis.

Stewardship is not simply an activity such as funding a mission trip, donating, or volunteering. Instead, it is the lived expression of a whole-life commitment.[14] It is not something we "do" or "contribute"; it is who we are. Membership in a community demands a specific vocation, that is, a specific commitment to advance the good of the whole, within our particular commitments within the organs of society. Each of us has a purpose within social organs that in turn possess a larger, God-given purpose.

The French philosopher Blaise Pascal said, "God established prayer … in order to communicate to his creatures the dignity of causality."[15] Such dignity is also actualized whenever we act. The human capacity to act is to be seen as one of God's first graces: "The Lord God then took the man and settled him in the garden of Eden, to cultivate and care for it" (Gen. 2:15).

[13] Novak, *Spirit of Democratic Capitalism*, 165.

[14] See Stephen Grabill, "The Church's Call to Steward God's Mission in the World," *The Gospel Coalition*, August 19, 2014, https://www.thegospelcoalition.org/article/the-churchs-call-to-steward-gods-mission-in-the-world/.

[15] Pascal, *The Thoughts, Letters, and Opuscules of Blaise Pascal*, 399.

Solidarity

Solidarity is a principle that affirms the bonds we share with other human beings. It invites us to value others as individuals. All human beings share a common human bond by their nature, but we need to consciously and freely actualize that bond by the choices we make in regard to others.

Solidarity must not be confused with mere sentimentality or with "feeling sorry" for people. It is not a dry and empty affirmation of the need to help people—one that is given by virtually everyone but is often followed by inaction. As Pope John Paul II stated, solidarity "is not a feeling of vague compassion or shallow distress at the misfortunes of so many people, both near and far. On the contrary, it is a firm and persevering determination to commit oneself to the common good; that is to say to the good of all and of each individual, because we are all really responsible for all."[16]

Solidarity is a virtue by which we fulfill ourselves by connecting with others in a personal fashion. That is, the good of others is necessarily included among the moral goods we seek to realize when we act. When I go to work to make money, I work not just to satisfy personal needs or wants but often also to feed my family, care for them, and fulfill my obligations toward them. My attitude of solidarity moves me to act on their behalf. That is why the reciprocity that follows from the virtue of solidarity must not be coerced: when we freely choose to fulfill our obligations to others, we perfect ourselves. Solidarity is then an attitude, a readiness, a moral habit, and a commitment to fulfill our obligations to others. When people work and strive together, they join in the subjective moment of jointly dirtying their hands and that transitive act builds an intransitive good: the good of community.

A misunderstanding of solidarity must be avoided. Solidarity does not mean taking over tasks and duties assigned to others, in a form of cheap paternalism. As Pope John Paul II wrote as a philosopher prior to his papacy, "Solidarity is to some extent a restraint from trespassing upon other people's obligations and duties, or from taking over as one's own the part that belongs to others."[17] As solidarity is a virtue that must be actualized,

---

[16] John Paul II, encyclical letter *Sollicitudo Rei Socialis* (December 30, 1987), §38.

[17] Karol Wojtyla (John Paul II), *The Acting Person* (Dordrecht: D. Reidel, 1979), 341; as quoted in Samuel Gregg, *Challenging the Modern World: Karol Wojtyla/John Paul II and the Development of Catholic Social Teaching* (Lanham, MD: Lexington Books, 1999), 210.

that must be self-realized, we must allow people to fulfill themselves morally by realizing their own commitments.[18]

Paternalism might move people to offer never-ending lines of material support, under the belief that the poor are incapable. It might move others to believe that the poor have nothing meaningful to share spiritually or intellectually. Or it could take the form of the poor passively watching someone labor for their benefit, reinforcing the belief— theirs, and perhaps the benefactors'—that they are indeed helpless. Finally, it might make the giver think that he is absolutely necessary in a managerial position—to lead, to decide, and ultimately to control. Each one of these paternalistic attitudes is harmful to any poverty-alleviation effort.[19]

Solidarity is not about saving the poor from the struggles of everyday life. It is instead to be willing to have true compassion, that is, to suffer with them. One of the reasons for a "rescue" attitude among those attempting to serve the poor is the realization that freedom is a burden that awakens our vulnerability. The "shock of accountability" is real. Freedom always challenges us, and we might want to save the poor from the quest. Resist that temptation!

Not engaging in that necessary struggle within the self gives way to an anti-self that lives in an underworld of self-doubt that feeds on our pity and eventually creates resentment and encourages isolation. Solidarity means to be there with the poor and believe in them, while finding ways to assist and support them in a journey only they can take.[20]

Too many times we hear of churches going on mission trips to foreign lands and inundating these areas with goods, with no regard to unintended consequences. So many crusades to dump "stuff" on people have generated never-ending requests for more, and eventual resentment on the part of givers, who abandon the mission, defeated by frustration and tired of ineffective ways of serving.

A few years ago I was working for a small mission church in the inner city. At a meeting one staff member told of her experience with a nearby migrant camp, populated mostly by Guatemalans. The ladies there had an

[18] See Gregg, *Challenging the Modern World*, 208–2110.

[19] See Corbett and Fikkert, *When Helping Hurts*, 109–113.

[20] For an excellent discussion of vulnerability among black Americans, see Shelby Steele, *The Content of Our Character: A New Vision of Race in America* (New York: Harper Perennial, 1990), chap. 3.

open common area with flat rocks and would go there every day to hand-wash clothes using the rocks. Mission staff were outraged at the sight and immediately mobilized to raise funds to build them a shed with two brand-new washing machines. They were so proud of the accomplishment!

Excitement turned into puzzlement as days went by and no one was using the machines. After asking why, they found the answer. The women loved to gather together and wash the clothes by hand, as it was their tradition. It was a meaningful time of camaraderie and community. They did not need washing machines. If the staff had only asked, they might have discovered what these migrants' real needs were, instead of assuming the nature of their needs based on values or expectations that were not necessarily shared.

Solidarity allows us to participate in the struggle of the poor, not to take over or eliminate the struggle. When we attempt to take over the responsibilities that rightfully belong to the poor themselves, we stymy their self-realization and weaken their resolve to strive. We create incentives not to participation but to passivity: "If you want to take care of me, I'll let you." In the rational economic calculations of everyday life, it is vital that we create a motive for engagement, for if such a motive is not created, mankind's lower nature will triumph in the war of inclinations.

Bonding does not mean "to do for" but "to do with." Individuals as well as nations must be allowed to freely choose and pursue what is good for them, and we are to come alongside. We must recede to the periphery of action to avoid compromising the poor's capacity to choose the good by developing the strength of character and the practical skills needed to build a better life. Solidarity, then, stands on a determination to help others that moves us into action without compromising the autonomy of those we desire to help.

Here, prudence is necessary, as there will be times when we will intrude beyond our role. There are times of crisis when we will have to take a leap of faith and do more. This is when subsidiarity becomes the conscience of solidarity. Subsidiarity tempers the totalistic impulse and temptation to take over, to see a crisis in every situation and to rationalize our meddling and busybody engagement.

Remember that each of us has a life and we ourselves each have the primary responsibility for that life. "While it is true that humans are social animals, and that there are many vital mediating institutions in which humans live, move, and have their being," writes Michael Novak, "still, humans are not … fully plumbed by the institutions in which they dwell. Each experiences a solitariness and personal responsibility which renders him (or her) oddly alone in the midst of solidarity."[21] I am responsible for my life; no one else is. I am my brother's keeper, yes, but my brother is his own keeper first. Our task is not to take over but to become witnesses to the miracle of lives well lived.

If connection with the poor is short-lived, the quality of our information on how to help will be limited. Gabe Hurrish, a long-time development aid worker, tells the story of a representative of a big-money donor, who dropped into Ethiopia to learn what the people needed. The visitor pretended to listen to the villagers, but in the end it was apparent that he had his own preconceived ideas about how to help and was not going to take into account the feedback of the recipients of his largesse. Hurrish was worried that the representative's insensitivity would sour the people's view of his own mission among them, but he discovered that they were unfazed. The reason was that Hurrish did not fly in and fly out but instead lived for years among the villagers, sharing their hardships and joys. "I was overwhelmed by their generosity of spirit," he writes. "It was clear that what gave me influence in the community was not my own merit, expertise, or credentials. It was the fact that I was present over a long period of time and that I demonstrated commitment to the genuine welfare of the people rather than to my own agenda."[22]

Poor people apprehend whether the well-intentioned volunteer is there for the long run or just easing his guilt. Unfortunately, the latter attitude only facilitates transactions that might keep the poor fed but still in poverty.

Person-Centered Work: Respect for the Individual

Solidarity and bonding require that we understand that collective labels obscure information. Although it is possible to have a general picture about who the poor are, proxies often impede the targeting of the real and deeper human need. Here, we can benefit from the insight of economics through the principle of methodological individualism.

The praxis of poverty-alleviation must address the action of individuals, or it runs the risk of descending into a fraud that at times takes the form

[21] Novak, *Spirit of Democratic Capitalism*, 55.

[22] Gabe Hurrish, "Reflections on International Aid and Human Development (Part 1): Development Assistance Should Be Personal," *Freedom & Virtue Review*, March 3, 2023, https://freedomandvirtue.substack.com/p/reflections-on-international-aid.

of activism. We truly do not know much that is meaningful about the poor unless we actually get to know them *as individuals*.

The concept of the individual is not an empty abstraction, nor is it a denial of the reality of the social nature of a person. A person is connected to others, and his or her existence is mediated through communities. Self-sufficiency increases over time and involves a wide array of social institutions. The human person's independence is never total, as even the so-called "self-made" entrepreneur depends on the cooperation of others.

Yet, all action is performed by individuals. The character of the meaning of human action is determined by the acting person. We cannot visualize collective wholes, but we can certainly get to know and act alongside individual persons. Every individual belongs to multiple coexistent collectives, and through unity with the individual, we get a secondary glimpse of social reality.[23] The Austrian economist Ludwig von Mises articulated the principle of individual action in his classic study *Human Action*: "A collective operates always through the intermediary of one or several individuals whose actions are related to the collective as the secondary source. It is the meaning which the acting individuals and all those who are touched by their action attribute to an action that determines its character."[24] Shelby Steele has warned about what happens when we begin to think of collectives rather than individuals as the motors of human action. "Social victims may be collectively entitled," he writes, "but they are all too often individually demoralized. Since the social victim has been oppressed by society, he comes to feel that his individual life will be improved more by changes in society than by his own initiative. Without realizing it, he makes society rather than himself the agent of change."[25]

Respecting the individuality of persons means understanding that each of us bears the image of God in a unique way and that each of us has different skills, aspirations, temperaments, hopes, histories, fears, and vices. That is why poverty-alleviation efforts that consist of massive distribution of goods or bureaucratic systems that devolve persons into "clients" or numbers fail. They operate on the basis of deficient information and an incorrect anthropology. They lack the personal experience of encounter, even if they might exhibit efficiency in distributing benefits or items.

---

[23] For a discussion of methodological individualism see Mises, *Human Action*, 41–43.

[24] Mises, *Human Action*, 42.

[25] Steele, *Content of Our Character*, 14.

In a person-centered system, encounter facilitates the acquisition of direct information from an individual relationship. As this encounter is focused on the person, whatever internal feature that is relevant is readily available, but the success of our effort cannot simply be reduced to quantitative measurements.

In a group-centered system, general features and general criteria are necessary to address the complexity arising from the task of addressing what often are larger numbers. Group-centered action relies on proxies, because these serve the purpose of reducing reality to common denominators, thus depersonalizing those who should be considered individually.

Bureaucracy emerges as an efficient system to dispense aid. Believing that we already know the needs of the clients, if things do not work, external constraints on the group are easier to target and blame as culprits for whatever negative features are found within the group. Often, two externalities are offered as reasons for failure: insufficient resources and discrimination. If there is any problem with the intervention, it is that it did not occur soon enough or it was not comprehensive.

Respect for the individual person calls for an attitude of humility. We must be very careful in trying to change people when we are working with the poor. As Robert Lupton observes, that attitude might convey a message that is offensive: "I am ok. You are ignorant; I am enlightened. You are wrong; I am right."[26] Practicing effective compassion means treading the tightrope of, on one hand, recognizing and discouraging vice, indolence, and dependence; and on the other hand, being sensitive and humble as we encourage others toward positive change. We must at once be willing to bring moral judgment to bear and also be ready to admit that our judgments or applications of principles could be mistaken.

At the same time, it is not productive to hurl accusations of insensitivity, judgmentalism, or privilege at those who are involved in charitable work. The reality is that most people genuinely want to help, even if all they know how to do is to write a check. Even if they are still influenced by prejudices or fears concerning getting close to the poor, they try to assist one way or the other, and this should be affirmed. Too many books have been written about how American middle- or upper-class Christians do not understand the poor, do not know what poverty is, or do not appreciate how "privileged" they are. Maybe it is the activists who are the ones who do not understand

[26] Robert D. Lupton, *Theirs Is the Kingdom: Celebrating the Gospel in Urban America* (New York: Harper One, 1989), 6.

the reality of most American Christians. What many get from condemning lectures is a sense of being attacked, and that is not going to inspire people to pursue authentic encounters. Affirm and encourage everyone who is doing at least something to help those in need.

At the same time, we must remember that encounter is not optional. What is most important is not where we are on a spectrum of encounter but the *direction we are headed*. Here is where the creation of effective networks of influence is vital. Your entire church or non-profit community must become a network of influence.

"The key actor in history is not the individual genius but rather the network and the new institutions that arise out of that network," writes the sociologist James Davison Hunter. "I don't want to underplay the role of individual charisma and genius," he continues, but "my point is simply that charisma and genius and their cultural consequences do not exist outside of networks of similarly oriented people and similarly aligned institutions."[27] Networks of influence propose better ways of working with the poor, create incentives for a type of learning that leads to understanding who we are, and systemically foster a type of action that is rooted in the Christian tradition of service.

Service must become integral, instead of incidental, to the mission of your organization and grounded in the great commandment: "Love your neighbor as yourself" (Lev. 19:18). If you believe that your organization is already centered on the great commandment, ask yourself this: Are our systems of care reflective of the firm commitment of bonding with the poor? Are they transactional or relational?

Encounter with the poor is not optional. It is a necessary aspect of poverty-alleviation efforts. Encounter brings us face-to-face with the reality of suffering and, as importantly, with the reality of human dignity. People need people more than they need things.

[27] James Davison Hunter, *To Change the World: The Irony, Tragedy, and Possibility of Christianity in the Late Modern World* (New York: Oxford University Press, 2010), 38.

Remembering a Better Way: Personal Engagement

The concept of *anamnesis* can lend insight to our quest for effective compassion. This Greek noun, in its New Testament context, most commonly translates into English as "remembrance, a commemoration, [or] memorial."[28] It refers to an active remembrance of the paschal mystery. In our context, anamnesis invites us to rediscover the tradition of Christian service in early American history by remembering how our Christian forebears lived out their duties and by entering into that memory by emulating that commitment through our service to others, adjusted to the social realities of our time. Marvin Olasky describes the earlier approach to charity, one feature of which was bonding: "When applicants for help a century ago were truly alone, volunteers worked one-on-one to become, in essence, new family members. Charity volunteers … usually were not assigned to massive food-dispensing tasks, but were given the narrow but deep responsibility of making a difference in one life over several years."[29]

Dilapidated homes and desperate poverty may give us a sense of what people need. However, the history of Christian service to the poor reveals a commitment to an encounter with the poor that rejects the idea of environmental determinism. True charity proceeds one person at a time, with love, courage, and great respect for the dignity of each person as an image-bearer of the divine. The circumstances have changed, but the principle of the priority of encounter remains the same.

What type of bonding with the poor? Appropriate bonding with the poor is about developing relationships over time. These relationships are of friendship and, more importantly, of active and faithful presence. What is faithful presence? Primarily, it embodies the attitude of a witness, not of a "fixer" or antagonist. Bonding requires that we surrender the temptation of control and accept the role of influencer.

The witness-influencer offers a presence that imbues the relationship with a closeness that has the capacity to have an effect on the character, development, and behavior of someone while retaining the capacity to recede to the background, allowing the poor themselves to become the main actors in the drama of a life they build. Living out a life that is distinguishable

[28] *The New Analytical Greek Lexicon*, ed. Wesley J. Perschbacher (Peabody, MA: Hendrickson, 1990), 23.

[29] Marvin Olasky, "Seven Principles from a Century Ago," Acton Institute, https://www.acton.org/public-policy/effective-compassion/seven-principles-century-ago.

from the world of the poor without antagonizing that world is a daunting but necessary task.

This sort of influence must not be one where we become either defensive or condemning of the life and culture of the poor. We cannot view their world with a hostility that poisons relationships and tends to send people into "rescue mode." As James Davison Hunter advises, we must avoid a relationship with the world of the poor that is filtered "through an ethos of anxiety, anger, or fear."[30]

Sorting Out, Taking Sides

Do not be a fence-sitter. Know that the business of caring for others in civil society is not for the faint-hearted or the politically correct. There are "vanilla" ministries and service-oriented organizations all around us. They avoid controversy because all they want to do is help, without exploring too deeply the details of those who are being helped or the long-term effects of their efforts. The hard truth is that if you are not controversial in trying to serve the poor in America, you are likely part of the problem. You must be courageous and take sides.

In speaking of "taking sides," we are not talking about politics but about principles. Taking sides refers to having a clear and committed vision of what is the mind and the heart of service, instead of proceeding directly into action. To take sides you need relevant information allowing you to establish meaningful categorization. Some categories hide information, as when we lump all people with lower incomes under the broad label of "the poor." This category is so general (as most unuseful categories are) that it prevents us from fully ascertaining how to proceed.

Moreover, the category allows people to hide within the group in the hopes of obtaining at least the semblance of benefit, afraid that the light of individuality might spot some character blemishes in them. Let the light shine on the truth!

Other, more useful categories can assist us as starting points to go deeper into a personal relationship with the poor. Remember, human beings are acting persons and they eventually become what they believe and what they

[30] Quoted in "A Faithful Presence: Inaugural Symposium Speaker Challenges Christians to Examine Language of 'Changing the World,'" Seattle Pacific University *Response*, Summer 2013, https://spu.edu/depts/uc/response/new/2013-summer/features/a-faithful-presence.asp.

do. Certain narrowly construed categorizations help us sort out relevant information essential to reasoning about what type of approach we are to take in encountering those in need.

Sort out, yes, but in fear and trembling …

Some features are constant or invariant in all human beings, but other features are variant; they are dependent on attitudes, lifestyles, beliefs, and actions. They are moral. Invariant features might offer us data, but only variant features offer evidence.

When we fail to categorize based on variant features, we reduce the human person to a set of invariant attributes that we can easily target; thus we dump persons into the lame designations of "needy" or "poor." We stop with only one side of the coin of human dignity: intrinsic dignity. More often than not, these invariant features are biologistic: people need food, shelter, clothes, recreation, and grooming. We perceive that there must be some unplugged holes of need in the lives of the poor, so our approach is to go and plug them. Many people would agree that these efforts to meet basic biological needs are not enough, but they are preferred for two reasons: as a hook to bring people in and as a necessary first step to "lead people to Christ."

At face value these are commendable attitudes. Yet they are also landmines. It is possible to snag oneself with that hook. As meeting invariant needs is easier, it is very tempting to focus effort, time, and resources on these activities, relegating the more difficult—but ultimately more meaningful—tasks to a secondary role. It is easier to claim success in hooking people momentarily than to struggle down the arduous path of existential change.

The quest for success can reduce our efforts to the vanilla type of ministry prevalent in our society. Human beings are dynamic; that is, we change over time. Biology determines some of these changes. We know beforehand what those biological changes are and what human beings need at a basic biological level. But adaptive changes in human beings are those in which internal states within the person determine the change; that is, human beings are subjects of meaning. Simply put, the exact same input will not necessarily produce the exact same output across time, every time, for every human being the way it may happen in the interaction between, say, wind and sand.

Organizations can settle for the task of distributing supplies, feeding people, or connecting them with the apparatus of the welfare state. As government systems of care are bureaucratic by nature (as a way to respond to the complexity of large numbers), organizations run the risk of mirroring such bureaucracies or even becoming bureaucracies themselves, paid by government funds to deliver goods and services. Many a ministry has succumbed to the "easy" money coming from government grants to perform certain tasks. Bureaucracies kill the soul of organizations and are more concerned with self-perpetuation than with solving problems. In effect, they are invested in the very problems they are supposed to solve, as it is the existence of problems that gives them purpose.

Organizations ought to be aware of these pitfalls and intentionally avoid them by observing the following practices: (1) imbue projects with a type of service that highlights the full scope of human dignity; (2) dedicate greater human and material resources to tasks addressing variant human features; (3) systemically categorize people by placing certain valves within systems; and (4) continually assess and measure progress in terms other than numbers served and amounts of goods distributed.

A can of food can be an instrument of great good: it can feed the hungry, help the needy. Yet, it can also become a weapon that hurts people. When we detach reward from accomplishment, we might hurt the poor, impede their development, enslave them, and cloud their dignity. The approach described by the head of Gospel Mission in Washington, DC, may be tough love, but it is genuine *love*, rather than a sentimentality that neglects the inherent dignity of those being helped. "We challenge them," he says. "We don't pat them on the back and say it's society's fault. They have to own up to their own faults. There is no free ride. If a guy's drunk and he comes to the back door, he can come in and go to sleep but his bottle has to stay out. If he comes in and he's obnoxious, we have him walk around the block till he sobers up."[31]

A good example of systemic valves weeding out and categorizing people can be found in the work of a Joplin, Missouri, ministry called Watered Gardens. They define their ministry as "church-servant," and the vision they have for engaging the homeless and the poor includes compassion but one that is "relational" and "responsible." How is that vision translated into action? One example is their Project Worth, whose thrift store offers items of clothing that can be earned through hours of labor in the workshops they have created. Homeless men can dedicate several hours to work creating products—bracelets, necklaces, rescue bands, and coffee bags—which are sold to benefit the ministry. The time spent working side by side is also a great opportunity for staff and volunteers to join efforts in a labor of love and develop relationships. The homeless in this program are given more than

[31] Quoted in Olasky, *Tragedy of American Compassion*, 215.

just "stuff," they are given the gift of work, the opportunity to experience what an engaged life is in fulfilling the grace given by God in the beginning when he sent us to "cultivate the garden" (Gen. 2:15).

Such a system allows the homeless to make a choice and distinguishes between those who are willing to take a step toward healing and those who are looking for an enabler. The system does not prevent offering assistance to those who are not ready to take that leap; it simply identifies them, allowing the organization to move forward with better information.

Only after a careful and painstaking analysis, which includes the creation of program features that systematically sort things out, can the search begin to discover deeper human needs. We must remember, however, that grouping is a difficult task and that categorization has inherent, but necessary, risks. There is an interplay between parts and wholes that must be considered.

Grouping is a basic element of human perception of reality, whether we group things or people. Every group is composed of members with at least one common characteristic. Groups convey an identity feature that gives the other members a common and foundational trait. If we combine people on the basis of being poor, then we get a group of poor people. We risk obviating aspects of self that are variant because they do not fit the category of poor.

Beware false categorizations that ignore each person as unique and unrepeatable, capable of transcending our groupings. If the identity of a group is "poverty" or "victim," the result is invariance, immobility, depersonalization. Grouping is unable to provide a model for those types of change that transcend the category that marks the group, that transcend the general point of reference.[32]

Honestly ask yourself: Has my effort lost its marrow under the weight of the emotional attachment to the idea of help? Is the effort offering only lip service to principles, afraid to discern the deeper human need?

Instead of groups, we would do better to refer to *types*. As with groups, types are unified by a common characteristic and are made up of members, but the totality is called a class, or type. Yet the identity member or feature is not part of the group. An example is saying that mankind is the class of all individuals. Yet, mankind itself is not an individual. The category of type allows us to deal with each member on his or her own terms yet allows us to recognize common features. There are types of people who share the

[32] For a careful study of group theory, see Watzlawick, Weakland, and Fisch, *Change*, 5–7.

common denominator of "poor" but are not defined exhaustibly by that description.[33] Failures in poverty-alleviation efforts might be due in part to ignoring the difference between member and class, between the individual and the group.

[33] Watzlawick, Weakland, and Fisch, *Change*, 5.

11

Who Should Help? Honoring the Family and Other Basic Communities

The human heart longs for connection; belonging is primal and essential to human flourishing. Isolation, detachment, and loneliness harm a person's subjective sense of well-being. Affiliation grants the person a sense of connectedness and helps to create networks of support that are crucial for economic and social success. When relationships do not work properly, poverty ensues, because economics is ultimately about cooperation, collaboration, and mutuality. "Historically speaking," Samuel Gregg observes, when people "are able to connect themselves to networks of productivity, what you see is increases in wealth and better-quality lives for everyone, not just the elites in the very wealthy segments of society, but also the poor and the lower-middle class."[1]

Helping people reconnect with others can bring about reconciliation and reabsorption of individuals into the social fabric of a community. What are we trying to restore? We attempt to restore the person to a good relationship with God, with himself or herself, with others, and with the rest of creation.[2] In the context of society, we attempt to restore the poor to the full exercise of their humanity. Poverty-alleviation is not only about economics but is a multifaceted endeavor whose goal is restoration.

[1] "Samuel Gregg on Economics, Politics, and Moral Philosophy," *PovertyCure*, https://www.povertycure.org/learn/media/samuel-gregg-economics-politics-moral-philosophy.

[2] Corbett and Fikkert, *When Helping Hurts*, 54–55.

When surrogates neglect or obviate the natural bonds of community, they do harm. When questions about who should be helping in this case or why a person is not reconnecting with family and friends are not asked, we encourage troubled persons to avoid the painful but necessary step of humbly reaching out to those who have been significant in their lives.

Yes, we feel good when children smile at the sight of a brand-new toy truck or fancy new doll. But are we truly creating a lasting positive effect by bypassing the parents' place in providing for their children? Do we pay attention when the father is nowhere to be found because he is ashamed at the sight of strangers doing what he feels is his duty? Inherent in the creation of some systems of care is a strong support for interventionism and institutionalization.

Again, these are the kinds of questions that were routine in earlier days of charity. When individuals applied for assistance, Marvin Olasky notes, volunteers tried first to "restore family ties that have been sundered" and "reabsorb in social life those who for some reason have snapped the threads that bound them to other members of the community." Rather than offering help immediately, charitable organizations would ask the question, "Who is bound to help in this case?"[3]

At times we believe that unless we "do something," people will crumble. Yes, if you see a man on the side of the road, bleeding and hurt, you do not approach and tell him, "Be self-reliant!" The nonsense of that approach ought to be readily apparent to all.

But we must keep in mind the distinction between a crisis situation and the condition of poverty itself. In a true crisis, the receiver recedes momentarily to the periphery of action precisely due to his inability to help himself, whether partially or completely. The giver moves to the protagonist role momentarily; that is, the duration of the giver's intervention ought to be finite.

However, the term *crisis* has lost its bite. Everything is now deemed a crisis, requiring open-ended intervention leading to institutionalization of care. Crisis becomes a tool to acquire certain benefits of a first-order type, when what is needed is second-order change. Second-order change is the change that requires people to learn new approaches and new values, to do something fundamentally different from what they have done before. People fear second-order change because it is often irreversible.

Sadly, when the power to benefit is found in suffering, people are encouraged to expand the boundaries of what is deemed a crisis, leading them

[3] Olasky, "Seven Principles."

to portray their suffering in vivid colors and to use their victim status as a weapon. If we can get rewards for being an underdog rather than taking the painful steps of second-order change, being an underdog becomes a way of life. It becomes an identity to be nourished instead of a status to be conquered. Incentives matter, and when *crisis* becomes the term used for every unfortunate situation, people end up being hurt.

Ministries and service-oriented organizations fear second-order change because it is a leap into darkness, requires risk, and requires new skills and difficult tasks. Thus, crises of dubious urgency are easier to tackle and more emotionally fulfilling for the benefactors. The three stages of the creation of "crisis-mode" projects are: (1) the crisis—whatever the problem is; (2) the solution—the intervention; and (3) the program—the institutionalization of the solution.[4]

An authentic crisis is often difficult to tackle, while a fake crisis has the semblance of difficulty but is simple: People are going to try to benefit while escaping the tough choices, because human beings have the tendency to avoid pain or struggle.

THE CENTRALITY OF THE FAMILY

Of all basic communities, the family is most important; as the family goes, so goes the neighborhood, the city, and the country. As economist Jennifer Roback Morse tells us, "Marriage is a naturally occurring, pre-political institution that emerges spontaneously from society." That is, it occurs systemically and naturally and is not a creation of the state and the law. "The drive toward a legalistic view of marriage is part of the relentless march toward politicizing every aspect of society."[5]

This is one reason for saying that the family is the bedrock of civilization. It is that basic community where children are supposed to be nourished, educated, and assisted in becoming engaged and productive members of society. The family is also an intergenerational bridge, a carrier of the wisdom of the past as it connects with the present and reaches forward into the future. A healthy family is the foundation for thriving communities.

---

[4] See Sowell, *Vision of the Anointed*, 21–30.

[5] Jennifer Roback Morse, "Marriage and the Limits of Contract: A Libertarian Case," Hoover Institution, April 1, 2005, https://www.hoover.org/research/marriage-and-limits-contract.

The problem of agency does not apply only to the level of individual action, although individual action is the most fundamental. Collective agency is an essential part of life in families. When the family breaks down, communities suffer and the role of government tends to increase. Sound poverty-alleviation projects place the family at the center, respecting and guarding the role of this permanent and foundational institution. Too many charities and churches agree with these statements in principle but ignore them in practice and supersede the family and other basic communities by intervening at the first call for help.

Despite spending $1 trillion a year in poverty-alleviation—an amount larger than the entire GDP of a large majority of the world's nations[6]—the US continues to fail in attaining a meaningful decrease in poverty. A function of that failure is that poverty has become a norm that offers an economic quality of life that would be the envy of most people around the world. By meeting the material needs of single-mother-headed households without regard for the effect on fathers, poverty-alleviation efforts have both entrenched material poverty and diminished the overall quality of life in single-parent families.

The absence of married fathers from the home is a national shame, a crisis like no other. According to the US Census, the poverty rate for single parents with children in the United States in 2009 was 37.1 percent, while the rate for married couples with children was 6.8 percent. During the same period, being raised in a married family reduced a child's probability of living in poverty by about 82 percent.[7] Interestingly, out-of-wedlock births are occurring more and more not among teens but among young adult women. The fundamental reality of the situation has not changed since sociologist Orlando Patterson described it at the end of the twentieth century: "The evidence that unemployment is the major source of the more severe social problems among the Afro-American lower class is weak. The most serious of these problems is, of course, the rise in families headed by single women."[8]

---

[6] "Real GDP," *CIA World Fact Book*, September 28, 2023, https://www.cia.gov/the-world-factbook/field/real-gdp-purchasing-power-parity/country-comparison/.

[7] Robert Rector, "Marriage: America's Greatest Weapon Against Child Poverty," Heritage Foundation, September 5, 2012, http://www.heritage.org/research/reports/2012/09/marriage-americas-greatest- weapon-against-child-poverty.

[8] Orlando Patterson, *The Ordeal of Integration: Progress and Resentment in America's "Racial" Crisis* (New York: Basic Books, 1997), 32.

Out-of-wedlock births in America shot up in the late twentieth century and remain catastrophically high. A 1996 study summarized the trend: "Since 1970, out-of-wedlock birth rates have soared. In 1965, 24 percent of black infants and 3.1 percent of white infants were born to single mothers. By 1990 the rates had risen to 64 percent for black infants, 18 percent for whites. Every year about one million more children are born into fatherless families."[9] According to a report released by the National Center for Health Statistics titled "Changing Patterns of Nonmarital Childbearing in the United States," in 2007 four of every ten children born were born out of wedlock. The birth rate for unmarried women aged 15–44 years was 52.9 births per 1,000. The rate had increased 21 percent since 2002 and was 80 percent higher than the rate for 1980.[10]

Not all these children end up in single-parent homes; rather they often grow up in cohabitating households. Cohabitation, however, is a very unstable situation that often ends up as a single-parent household. The belief that cohabitation will somehow improve the quality of a subsequent marriage—as it provides a test of compatibility before commitment—is incorrect. Cohabiting relationships are relatively short-lived. After seven years, only about 20 percent of cohabiting couples who did not marry each other are still together. The cohabiters who eventually marry each other are as much as 46 percent more likely to divorce than people who marry but have not cohabited first.[11] Research in recent decades shows that cohabitation does not lead to more satisfying and stable marriages. Disadvantages suffered

---

[9] George A. Akerlof and Janet L. Yellen, "An Analysis of Out-of-Wedlock Births in the United States, Brookings Institution, August 1, 1996, https://www.brookings.edu/articles/an-analysis-of-out-of-wedlock-births-in-the-united-states.

[10] NCHS (National Center for Health Statistics) Data Brief, "Changing Patterns of Nonmarital Childbearing in the United States," Centers for Decease Control and Prevention, May 2009, http://www.cdc.gov/nchs/data/databriefs/db18.htm. As of 2021, the proportion of births to single mothers remained study at about 40 percent: "Unmarried Childbearing," NCHS FastStats, CDC, https://www.cdc.gov/nchs/fastats/unmarried-childbearing.htm.

[11] David Popenoe and Barbara Dafoe Whitehead, *Should We Live Together? What Young Adults Need to Know about Cohabitation before Marriage*, 2nd ed. (Piscataway, NJ: National Marriage Project, Rutgers University, 2002), 4, 6; Jennifer Roback Morse, *Love & Economics: Why the Laissez-Faire Family Doesn't Work* (Dallas: Spence, 2001), 64; Jan Stets, "The Link Between Past and Present Intimate Relationships," *Journal of Family Issues* 14:2 (June 1993): 236–60; Vijaya

by cohabitating families include a poverty rate that is at least four times higher than that of married families and a higher probability that children will exhibit anti-social behavior and eventually become single parents.

Brookings Institution scholar Ron Haskins' research finds that, "Controlling for other differences, children in female-headed families are more likely on average to enter school behind their peers in math, reading readiness, and socio-emotional skills—a gap our schools are often unable to close. As a result, these students are less likely to graduate from high school and less likely to enter, and graduate from, college."[12] These detrimental effects are often long-lasting. A recent major study conducted by prominent scholars at an array of prestigious institutions stated its conclusions modestly but nonetheless clearly: It found "a strong association between growing up in a single-parent family and childhood poverty. The links between family structure during childhood and adult poverty (i.e., the transmission of poverty intergenerationally) suggest a causal effect."[13]

Nonmarital childbearing creates poverty; offers less opportunity for social mobility; negatively affects the educational, social, and economic destiny of children; and leaves children behind. Regardless of money spent on poverty-alleviation programs, if the trend of broken families continues, we will continue to experience frustration and failure in our quest for success. It follows that marriage ought to be seen as an indispensable institution for any poverty-alleviation effort. Why then do we often bypass the family to assist individuals directly?

Intervening feels good, but it might be unwise if it lacks discernment. Marvin Olasky reminds us that in the past Christians understood that context is everything and that the purpose of charity is to restore individuals, not to

---

Krishnan, "Premarital Cohabitation and Marital Disruption," *Journal of Divorce and Remarriage* 28:3–4, (1998): 157–70.

[12] Ron Haskins, "The Crisis of Nonmarital Childbearing," in *2014 Index of Culture and Opportunity: The Social and Economic Trends that Shape America*, eds. Jennifer A. Marshall and Rea S. Hederman, Jr. (Washington, DC: Heritage Foundation, 2014), 45, https://www.heritage.org/marriage-and-family/report/index-culture-and-opportunity-2014.

[13] Greg J. Duncan, Jennifer Appleton Gootman, and Priyanka Nalamada, eds., *Reducing Intergenerational Poverty* (prepublication, uncorrected proofs of Consensus Study Report, National Academies of Sciences, Engineering, and Medicine) (Washington, DC: National Academies Press, 2023), 7, https://nap.nationalacademies.org/catalog/27058/reducing-intergenerational-poverty.

enable them. Olasky retells the wisdom of old, captured in declarations of the New Orleans Charity Organization Society in 1899: "Intelligent giving and intelligent withholding are alike true charity," and, "If drink has made a man poor, money will feed not him, but his drunkenness."[14]

Being afraid to discern is common in a society informed by political correctness and enamored with the idea of entitlement. It is not that difficult to cover such fear with a few Bible verses to justify our activities. Lacking discernment, however, ends up hurting the poor. Discernment is always necessary as the first step before action.

There are three ways in which lack of discernment can result in actually harming those we intend to help:

1. Action is necessary but is not taken. A solution is needed but action is not taken to work toward one. This concerns both the person in need and the organization trying to provide aid. People know what the problem is but are scared; they need support in taking needed steps. Organizations know what the problem is, but change is painful, so they continue to do what they have been doing even if it has not produced the desired results.
2. Action is taken when it should not be. When we do not discern, the mere fact that we "did something" justifies the activity. Systems of care focused on distribution of things often fail to discern the real need.
3. Action is taken at the wrong level. For example, we engage in first-order change activities when what is needed is second-order change.

As churches and other organizations discern how to better help the poor, it is imperative that they develop simple and practical ways to strengthen families and alleviate the burden of isolation they often encounter. There are a few things to consider when planning assistance for an intact family:

- Consult with them, dialogue, bring the parents into the decision-making and the process of assistance. Never bypass the parents to help the children.

[14] Marvin Olasky, "The New Welfare Debate: How to Practice Effective Compassion," *Imprimis* 24 (no. 9, September 1995), https://imprimis.hillsdale.edu/the-new-welfare-debate-how-to-practice-effective-compassion/.

- Demand of the parents that they be involved. Do not become surrogates who engage in activities that the parents ought to be doing. Do not enable parents to surrender their responsibility. Practice "intelligent giving and intelligent withholding."
- Develop a plan for family independence while providing assistance. Do not offer assistance without a plan for that family to eventually become detached from the gift. For example, if in year one a family needs Thanksgiving food, develop a savings plan with the family for year two. That savings plan can be administered by the church by opening a savings account and alternatives to work (if necessary) for the family to earn and save.
- Celebrate marriage. Make it clear in your relationship with poor, intact families that you honor their commitment.

If there is not an intact family, then the following points should be kept in mind:

- Avoid both the attitudes of condescension and approval. There is harm done when those trying to help a single parent attack the person. The opposite is also detrimental: conveying approval by avoiding the question of marriage altogether. Remember, we are to convey our support for integral liberty.
- Mentor. As children from single-parent homes are more likely to become single parents themselves, provide opportunities to model marriage by offering wholesome, intact families as mentors who will offer children a positive glimpse into what family life is within an intact family.
- Don't abandon the ideal. Some scholars have looked at single-family households, especially among Blacks, and have tried to minimize the problem associated with broken homes.[15] These families have been described as authentically African examples of energetic, cooperative urban villages where mutual aid from extended family networks was the norm, in contrast with the Western, nuclear-family, hyper-individual tradition. Understand

---

[15] See Carol B. Stack, *All Our Kin: Strategies for Survival in a Black Community* (New York: Harper & Row, 1974); Joyce A. Ladner, *Tomorrow's Tomorrow: The Black Woman* (New York: Doubleday, 1971); Robert B. Hill, *The Strengths of Black Families* (New York: Emerson Hall Publishers, 1972).

that these racially biased ideas are detrimental to what is best for children—for *all* children of *every* race.

KEEP IT "REAL"

We live in the age of utopia. Grandiose plans and comprehensive solutions are offered to us at every turn. Gurus and sages promise a new age of superior consciousness. Planners plan and then plan some more to control the complexities of life; they impose dire consequences on society as they erect the structures that will supposedly bring about heaven on earth. The idea that we can "end poverty" is an enticing proposition, leading, as all utopias do, nowhere. As Robert Ardrey says, "While we pursue the unattainable, we make impossible the realizable."[16]

Frustration and "compassion fatigue" are often the result of unattainable expectations. The struggles of poverty are real and need attention, but not every struggle is a negative situation. In fact, the struggle for a better life can be seen as a prerequisite for achieving an improved state of affairs. Remove the struggle and you remove the most efficient instrument for self-realization.

Discernment must start with humility about our capacity to help others. Remember, there is a savior, and it is not you!

The Utopia Syndrome

A good practical test to discern whether your project is on the right track is asking whether it is absolutely necessary. Have you built into the processes of your endeavor an end to your *program*—even if you do not perceive an end to the *problem*? If the answer is no, you might reconsider the entire project. Here, the principle of subsidiarity that we explored is crucial: interventions ought to be narrow and limited, both in scope and duration.

Not having a narrow path creates several negative incentives. Those receiving help get accustomed to being on the receiving end. Those serving eventually get frustrated by the seemingly never-ending exercise. Exhaustion causes people to give up. Eventually people resent the receivers of benefit. There is no urgency to motivate full engagement when the program is open-ended. Donors eventually leave to support other endeavors. Often,

[16] Robert Ardrey, *The Social Contract: A Personal Inquiry into the Evolutionary Sources of Order and Disorder* (New York: Atheneum, 1970), 3.

evaluation descends into quantitative assessments at the expense of qualitative ones.

If your project is suffering from some of these negative incentives and your efforts seem to be a perpetual cycle of "giving stuff away," be aware that you might be experiencing a strain of the utopia syndrome.[17] If your goal is to end a condition and that condition does not seem to disappear, your project might go on forever. As utopias are first and foremost ideas in the mind with no necessary reference to reality, they can go on forever, as the dream never ends. Activism, as we shall see, can become a type of utopia where we attempt to hammer a vision into reality. The world is full of examples of utopian hammers whose tips are stained with blood. Once the vision becomes truer than reality, evil can be justified in a quest for the ultimate solution. Remember: "By any means necessary" is a dangerous moral principle.

Conversely, there is another common variation of the syndrome, one with a certain modern allure best described in the aphorism "It is better to travel hopefully than to arrive."[18] Since the goal is distant and the journey long, we procrastinate, professionalize, and bureaucratize. Such a journey invariably requires rules, sequences, preparations, staff, lots of money, and the constant tweaking of processes. Instead of reexamining the premise, we tinker with the model, not overly worrying about progress toward what is an unachievable goal.

There is an uncomfortable question that is too rarely asked: Should we be doing this in the first place? There are a number of reasons why we do not often hear that question. Perhaps a project has become someone's "baby." Maybe a recognition of failure after so much investment is simply unbearable. Or possibly an organization's programs are guided by the natural but not very compelling nostrum "But this is the way we have always done it!"

Projects whose goal is to restore one person at a time instead of to maintain or manage a situation for large numbers of people can better avoid the pitfalls of utopianism. Anti-utopian systems, which are more likely to bear fruit, focus on individuals or specific families; restoration rather than management; and processes rather than products. They also set deadlines instead of operating on open-ended timeframes. "The proper aim of giving," says C. S. Lewis, "is to put the recipient in a state where he no longer needs

[17] Watzlawick, Weakland, and Fisch, *Change*, chap. 5.

[18] Watzlawick, Weakland, and Fisch, *Change*, 49.

our gifts.... Thus a heavy task is laid upon Gift-love. It must work toward its own abdication. We must aim at making ourselves superfluous. The hour when we can say 'They need me no longer' should be our reward."[19]

As Jayakumar Christian warns, those serving the poor can acquire a "god complex," a subtle and often unconscious sense of superiority based on their economic advantage.[20] They can end up believing that their economic success grants them the right to decree what is best for the poor, as they have become successful on their own merits. The god complex can lead to disdain for those perceived as unable or unwilling to change.

In these situations, the expectation is utopian from the get-go: "We go there, we teach them, they change." The commitment is also short-term, with no intention to bond with those in need. When one bonds with people, one stays for the struggle. Instead, from the beginning, it has been a sort of "drive-by compassion."

The Savior Complex

Another dysfunction of charitable action is the "savior complex," which is based not on a subtle sense of superiority but on collaborating with the emotional circumstances that trap the poor in poverty. This can be done by moving to live among the poor, joining campaigns to change structures, or offering never-ending support programs.[21] The savior complex is a sort of environmental determinism in which the external circumstances of society determine the state of the poor's lives, leading those with a savior complex to believe that intervention to change those conditions is the answer. The activists believe they can and should save the poor because it is "unfair" that they do not enjoy the economic advantage everyone deserves.

Activism to change social structures can become a variation of the savior complex, by which the successful feel guilty for their success and "privilege" and transfer that guilt to the structures of society that assisted them in becoming successful but apparently excluded others. As poverty is often entangled with race, "white guilt" is a common form of this disorder.[22] The "privileged" one feeling guilty is seeking vindication and reclaiming

[19] C. S. Lewis, *The Four Loves* (London: Geoffrey Bles, 1960), 63.

[20] See Corbett and Fikkert, *When Helping Hurts*, 61–62.

[21] Corbett and Fikkert, *When Helping Hurts*, 61.

[22] For a discussion of white guilt, see Steele, *Content of Our Character*.

innocence. The poor get at least a mirage of benefit that ties their identity to that of a victim. In the end, the one who seeks innocence remains in control by offering benefit, and the victim sees benefit in remaining a victim and not releasing the guilty from his condition.[23]

Ironically, this type of activism often engages in support for the very structures and modes of dependency that keep the poor from engaging in the activities that hold promise for getting them out of poverty. Out of guilt for one's own success—and for a past described as oppressive—it is very easy to move to support government entitlements for the deprived, avoiding the necessary question of whether or not that is the right path. Helping people lock themselves to the manacles of government programs ought not be an activity of ministries and non-profits. As we saw earlier, government programs do not help in reducing poverty.

The savior complex in the form of activism offers the materially poor a reason to see their condition as the result of forces outside of their control. It offers an alibi for one's condition as, after all, the condition is caused by "those people in power." Instead, if activism is to be used as a main activity it ought to be to open avenues for entrepreneurship and economic and civic engagement that can assist people in their quest for independent lives.

Around the world, activism in the political realm often centers on "caudillos" and vanguards of enlightened ones who often come from economically advantaged circumstances. Entire congregations are at times lured by the savior complex and a common thread of the complex in the form of social activism. Extremism is a temptation that should be avoided but that often becomes an expression of activism. Activism is performed on behalf of "empowering" the poor but can become a distraction from truly seeing the poor as subjects of meaning instead of objects moved by external forces.

One means of countering the savior complex is to face the truth that scarcity is real. There is limited time, money, energy, and resources to accomplish certain tasks. Scarcity implies opportunity costs; that is, the idea that with every action or decision there is another action or decision we must give up. It also implies cost–benefit analysis; that is, the reasoning one undertakes to make a decision for one course of action rather than another under a condition of scarcity. Economics is essentially the study of the decisions people make in the face of scarcity.

We must understand that reorganizing unjust structures will not accomplish much if the problem is a failure to create wealth. "The first lesson

[23] Steele, *Content of Our Character*, chap. 1.

of economics is scarcity: there is never enough of anything to satisfy all those who want it," says Thomas Sowell. "The first lesson of politics is to disregard the first lesson of economics."[24] A bias toward political activism reflects a belief that the elimination of poverty is merely a matter of political will. This removes the focus from wealth creation—which is a more effective strategy to alleviate poverty—but even more importantly it diverts attention from the poor themselves, who must be empowered to become their own saviors.

Discernment is essential if those who truly want to help the poor are to avoid the pitfalls of emotionalism that sends many on rescue missions that often end in activism or other extremisms. Discernment about when to help can be counterintuitive. Because some needs seem obvious, it is understandable that we become anxious to help.

But we always need to reflect on how effective this compassion is, in light of the principles outlined above. When an organization is focused on creating comprehensive "cradle to grave" networks of support that assume that needs are always increasing and never receding, they feed on need and become invested in the very problem they are supposed to be solving. If poverty is what brings the money in, who wants fewer poor people?

In its extreme form, the savior complex can be a destructive force, as history demonstrates. Vladimir Ilyich Lenin adapted Marxism to the socio-economic and political conditions of Imperial Russia (1721–1917). Lenin coined the phrase "vanguard of the proletariat" to refer to the Communist Party as the leader of the workers' movement. These were the more enlightened workers who understood class consciousness properly and were fit to lead. "Vanguardism" has come to mean frontal leadership within a movement, and its expressions can be found in many contexts. Simón Bolívar is probably the most important caudillo in Latin American history. Socialist leaders favor associating their cause for "liberation" with the image of Bolivar. The term *caudillo* translates into English as leader, chief, or even as dictator or strongman. The caudillo was a charismatic populist leader battling the oppressor.

Most poverty-alleviation efforts start with a genuinely good intention, one that becomes a powerful incentive to separate action from reason. To reason about *whether* we should help and also *how* to best serve seems cold-hearted. Instead, the impulse to help insists that we should love people

[24] Thomas Sowell, *Is Reality Optional?: And Other Essays* (Stanford: Hoover Institution Press), 131.

by serving them, moving quickly into action. We tend to believe that helping is a simple equation: Heart (caring) plus muscle (effort) equals service (benefit). Again, it is important to resist the lure of such simple equations and be sure that careful thought precedes action.

THE LIMITS OF "ROOT CAUSES"

To avoid utopianism, it is important to focus on what can realistically be accomplished in the present. One corrupting element in the field of poverty alleviation is inordinate concern with "root causes." This is not because there is no justification, in an academic sense, for positing root causes. All contemporary problems have complex causes, and any comprehensive understanding of them must take into account a long history and a variety of factors.

Yet, this very complexity can be employed in ways that are counterproductive, if we are truly concerned about empowering the poor. Complicated theories about the past will always be partial, because the human mind does not have boundless capacity to unscramble the eggs in the omelet of history. We do not know how to put in place every element of a long-ago past to find the ultimate answer to the problems of human existence. If we believe that we have fully understood the dynamic of causation regarding poverty, then we will be inclined to believe that we also possess the knowledge to prevent it. Arrogance about the human capacity to reason is at the heart of many failed attempts to "fix" things.

We do not always know why things happen, but so much effort and money are spent on "experts" and "gurus" who pretend to know why people find themselves in the mess they often find themselves in. We assume that unless we find the root causes of events or conditions we are doomed to fail in helping others. Discard that myth.

The most successful projects use trained volunteers and simple methods to deal with the *what*, not the *why*. We concentrate on the effects and not on the presumed causes. This practical attitude does not discard the importance of understanding; it simply operates on the principle that we can help to create change without pretending to comprehend the entire chain of causation behind the problem—a knowledge of which must always remain partial in any case.

We do know one thing, however. Spontaneous change works better.

By spontaneous change we mean the type of problem resolution that occurs in the ordinary course of life, without expert knowledge, sophisticated theories, or concentrated power.[25] Projects that allow people to make choices for themselves and simply offer an open-ended realm of possibilities, instead of a deliberate system of care, often work better. "When my goal is to change people, I subtly communicate: Something is wrong with you; I am okay. You are ignorant; I am enlightened."[26]

The Quest for Justice

Social justice advocates often fall prey to the pretense of knowledge. As we saw in chapter 5, the term *social justice* is elusive at best, and most people demanding social justice are really seeking what Thomas Sowell calls "cosmic justice," a type of justice that does not exist nor can be brought to bear in the here and now. What we would do if we were God or omnipotent is irrelevant to what we can do now. The desire to equalize everything is a sort of cosmic justice that never attains the goal. "The rhetoric of clever people often confuses the undeniable fact that life is unfair with the claim that a given institution or Society is unfair."[27]

The term *social justice*—as with *economic justice*—is commonly used as a synonym of what was classically known as distributive justice. In practice, these three concepts pertain to income redistribution. Additionally, the term unfortunately has become synonymous with a certain kind of political activism, which has rendered its operational meaning as "We need a law against that."[28] The application of these ideas to a market economy is dubious because, as Fredrick Hayek stated, "There cannot be distributive justice where no one distributes."[29] The loss of the traditional understanding of these terms has brought nothing more than confusion and antagonism.

---

[25] Watzlawick, Weakland, and Fisch, *Change*, chap. 7.

[26] Lupton, *Theirs is the Kingdom*, 6.

[27] Thomas Sowell, "The 'Equality' Racket," *National Review*, January 6, 2015, https://www.nationalreview.com/2015/01/equality-racket-thomas-sowell/.

[28] Michael Novak, "Defining Social Justice," *First Things* 108 (December 2000): 11–13.

[29] Friedrich Hayek, "The Atavism of Social Justice," in *New Studies in Philosophy, Politics, Economics, and the History of Ideas* (London: Routledge & Kegan Paul, 1978), 58.

It is time to take a closer look at the classic definition of justice: "Rendering to each one his own."[30] That is, justice is a personal virtue by which I order my personal relations according to what is right. In the words of Joseph Burke, "Justice pertains to what is owed to a person, and justice is satisfied when each gives what he owes and receives what he is owed."[31] This understanding is consistent with the main stem of Western thought, which was ably expressed by St. Thomas Aquinas: "Now each man's own is that which is due to him according to equality of proportion. Therefore the proper act of justice is nothing else than to render to each one his own."[32]

When an intelligent assessment of the real needs of the poor is absent, reason is instrumentalized. In other words, we use our rational capacities to create effective systems of delivery, not to discern first principles and action principles. Action separated from a knowledge of the proper ends of human action allows for rationalizations controlled by emotionalism.

We are called to a loving and generous concern for the poor, what is sometimes called "having a heart for the poor." A heart for the poor is essential, but we must beware of the temptation of collapsing all elements of support for the poor within that single, emotion-driven phrase. We must ensure that our poverty-alleviation efforts do not become, in philosophical terms, Humean—utilitarian (see chapter 5). They should not have as their purpose to make us "feel good," while the poor themselves become a tool to that end. This is the danger we court when we are less invested in identifying what is rational and ought to be done (that is, what form of the good is at play and how we can actualize it) and more concerned with devising means or responding to sympathies.

In such cases, passions motivate action. Our passions include our desires, our appetites, and our whims. They do not respond to reason. Reason becomes the servant of our passions. Good intentions become sovereign rulers over the manor of service. We must reject such foundations because good intentions are not enough.

---

[30] Thomas Aquinas, *Summa Theologica* II-II, q58, a1.

[31] Joseph Burke, "Distributive Justice and Subsidiarity," *Journal of Markets and Morality* 13 (no. 2, Fall 2010): 297–317.

[32] *Summa Theologica*, II-II, q58, a11.

12

The Missing Piece: Sound Economics

We need to move away from thinking about poverty and the causes of poverty, and start to move to the real question: What causes wealth?

—Michael Matheson Miller,
PovertyCure[1]

Of all the economic systems mankind has developed, none has so revolutionized the lives and economic aspirations of ordinary people as the free-market economy. In spite of this, many of those who seek to help the poor condemn this system and advocate for more active government intervention to curb it. Much of this skepticism of the market stems from misunderstanding the source of economic dysfunction and inequity. Many ills attributed to "the market" are actually distortions of the market that have been introduced by government interventions. In any case, it behooves those who wish for the economic empowerment of others to understand how the economy works and to appreciate the indispensable role of entrepreneurship in bettering the lives of the poor.

---

[1] Michael Matheson Miller, *PovertyCure* (Grannd Rapids: Acton Media, 2012), DVD.

Human Action

The science of economics is an attempt to determine the best use of scarce resources for meeting human needs. Scarcity is a reality: we have limited material resources with which to work. However, when intelligence and work are applied to the material world, calculations go beyond mere material resources. The human person is a creative being, and it is in the consideration of that creative power that we must find a remedy to poverty. There is a self-evident axiom we often ignore in our well-intended quest to help the poor: Humans act.

For too long, people have focused on the wrong question: What is poverty? Economic improvement comes about by understanding the processes, incentives, and attitudes about the human person that form the unspoken foundation of our activity. In his magnum opus, *Human Action*, the economist Ludwig von Mises tells us that contentment or satisfaction is the state that cannot produce any action. It does not lead to active participation and creativity. "Acting man," he contends, "is eager to substitute a more satisfactory state of affairs for a less satisfactory."[2]

Man is not only *Homo sapiens* but also *Homo agens*, "acting man." Purposeful action is uniquely human. Herein lies the key to every sound poverty-alleviation effort that goes from mere desire to help to a determined effort to create true and lasting change: "The incentive that impels a man to act is always some uneasiness."[3] Those who wish to thrive in a dynamic economy must avoid resting on their laurels. "It is certainly true that the necessity of adjusting oneself again and again to changing conditions is onerous," says Mises, "But change is the essence of life."[4]

Although it sounds counterintuitive, every system of care must be based on a set of incentives that create a burden that must be lifted. The poor must come to the realization that they should not be content with their present state of affairs. This is what will impel them to act to change things. The institutional arrangement we create must be one of liberty and of action. It must not be based on the satisfaction of unmet needs by a bureaucracy but instead on the creation of a dissatisfaction that leads to effort and change.

Incentives are needed because the actual situation of humanity is one in which human nature is afflicted by corruption and by an inclination toward

[2] Mises, *Human Action*, 13.

[3] Mises, *Human Action*, 13.

[4] Mises, *Human Action*, 848.

passivity, self-deception, vice, and conformity. The poor deserve more than long lines of degrading treatment. Systems that do not emphasize the virtue of work are often hierarchical, in which some are "superior" and have the resources while others wait in line to receive aid.

Unfortunately, ameliorative efforts often conflate a crisis situation of need with the condition of poverty itself. Incentives are often ignored because incentives do not produce the immediate results we expect when operating in crisis mode. Incentives allow space for failure because, after all, they are not commands. That seems unacceptable when everything is a crisis and we are more invested in how we feel than in the long-term results of interventions.

With command systems of care—as with command economies—control is not surrendered by the experts or the "do-gooders" at the helm. They are inherently top-down approaches because those at the top "know better." In contrast, systems based on economic incentives recognize that what matters more is not a desire to help the poor but a commitment to allow the poor to decide for themselves. It also means that those who intend to help must take into account the totality of a beneficiary's behavior—and history—and not fall prey to his or her talk of changing.

Food Security for America is one of those charities that get it right. Based in Atlanta, it assists various organizations in establishing food co-ops in the form of "food buying clubs" where the poor are able to pay for the food they receive at minimal prices. The incentive is the opportunity to meet needs with a sense of pride and ownership.

Realized acts, not asserted needs, bring about economic benefit.

The dignity of causality that we previously discussed is what allows people to connect cause and effect, means and ends, accomplishment and reward. Built–in, that is, systemic, incentives assist in the creation of such connections. In essence, every poverty-alleviation program ought to have these components:

- A vision of ends (an exit strategy, if you will). What state of affairs is the desired state and ultimate goal?
- A specific set of means. A method, a course of action, or an instrument by which an act can be accomplished or an end achieved.
- A simple, meaningful activity.
- A set of incentives. Built-in incentives to motivate human action.

- A set of rewards. Those being helped must understand that it is the action they take on their own behalf that removes the uneasiness of their former state. Rewards must always be at the end of the exercise, and they must always be tied to human action.

Incentives emphasize the dignity of work. It is often the case that those immersed in poverty-alleviation efforts think that requiring work is an imposition. We should not "make the poor work" for what they receive, this thinking goes. But carefully crafted systems of care that are based on the dignity of the human person do not *make* anyone do anything. They are created with the gift of work as an indispensable *opportunity* given to the poor. Instead of "making people" stand in line, they engage the poor in the entire exercise of receiving support.

Public service and charity have long engaged in activities that transfer goods or offer services, but the outcomes of such systems are often unexamined. Those closer to these activities will admit their frustration at the interminable lines of distribution that incentivize dependency and destroy personal initiative. "For all our efforts to eliminate poverty—our entitlements, our programs, our charities," Robert Lupton writes, "we have succeeded only in creating a permanent underclass, dismantling their family structures, and eroding their ethic of work."[5] It is precisely because the truly struggling poor work that we can learn from them about the dignity of work. Work offers people a sense of identity and dignity. A lack of work contributes to poverty, crime, homelessness, domestic violence, substance abuse, unwanted pregnancies, divorce, and suicide.

This opportunity to work is what helps to make the previously mentioned Worth Shop at Watered Garden Ministries a model charity. "We are all created in God's image," the project's home page says. "Not one of us has any less value than another, and yet, many of the poor we meet at Watered Gardens have been told for years they have less value or are of no worth." The Worth Shop "offers an opportunity for the poor and homeless to be creative and endeavor to build products that go to market." This opportunity "provides a reawakened sense of value as dignity is preserved and the cycle of dependency on handouts is broken."[6]

[5] Lupton, *Toxic Charity*, 3.

[6] Project Worth, Watered Gardens, https://wateredgardens.org/services/project-worth.

Failing to understand that work is the actualization of human dignity, many poverty-alleviation efforts end up mimicking the bureaucratic and dependency-inducing systems of government. Christian organizations must choose: Are they committed servants in faithful presence among the poor, or are they the hired hand of the state? Those who choose the latter should be clear-eyed about the fact that the aim of the state is not always the welfare of the people. The nineteenth-century French economist Frédéric Bastiat articulated the friction between charity and the state. "In fact, it is impossible for me to separate the word *fraternity* from the word *voluntary*," he wrote. "I cannot possibly understand how fraternity can be legally enforced without liberty being legally destroyed, and thus justice being legally trampled underfoot."[7]

The role of enterprise and economic freedom is essential for promoting the dignity of work and the creation of opportunities. The free-market system is the best economic system available to us in our quest to find solutions to poverty. "The record of history is absolutely crystal clear," avers Milton Friedman, "There is no alternative way, so far discovered, of improving the lot of the ordinary people that can hold a candle to the productive activities that are unleashed by a free enterprise system."[8] We must reject the erroneous conclusion that the market is about winning by defeating others. This is a crass misunderstanding of what a free economy offers.[9] As Theodore Malloch has argued, "The free economy is not the enemy but the friend of social capital. [It] is an accountable economy, in which the cost of risk falls on the one who takes it, and in which reward comes to those who pay their debts and who deal openly and justly with their fellows."[10]

A loving and generous concern for the poor demands a recognition that individuals have the rational and moral capacity for self-realization and that the free-market economy is the system that empowers them to actualize such dignity. When we begin to look at economic freedom as a suitable context

[7] Bastiat, *The Law*, 22.

[8] Milton Friedman, TV interview with Phil Donahue, 1979, as quoted in Jessa Potvin "Capitalism, Greed, and Self-Interest," Palmetto Promise Institute, August 19, 2016, https://palmettopromise.org/capitalism-greed-and-self-interest/.

[9] For an instance of the view that market economics means winning at the expense of others, see Lupton, *Theirs Is the Kingdom*, 23–24.

[10] Malloch, *Doing Virtuous Business*, 15.

for the creation of wealth, we begin to see the market as a community of cooperation rather than a system based on greed and antagonism.

Moving from paternalism and aid to respect and enterprise requires that we stop imagining new economic systems that have no basis in reality. Engaging in an experimental utopian quest for a new economic system detracts from the good that is realizable in the here and now through economic freedom and enterprise.

Here is where we can—and must— redefine what we have been calling "poverty-alleviation" efforts with the use of a forward-looking, open-ended, empowering term: wealth-creation incentives.

WEALTH-CREATION INCENTIVES

Honest competition within a moral framework creates opportunity for the poor. Paternalistic systems based on subsidies and relief deny the working poor, self-sacrificing and tenacious as they are, the right to engage in activities that create opportunities for a better life.

The quintessential myth of poverty-alleviation is that the poor will crumble under competition because the free-market system is intentionally rigged to keep the poor in the bondage of poverty. In effect, what we have seen in America is the opposite: Paternalistic systems that eschew the rigors of the market enslave the poor by creating incentives to remain in poverty while being reasonably well-fed.

Our answer to the struggles of enterprise, which involve risk and failure, should not be to attack the system or to envision that tinkering with it will create the ever-elusive grand day of discovering a better one. Our answer ought to be a reaffirmation of our trust in a system that has demonstrated that it works well and a reaffirmation of our long-term commitment to walk side by side with the poor.

Although relief is necessary under certain circumstances, unless we recognize economic initiative, the dignity of work, and the entrepreneurial vocation as the normative avenues for integral human fulfillment, we will not help the poor in any meaningful way. The connection between reward and accomplishment is the key in transforming our service from poverty alleviation into wealth creation. More importantly, it will serve well our effort to assist, in subsidiary fashion, in the journey of individuals to integral human fulfillment.

Whenever the connection between reward and accomplishment is lost, harm is done. The beauty of systems of care that emphasize market-driven, work-encouraging, and wealth-creating incentives is that they view the poor not as helpless children but as capable persons. These systems fight the anonymity of the label "poor" in favor of the profoundly personal reality of one-on-one engagement. A wonderful thing will happen as a result. We will stop thinking of the poor as mouths to be fed, bodies to be clothed, or lazy people looking for an enabler. We will begin to see them as potential producers, active participants, and partners in a joint enterprise.

It is important to fight the temptation of viewing the economy as a zero-sum game where wealth is fixed and the pie has been placed at the table of distribution to be sliced, with your task being slicing a tiny portion to give to "the little people." As philosopher Michael Novak warns, "The aftertaste of affluence is boredom."[11] Beware of the boredom of affluence leading you to an attitude about the poor that may cause you to self-flagellate and attack the very system that helped you become affluent. Instead, share that knowledge and open those doors for others.

One important practical point for individuals and organizations to keep in mind is to promote the idea of business as a calling and the entrepreneurial vocation. Reject the idea of business as greedy, vulgar, philistine, and morally suspect.[12] Entrepreneurs are not villains but people responding to a call to use insight, intelligence, innovation, and work to improve the world. Emphasize the virtues of enterprise. To become creators of wealth, individuals need a set of virtues. Among them are the following:

- Sensitivity. An awareness of one's surroundings and the needs of others.
- Insight. Looking beyond the obvious.
- Bravery or Courage. It takes guts to take risks.
- Creativity. "An inclination to notice, the habit of discerning, the tendency to discover what other people do not yet see."[13]
- Building community. Against the common idea that entrepreneurs are lonely sharks, enterprising businesspeople almost always create natural systems of cooperation. Entrepreneurs work with people and for people. Many of those who cooperate with them

[11] Novak, *Business as a Calling*, 6.

[12] See Novak, *Business as a Calling*, 6–10.

[13] Novak, *Business as a Calling*, 120.

are not known to them, as the creation of even a simple pencil involves multiple networks across the oceans.[14]

- Practical Realism. Common sense, prudence, and an openness to learn from experience are essential to the entrepreneur. Although creative and prone to taking risks, the entrepreneur is also practical and understands the need to develop habits of mind and of action.
- Enjoyment. Yes, the entrepreneur finds pleasure in the challenge of enterprise.
- Ethics. Ethics is more than rectitude and respect for norms and law. Ethics involves taking seriously the internal moral imperatives of enterprise: honesty, leadership, patience, perseverance, discipline, justice, forgiveness, compassion, humility, and gratitude.[15]

Personal Responsibility

A sense of personal responsibility is imperative if those in need are to realize their human dignity by engaging in the wealth-creation potential inherent in the market. Each human person is on a journey that he or she alone must tread. Rescuing people from their own mistakes at every turn animalizes people and renders them incapable. Systems that respect people understand that they at times will fail, that they will experience alienation, anomie, loneliness, and even nothingness. These are, in effect, radical experiences of human liberty that highlight the challenges before us as well as the possibilities ahead.

It is precisely that experience of nothingness, that reality of struggle, that allows people to make transcendent choices moving them toward wholeness. Humility is essential to accept that fact, and adherence to practical principles is necessary to resist the temptation of interventionism. The task of helping others is not the task of defining for others the whole of life. Instead, creating a program that establishes practical structures of cooperation that respect the moral capacity of the poor is the best practice in creating sound programs. To put this best practice into effect, keep in mind the following guidelines:

---

[14] See Leonard E. Read, *I, Pencil: My Family Tree as Told to Leonard E. Read* (Irvington-on-Hudson, NY: Foundation for Economic Education, 2010).

[15] See Malloch, *Doing Virtuous Business*, chaps. 4–5.

- Dialogue with participants is essential. Constant discussion allows us to know what is important to others and how to create projects that are practical and meaningful. An example of active dialogue is found in the ministry of Tenth Presbyterian Church in Philadelphia, in which volunteers hold Bible studies in the city's prisons and nursing homes. Church members host a weekly meal for homeless men and a weekly worship service with patients at an AIDS hospice. It is a very simple way of forming community through encounter and dialogue.[16]
- Commit to preserve the sphere of personal responsibility as inviolable. Guard jealously the systemic incentives that foster personal responsibility. Many a ministry has succumbed to the whining of those looking for an enabler or the emotion-driven insistence of volunteers and neglected the need for accountability on the part of recipients.
- Take your time in creating viable business ventures. Entrepreneurship is often about failure after failure until success is achieved. If commitment to the idea of enterprise is exclusively utilitarian, and not an intrinsic value, it will soon be abandoned.
- Commitment to the principles of freedom, enterprise, and individual responsibility becomes a type of civic faith rooted in the nature of human beings and the possibility of practical cooperation. The networks of community and social cooperation that spring from your commitment to these principles prepare the ground for a closer encounter. To quote Michael Novak again, discussing the free-enterprise system: "Too low a system for angels, it seems not to be too high for humans as they are. It stretches them a little."[17]

In the end, remember that every human action is part of a narrative. Work and enterprise place faith in a narrative that believes in the radical human capacity for creativity, invention, action, and risk. To make our compassion effective, to truly help those in need, we must embrace this faith. We must believe.

---

[16] "History," Tenth Presbyterian Church, https://www.tenth.org/mercy/history/.

[17] Novak, *Spirit of Democratic Capitalism*, 67.

Selected Bibliography

Ballor, Jordan J. *Get Your Hands Dirty: Essays on Christian Social Thought (and Action)*. Eugene, OR: Wipf & Stock, 2013.

Borders, Max. *Super Wealth: Why We Should Stop Worrying about the "Gap" between the Rich and Poor*. Sioux Falls, SD: Throne Publishing, 2012.

Brooks, Arthur C. *The Road to Freedom: How to Win the Fight for Free Enterprise*. New York: Basic Books, 2012.

Claar, Victor V., and Robin J. Klay. *Economics in Christian Perspective: Theory, Policy and Life Choices*. Downers Grove, IL: IVP Academic, 2007.

Corbett, Steve, and Brian Fikkert. *When Helping Hurts: How to Alleviate Poverty without Hurting the Poor... and* Yourself. Chicago: Moody Publishers, 2009.

Cox, Michael, and Richard Alm. *Myths of Rich and Poor: Why We're Better Off Than We Think*. New York: Basic Books, 1999.

Donohue-White, Patricia, et.al. *Human Nature and the Discipline of Economics: A Personalist Anthropology and Economic Methodology*. Lanham, MD: Lexington Books, 2002.

Favale, Abigail. *The Genesis of Gender: A Christian Theory*. San Francisco: Ignatius Press, 2022.

George, Robert P. *In Defense of Natural Law*. Oxford: Oxford University Press, 1999.

Gilbert, Neil, and Paul Terrell. *Dimensions of Social Welfare Policy*, 5th ed. Boston: Allyn and Bacon, 2002.

Gregg, Samuel. *Challenging the Modern World: Karol Wojtyla/John Paul II and the Development of Catholic Social Teaching*. Lanham, MD: Lexington Books, 1999.

Gregg, Samuel. *The Commercial Society: Foundations and Challenges in a Global* Age. Lanham, MD: Lexington Books, 2007.

Gregg, Samuel. *On Ordered Liberty: A Treatise on the Free Society*. Lanham, MD: Lexington Books, 2003.

Hayek, F. A. *The Fatal Conceit: The Errors of Socialism*. Chicago: University of Chicago Press, 1991. First published 1988.

Hittinger, Russell. *The First Grace: Rediscovering the Natural Law in a Post-Christian World* Wilmington, DE: ISI, 2003.

Hunter, James Davison. *To Change the World: The Irony, Tragedy, and Possibility of Christianity in the Late Modern World*. New York: Oxford University Press, 2010.

Lupton, Robert D. *Theirs Is the Kingdom: Celebrating the Gospel in Urban America*. New York: Harper One, 1989.

Lupton, Robert D. *Toxic Charity: How Churches and Charities Hurt Those They Help (And How to Reverse It)*. New York: HarperCollins, 2011.

Malloch, Theodore Roosevelt. *Doing Virtuous Business: The Remarkable Success of Spiritual Enterprise*. Nashville: Thomas Nelson, 2008.

Morse, Jennifer Roback. *Love & Economics: Why the Laissez-Faire Family Doesn't Work*. Dallas: Spence, 2001.

Mises, Ludwig von. *Human Action: A Treatise on* Economics. Auburn, AL: Mises Institute, 2008. First published in English in 1949 by Yale University Press.

Novak, Michael. *Business as a Calling: Work and the Examined Life*. New York: Free Press, 1996.

Novak, Michael. *The Spirit of Democratic Capitalism*. Lanham, MD: Madison Books, 1991. First published 1982 by Simon and Schuster.

Olasky, Marvin. *The Tragedy of American Compassion*. Washington, DC: Regnery, 1992.

Patterson, Orlando. *The Ordeal of Integration: Progress and Resentment in America's "Racial" Crisis*. New York: Basic Books, 1997.

Pluckrose, Helen, and James Lindsay. *Cynical Theories: How Activist Scholarship Made Everything about Race, Gender, and Identity—and Why This Harms Everyone*. Durham, NC: Pitchstone, 2020.

Rector, Robert, and William Lauber. *America's Failed $5.4 Trillion War on Poverty*. Washington, DC: Heritage Foundation, 1995.

Reed, Lawrence W. *Are We Good Enough for Liberty?* Ottawa, IL: Jameson Books, 2018.

Reed, Lawrence W. *Great Myths of the Great Depression*. Midland, MI: Mackinac Center, 2010. First published 1981.

Rommen, Heinrich A. *The Natural Law: A Study in Legal and Social History and Philosophy*. Translated by Thomas R. Hanley, OSB. Indianapolis: Liberty Fund, 1998. First published in German 1936.

Röpke, Wilhelm. *A Humane Economy*, 3rd ed. Wilmington, DE: ISI, 1998. First published 1960.

Santelli, Anthony J., Jr., et.al., *The Free Person and the Free Economy: A Personalist View of Market Economics*. Lanham, MD: Lexington Books, 2002.

Sirico, Robert. *Defending the Free Market: The Moral Case for a Free Economy*. Washington, DC: Regnery, 2012.

Sowell, Thomas. *The Vision of the Anointed; Self-Congratulation as a Basis for Social Policy*. New York: Basic Books, 1995

Steele, Shelby. *The Content of Our Character: A New Vision of Race in America*. New York: Harper Perennial, 1990.

Stone, Deborah A. *Policy Paradox and Political Reason*. Glenview, IL: Scott, Foresman, 1988.

Tanner, Michael D. *The Poverty of Welfare: Helping Others in Civil Society*. Washington, DC: Cato Institute, 2003.

Townsend, Peter. *Poverty in the United* Kingdom. London: Penguin, 1979.

Washington, Booker T. *Up from Slavery: An Autobiography*. New York: A. L. Burt, 1900.

Watzlawick, Paul, John Weakland, and Richard Fisch. *Change: Principles of Problem Formation and Problem Solving*. New York: W.W. Norton, 1974.

About the Author

Ismael Hernandez is the founder and president of the Freedom & Virtue Institute. He worked in an inner-city ministry in Florida for fifteen years before he founded the Freedom & Virtue Institute in 2009. He regularly lectures for the Acton Institute in Grand Rapids, Michigan, and has lectured for the American Enterprise Institute, the Heritage Foundation, the Foundation for Government Accountability, and the Foundation for Economic Education. His writings have appeared in *Religion & Liberty*, *Crisis*, *World*, *The Vital Center*, the *Washington Times,* and *Schweizer Monat* in Switzerland. He is the author of *Not Tragically Colored: Freedom, Personhood, and the Renewal of Black America* and of an essay in the forthcoming *A Pathway to American Renewal: Red, White, and Black* (vol. 2). He holds an MA in political science from the University of Southern Mississippi.

Index

www.ingramcontent.com/pod-product-compliance
Ingram Content Group UK Ltd.
Pitfield, Milton Keynes, MK11 3LW, UK
UKHW022025190726
13853UKWH00005B/2120

9 798218 441043